LEFT TURN, RIGHT TURN

LEFT TURN, RIGHT TURN

Jana Meehan

Book design copyright 2014 by Marquee Publishing
All rights reserved.
Published by

⬤Marquee Publishing

3901 Berger Ave. • St. Louis, MO 63109
www.MarqueePublishingLLC.com• 314-202-2035

You Go to the Bathroom © Clinton Gallagher, 1982

Published in the United States of America
© 2014 Marquee Publishing

ISBN: 978-0-615-99158-0

1. Fiction/Suspense/Family/Youth/Drug Abuse

Acknowlegdments

I offer special thanks to these folks whose contributions to this work make it better:

Laine Boyd

Charlie Everingham

Clint Gallagher

Jo Skabo

Robert Subert

For Inge, my Friend

COMING SOON
FROM JANA MEEHAN

Provisions

Tim and Theresa Shelton have been out of work for a long time. In a last ditch effort to find a job in a city a long drive away, the two meet a group of nightclub singers whose kindness and care give the Sheltons a new perspective on the nuances and community formed by being poor.

As the two battle their financial woes and fears, a burgeoning friendship forms, and the faith of their new friends offers a lifeline in a new city.

Tim's view of life, death, and God Himself begins to change, however, when Theresa is in a car accident and faces life-threatening injuries, the pressure mounts and faith is tested.

Meanwhile, the leader of the Cole Renshaw Trio and his wife face their own domestic worries with money and family relations. This story of love, faith, and struggle hits home with many, and leaves a lasting message that there is faith, hope and love, these three.

CHAPTER 1

The best-laid plans of mice and teenage boys often go awry, according to Joe MacDonald. The plan was to spend his summer vacation hanging out with his buds, getting a little wasted, scoring with a girl or two, and generally chilling. Two things stood in the way: his father and his own big mouth.

Note to self: While articulating your plans in so many words, don't allow yourself to be overheard by your hard-ass father, whose purpose in life is to separate you from any kind of a good time.

Joe's father, also named Joe, was a St. Louis stockbroker with a major brokerage downtown . He worked hard, and was out of the house for commensurate periods of time each week. The distance between father and son was physical and emotional. Young Joe felt like he hardly knew his dad.

When the announcement was made that the boy was to go to his grandparents' farm for the summer, young Joe's reaction was one of unsurprised resignation. Clearly, Dad wanted rid of him. Dad always wanted rid of him. Joe was an add-on and a nuisance. He should never have been born.

Admittedly, some of Joe's own behavior widened the chasm between him and his father. After his mother's death, Joe began acting out to get his dad's attention. There had been drinking and delving into recreational chemicals. He boosted a car when he was sixteen, and engaged in other behaviors that a reasoned person would only describe as pure idiocy.

At fifteen, some guy he had met offered Joe ten bucks to knock on a stranger's door, scream threats at the stranger, promise to kill him, and then run for the hills. That would be a huge hoot, wouldn't it? Great, harmless fun.

The ten bucks looked good to Joe until federal marshals knocked on the front door and took Joe away, charged with threatening a witness in a federal criminal case.

His father had gone to the authorities, paid bail, and pleaded stupidity on behalf of his wayward kid. Lesson learned, but it did little to heal the rift between father and son.

Joe got along better with his stepmother, Liz. A svelte blonde beauty in her forties, Liz had joined the family five years after Joe's mother died in a terrible accident. Liz's appearance in the boy's life was a welcome comfort, even if it made the emptiness both more and less pronounced.

Why, Joe had often wondered, did Dad have time to date, form a serious relationship, and eventually marry a woman like this when he never, found time to notice his own son was alive? Don't tell me, his reasoning went on, that parents naturally love their children. Obviously not all of them do.

Liz knocked on the boy's bedroom door after his father's announcement had driven him in anger and hurt to his private quarters.

"Hey," she said when he gave permission for her to enter.

"Hey," he intoned.

"This isn't all bad, you know. Your grandparents are great folks, and you may find you have a lot to do there. It could be fun. And you like animals, and they have lots of animals."

"Yeah, okay."

"Joe, talk to me. I know you're hurt by this and you think it will waste your whole summer, but give it a chance."

"Hurt? Hey, I'd love to just be hurt. The problem is that I'm not hurt, and I'm not surprised. Him doing this is just another example of trying to get me out of his way. If it was the first time he dissed me, I might be hurt. But it's the millionth time," Joe complained. "Plus, okay, some of it is my fault. I've done stupid stuff, but you gotta ask yourself about the chicken and the egg."

"Why do I have to do that?"

"You have to wonder if I do stupid things to get his attention, or if I've given up on getting noticed and just do stuff to be doing it."

"What do you mean?"

He stared at her for a moment, appalled that she had raised such a question. "Liz, he's at work all the time. If I won the freaking national basketball title, he wouldn't even notice. He hardly knows I'm alive."

"Joey." Liz rested her hands in her lap for several moments and considered what else to say , as Joe sorted his tee shirts and stuffed them in a cardboard box.

Liz finally spoke. "Joey, you've had some problems. Three weeks ago, the police brought you home from a party so stoned you couldn't walk on your own. Before that, I came home and found you in bed with a girl. My bed! Do you know how disrespected I felt when you did that?"

"Sorry."

"Sorry is not the point."

"Then what's *is* the point?"

"Did you ever think your dad just wants you to succeed and do well, and that maybe some of your friends don't have your best interests at heart?"

"Maybe they don't," he spat angrily. "But at least they have some interest in me. He doesn't. I'm just a headache he's putting off on somebody else."

Liz switched gears. "The glass is more than half-full, Joey. Your grandmother Inga is a terrific cook— much better than I am. She's an Old-World German, and she cooks like one. She has some tales to tell if you ask her. She grew up in Germany during the Nazi era."

"Really?" Joe asked, turning toward her. "Did she meet actual Nazis?"

"I don't know if she met actual party members, but she had a German soldier living in her house at one point. And her mother was forced to hang a swastika outside the window to keep from getting into trouble.

"Wow."

"And your granddad has a different take on the world that you may get a kick out of," Liz continued. "He grew up in Oklahoma. He's been a farmer since he was a kid. You could learn a lot from him."

"I'm not interested in farming," Joe stated.

"Of course not, but you're interested in people, aren't you? And you're interested in how they think and what they do. Grandpa Joe sees from a different perspective. Get him talking.

"This is a new adventure, Joey. Look on it as a chance to explore new experiences a little and get to know another part of your family.

"I'll miss you," Liz concluded. She hugged the boy.

As Joe packed, he examined his memories of his grandfolks and their farmhouse. They were scant and fading, but he searched the dimness.

Joe's father had moved to St. Louis right out of college, and had married Anne shortly thereafter. Gramps, the first Joe in the MacDonald dynasty, had expected his son to take over the farm, and was disappointed when his son announced his intention to be a stockbroker in the big city. Harsh words were exchanged, but in the end, Gramps had reluctantly accepted that he couldn't force a man to be a farmer. But the strife had left a bad taste in both men's mouths. Joe II hadn't been back home since.

Joe III remembered visiting for a short time prior to the time of his mother's death, but had only vague memories of the small burg out Highway 36, an hour west of Hannibal, Missouri.

His stepmother had contacted the grandparents about the summer-long visit that was about to ensue. Joe had no knowledge of his father ever communicating with his own parents at any time in his life.

Sad, he thought. But his dad had never been a great communicator. What did Liz see in him? Liz was as approachable and easy as a female could get, in young Joe's opinion.

He dreaded the three months ahead, but had too much pride to linger where he wasn't wanted.

Sure, he took the onus for bedding some girl in his dad's bed, and he probably shouldn't have attended four or five really cool parties where the beer flowed and the bud was toked freely. But what did his father expect? It's not as if any notice would've been taken if he'd stayed home with his face in a book or something.

It was a Monday morning in early May when Joe, his father, and Liz drove Missouri State Highway 61 north to Hannibal, then west on Highway 36, into dingy, depressing Sylvia, Missouri. All of the businesses were closed or filthy-looking, with faded, inadequate signage and dirt or gravel parking lots. Few cars were visible; the scarce vehicles in view were pickup trucks. The men on the streets wore overalls — almost to a man, and Joe sensed that he was in some other world.

The three drove through the apparent near-ghost town until Joe's father spouted off. "This is going to build your character, working on a farm for the summer. You'll come home in September more of a man."

Young Joe listened to the bromides stoically, but he recognized that his father was speaking out of guilt.

He should feel guilty, the boy mused. This was just wrong.

Joe also took the remark about being more of a man as a personal insult. What manliness did he lack in his father's view? He clenched his jaw.

Joe wasn't one to eschew self-examination. A nagging voice in his head acknowledged that some of his stupid teenage behavior might be perceived as immature and lacking in character. A thought flitted by in a moment: why did he boost that car?

It was shocking and pathetic, though, Joe also mused, that Liz, in the front seat of the MacDonald SUV, had a hand-written page of instructions how to get to the farmhouse. It seemed his father had forgotten how to find the very home in which he was raised.

Joe rolled his eyes at the thought.

The three came out of town on another two-lane highway that headed south. They were enveloped in cornfields as far as they could see, with occasional patches of something else that Joe concluded was a soybean crop. Dust clouds formed behind the SUV, but in front of it, the vista was green and sunshiny. The three took several turns down increasingly narrow dirt roads until at last they turned around a corner and saw a huge willow tree in the front yard of a two-story white frame house. His father pulled in front of the house. A screened-in front porch sported a weather-beaten look.

Exiting the car, Liz approached the house ahead of Joe and his father. She opened the loose, wobbly door and held it for the other two. The three stepped through the screened porch, past an ancient red settee, and plethora of potted geraniums. Liz knocked on the inner door.

It took a few moments for the door to be opened. Inside, Joe saw his grandmother for the first time since he was five years old. His memories of her were hazy. He didn't recognize the woman before him at all.

"Hello!" she greeted the three. Her voice bore a thick German accent, but it also had a light, high, musical tone that was incongruous against the accent, and like no human voice Joe had ever heard. He likened it to a xylophone being played by someone who knew how to do it.

His grandmother was still blonde, but her locks were graying around the edges. She was portly, but not fat. Her piercing blue eyes were small and alert. The word shrewd popped into Joe's mind. As his grandmother gazed at the three visitors, he thought she looked wise, thoughtful, and completely aware, as if nothing could surprise her. She had already seen it all.

When his father stepped into the room, both he and Inga halted their movements, gazing at each other. Joe sensed a tense dynamic. Neither adult knew what the other was thinking, though it seemed clear to Joe, from the looks on their faces, that his dad expected anger and rejection, and his grandmother expected cold indifference.

They were both wrong. Each paused, waiting for the other to make a move. It was Joe's strong, astute-looking grandmother who blinked.

She raised her arms and wrapped them around the neck of her son with a fierce hug that lasted a long time. Joe's father returned the tight embrace, exhaling in relief. Behind her head, his eyes squinted shut, and Joe was puzzled to see his father try to contain his tears.

Joe's grandmother made no such attempt. Her tears flowed, and when she broke the hug, she gazed into her son's eyes with a mother's love and devotion.

Joe watched this encounter and noted that his father's inability to love his own child wasn't learned from this woman.

A twinge of envy washed over him for a moment. He was ostensibly part of this family, he thought, but not part of this.

The woman patted his father's face and chest, placed her hands at his side and rubbed, hugging him again. Then she stepped back and looked at her son again.

Abruptly, as if remembering her manners, she turned to Liz and offered a welcoming hand to her.

"You must be Liz," she chirped in her high-pitched voice. "So glad to meet you after all those phone calls."

Liz smiled. "It's so nice to meet you, Mrs. MacDonald. Your directions were perfect."

"They should be, I guess," the older woman replied with a smile. "I've lived in this town for forty years. And you are to call me Inga." Her smile was warm, Joe thought, but her eyes remained sharp.

At last, she turned to her grandson. "Hello, Third," she said. Her musical voice belied her coolness. "I won't be surprised if you don't remember me at all. You haven't been here since you were a small boy." She reached for his hand and clasped it. Joe hadn't been called "Third" since his early years of grade school. This would take some getting used to.

"Nice to meet you—um, I mean, nice to see you again." Could he sound any more lame, he scolded himself. But his grandmother's eyes twinkled as she seemed to sympathize with his discomfiture.

"Your grandfather will be in from the barn soon, Third. Then we'll eat. I've made a nice dinner for us." Inga looked around at everyone. "Sauerbraten and spargel for the start of spargel season, and old-fashioned baked potatoes will be on the table as soon as Joe comes in the house. If you want to use the bathroom, it's through there," she announced, gesturing to a door adjacent to the kitchen.

"It's good to see you, Momma," Joe II said humbly. "It's good to be home."

"You are welcome in this house, Joseph," his mother said. "You always have been."

Joe's father paused before exiting to the bathroom, as if he had something else to say. Joe could sense his objection and his choice to demure.

Inga continued, "Why don't we all sit down in the living room? Does anyone want anything to drink before dinner?"

Seventeen-year-old Joe resisted the urge to ask for a beer. Instead, he followed his grandmother and Liz into the living room where they found comfortable seats.

The living room was old and worn, Joe noted. The furniture was from another era, and an old space furnace sat near one wall. The stovepipe extended from the top of it, turned right, and vented out the wall. Joe had never seen such a contraption, and felt like he had entered a time warp.

Inga excused herself to the kitchen, and the boy whispered to his stepmother, "What in hell is spargel?"

"Asparagus, I think," Liz responded. "I'm betting they grow it right on the property."

"Great. I hate asparagus."

"You only hate it out of a can. I do, too. It's really good fresh, and I bet you've never had it that way," Liz explained, smiling at him.

"We'll see."

"So, we will."

"You're enjoying this," Joe objected. "I'm miserable, and you're having a great time! And why does she call it dinner when it's lunchtime?"

"That, I don't know," Liz admitted. "But let's just roll with it, okay?"

Joe sat quietly, looking around. The living room was full of furniture—antiques, he guessed—from a past he didn't know. End tables sported elaborate table lamps whose bodies and shades were rendered of what appeared to be hand-painted porcelain.

Doilies covered everything. Joe had never seen so many. Come to think of it, he mused, he might not have ever seen a doily at all, except in photos in history books.

A large doily decorated the back of every upholstered chair. They adorned every table and protected each surface from the feet of the lamps and knickknacks.

"Those look like authentic Dresdens," Liz commented, standing to examine some of the figurines that filled a curio cabinet. "Oh, wow!"

"What are authentic Dresdens?" Joe asked, not really caring.

"Dresden figurines are famous," Liz replied. "They were made before the war in Dresden, Germany. They're quite detailed and exquisite. Take a look. The artists used actual lace covered in porcelain to make these wide, fluffy petticoats on the figurines' dresses. When they were fired, the lace burned away but left these incredibly delicate details behind.

"I think the place where they were made was torn up by bombing. You can't get them anymore. They're quite rare. And beautiful." She returned to her seat without touching any of the treasures.

Joe, uninterested, remained in his own thoughts.

The room was decorated in forest green and beige, an awful combination, Joe thought. It was well-lived in.

Behind the couch, an ancient photo hung of a young man from the 1920s with short hair parted in the middle. He wore an old-fashioned-style of suit coat and a peculiar-looking cap. His pose was formal and stiff, Joe thought. "I wonder who that is," he remarked to Liz, gesturing at the photo.

"No idea. Probably one of your ancestors."

"Hmm."

Liz and Joe heard voices from the back of the room. The sound came from the other side of a door Joe had not noticed before.

"That must be your grandfather coming in," Liz said.

Joe didn't say anything. For no reason he could understand, he felt a nervous, unexpected trepidation.

He heard his grandmother's voice, but he couldn't make out her words. He assumed his grandmother had told her husband that the guests had arrived.

Grandpa Joe stepped into the living room. He was a tall, muscular man, aged, with a barrel chest and a stomach that spilled over his belt. Twinkling blue eyes highlighted a fleshy face, framed by a shock of white hair. Thick, wire-rimmed glasses perched on his nose.

As Joe gazed at his grandfather, the older man saw him and blinked several times. He stood, unmoving, while his eyes adjusted from the sunlight outdoors to the dimness of the room. When his eyes focused, Grandpa Joe marched assertively to the boy, took him by both shoulders, and lifted him off his feet.

A startled Joe felt both afraid and annoyed, but before he could react in any way, his grandfather bellowed with joy, "Third! Welcome! Welcome! Great to see you, boy." He threw his arms around Joe and hugged him hard and long. The hug unnerved Joe further.

Liz stepped forward to greet the father-in-law she had never met.

The man broke the suffocating hug and held Joe back by the shoulders, looking at him. "I know you don't remember me, son, but I sure remember you. I sure do. What a strong young man you've grown into. You look good. Tall and strong. You play sports, son?"

"I play a little basketball," Joe replied, warming a little at the mention of sports.

"Really? How's 'bout that? We've got a high school team here in town that went to the state finals last season."

"Cool. That's good. Um, this is my stepmom, Liz."

"Oh, good God, where're my manners?" Grandpa Joe chided himself. "I got so excited about my grandson, I was damned rude to you, lady. Joe MacDonald." With the statement of his name, he reached for Liz's hand and pumped it.

"Liz MacDonald," she replied, smiling. The man grinned at her, eyes twinkling.

"Let's go in and see if Inga has dinner on the table. Bet she does." He draped his hand on his grandson's shoulder as he led the two into the dining area.

The room with a large table and chairs was a step down from the kitchen. The entry door was wide and welcoming, and the table was set with china and silverware. A bouquet of flowers formed the centerpiece. As the three entered the room, Joe noticed that his father was already seated next to an empty chair for Liz. He must have gone into the kitchen straight from the bathroom, Joe mused. Typical. He couldn't expect his father to come get his son.

Inga was removing the centerpiece as the three stepped down into the room.

"Those are lovely flowers, Inga," Liz remarked. "Why move them?"

"They are pretty," Inga agreed. "But it's important for us to see you all without obstructions. It's such a rare visit."

Green must be someone's favorite color, Joe thought. The walls were covered with bead board, painted a dull pea green that Joe disliked.

The table seated eight. Grandpa Joe took his seat at the head of the table. Liz and Joe's father sat together on a wide side of the table, and Joe sat across from Liz, adjacent to his grandfather, refusing to look. He scarcely looked at his father.

Liz leaped up to help when she saw Inga step down the stair with bowls of hot food. Turns out, asparagus was only one of four vegetables offered, and Joe ate hungrily with growing assurance that this may be the best meal he'd ever had. He had always thought that German food was not to his liking, but now thought he may have judged in haste.

As the five dug in, Grandpa Joe attempted small talk. He explained about the hardness of the ground following a dry winter, and the goings on in the community with the drug trade and the decline of family farms in the region.

"Drugs up here?" Joe's father wanted to know. "I thought most of that was concentrated in the cities."

"The kids up here cook their own," Grandpa explained. "It's called methamphetamine, and it's dangerous stuff. Instantly addictive and impossible to break away from."

"Oh, yeah. That's in the city, too," Joe's father said, "and south of St. Louis in the middle and west of the state. It's bad news, for sure."

"The newspaper had a story this week about a kid who blew most of his face off cooking it," Grandpa went on. "The article's still around here somewhere. It's got a picture of the guy, all burned up."

Inga had taken a seat next to Third. She ate quietly, but her sharp gaze switched from her son to her husband and back with interest.

The exchange of small talk continued for some time, while Joe observed the dynamic between the two older men. Neither was comfortable. Both were stiff and stilted in their words and body language. They were attempting, he reasoned, to pretend like the last twenty years of bad blood had never occurred. Like they talked every week about the weather, the ballgame, and the meth. Why, he thought, don't they talk about what's really on their minds, and get it over with?

"Third tells me he plays some basketball," Grandpa said, changing the subject. He turned to the boy and continued, "You any good?" The words could have sounded like a disparagement, but the broad, accepting smile on the man's face was encouraging to young Joe. He returned a confident smile.

"As a matter of fact, Gramps, I am." He tried out the term "Gramps" to measure both how the old man reacted to it, and how it tasted in his own mouth. "I score on average twenty-three points in a game, or at least I did last season, and I'm the team's leading defender."

"You play point guard?" Gramps asked.

"Yes."

"Joey is also the team captain and leading scorer," his father interrupted.

Joe turned to his father and said with a forced calmness that was almost menacing, "I guess Liz told you that, otherwise you'd have no way of knowing it. I wasn't sure you knew I even played. You've never been to a game, and you've never asked me one question about it."

Middle Joe's mouth came open, but then shut as he swallowed hard and looked away.

Joe didn't care that he had humiliated his father in front of his grandparents. He knew he had been rude, but if the other two men didn't want to acknowledge the family dysfunction, then he, himself, would step to the free-throw line.

"Apple strudel!" Inga chirped her awkward segue in a voice louder than necessary. "With cinnamon ice cream!" She rose from her chair and exited to the kitchen. Liz followed her.

The three men fell silent. Resentment hung over them like hot, wet air in a badly ventilated laundry room.

Middle Joe was the one to break the silence. It seemed like he forced every syllable, and the effort was too much for him.

"Joey, listen to me." He paused, catching his breath. It seemed to the boy that there was nothing to listen to. The man didn't know what to say. Silence followed for a long moment while his father formed his words. "I think the flaw in my life is that I care about you too much, and you look so much like your mother, it's all I can do to look at you —"

Third cut in rudely. "Why did you have a kid, Dad? Why didn't you just work your stupid job and go to your stupid meetings and forget all about kids? You don't want me, and now you've succeeded in getting rid of me, at least for the summer. Good work!" Young Joe's face twisted with impending tears, but he fought them back. He realized that his behavior looked awful to his grandfather. He also realized that this was the point in the discussion where he would typically storm off to his room and slam the door. But he was two hundred miles from his room, and there was nowhere to go.

The room was heavy with a pregnant silence for what seemed to Joe like an eternity.

Grandpa Joe broke the impasse. "What there is between a father and his son can't be reckoned by just anyone. You have to be a father to understand. What no one seems to grasp is that time is short. A man only has so long to live, and in that short time, he has to make as much peace as he can with sons, fathers, wives and mothers. The trick is to get all that done while you still have time to live in the peace you've made."

More silence at the table. Young Joe fidgeted with his teaspoon, staring at it. His father said nothing.

Presently, Inga and Liz came in from the kitchen with bowls of warm strudel and ice cream. They set a bowl down at each place setting, and sat down with the men. But the heaviness in the air was lost on no one. The five ate quietly.

CHAPTER 2

"What I Did on My Summer Vacation" wasn't an essay Joe looked forward to having his friends read this fall. What I Did would most likely be shoveling chicken droppings.

The first morning of his visit started early. Joe's grandmother woke him at six, and told him Gramps was already in the barn working. Gramps would need Joe's help until about seven, when they could come in for breakfast. Joe jumped out of bed — the bed his father had slept in all of his young life — dressed, and went outside. He was handed a shovel and shown the chicken pen.

Joe wasn't that wild about the large flock of chickens. They weren't cuddly, and smelled awful. The chickens were Inga's turf. The egg-producing feature of the farm was her cottage business. But, he shoveled as asked.

The hour before breakfast featured an introduction to the MacDonald livestock that pleased the young man.

Joe liked the orange tabby cat in the barn, Marylou, who had just had a litter. The old dog, Lady, white and black, long-haired with feathers on her legs, was gentle and a lover of all treats.

When Gramps called Lady, and introduced her to Joe, Joe fell to his knees on the ground and wrapped his arms around the dog.

"Is this a Dalmatian?" he asked, observing the white coat with black spots.

"No, this is an English setter. She and I used to hunt quail when my eyes were good enough. Setters are retrievers, and she was a good one."

"I've always wondered why they don't eat the stuff they bring back."

"I guess they would without proper training. See, you train the dog by wrapping bird feathers and a wire around a small block of wood. The wires will cut into the dog's mouth if she bites down too hard on the feathers, so she learns to not do that. She brings the block back without chewing it, and when she's good at that, you take her in the woods," Gramps explained .

"She's pretty," Joe said, petting her. Impulsively, he rubbed his cheek on the top of her head and was rewarded with a lick to his face. He grinned and scratched her ears.

"Lots of folks confuse English setters with Dalmatians," Gramps went on, "but Dalmatians are short-haired and not as sweet-natured. And they got a tendency to go deaf."

"Really? Why?"

"Bred too high, I guess."

"What do you mean?"

"Well, seems like if a breed of dog becomes popular, like Dalmatians did some years ago, breeders start breeding their dogs with their own littermates or their own mothers or fathers. The inbreeding causes genetic flaws just like it does in people. That's why the law says you can't marry your cousin."

"Gotcha."

"The opposite is also true, I think," Gramps continued. "When folks marry, and have kids with someone who is real far away from them genetically, the kids turn out stronger, seems like. Seems like when whites have kids with blacks, the kids are smart and beautiful quite a lot o' the time."

Every word the old man spoke was a revelation to Joe. Not only the content, but the source. The old man spoke in a countrified dialect that Joe considered "hick" — the dialect of an uneducated lowbrow. But the things Gramps said struck Joe as smart, aware, and worldly-wise.

Joe also made the acquaintance of Susie, the very pregnant Holstein . She stood among many sister cows, grazing in a fenced meadow on the west side of the property, but only Susie acknowledged the humans. As Grandpa Joe approached the fence, he gave off a loud, shrill whistle. Susie looked up, saw her keeper, and strolled toward him with her belly protruding and her long, stringy tail flailing in the air. When she saw the younger man, however, she stopped and looked distrustful.

"She'll have to get to know you real well before she'll come when you call her," Gramps explained.

"I've never heard of a cow that would come when you call her," Joe replied with wonder.

"That's 'cause you haven't met Susie."

Once animal introductions were in place, the two wrapped up a few more chores before Gramps gestured for Joe to follow him back into the farmhouse. Joe looked at the house as he approached it. It was of vintage 1940s construction, and had seen a lot of wear. The two-story frame was painted white, but needed a fresh coat. Joe noticed the uneven wood floor on several levels to step up or down . This suggested to him that the house may have started out much smaller and had had additions built over the years. As they walked toward the back door leading to the kitchen, Joe tried to imagine his father growing up here, sleeping every night in the room Joe now occupied. He envisioned his father with a smooth complexion and compared his appearance to the weathered, sunburned wrinkles and scars on his grandfather's hands and face. He pictured his father in the white shirts, conservative striped neckties, and business suits that comprised his current uniform, and compared them to the plain front-pocket tee shirts the older man wore under his worn overalls.

Nope, he couldn't picture it. He couldn't imagine that the two men were connected by blood or in any other way. The incongruity was laughable.

He was learning fast that Gramps was easy and approachable, affectionate and kind. He smiled often, laughed easily, and seemed interested in his grandson. That added to the differences. Joe realized that he already liked the old man. Part of the attraction might be by default, he knew. He might like his grandfather just *because* he was so far removed from his father. It might be that the fondness he was starting to feel was nothing more than vindictiveness against his own dad. But he wouldn't let his grandfather know.

Inside the house, Inga was completing breakfast. Joe learned the evening before that Grams' cooking was a good thing. This morning, she was setting a bowl of scrambled eggs on the dining table in the pea-green dining room, along with a plate of bacon, biscuits and gravy.

This time, the centerpiece remained as the three gathered at the end of the long table.

"How did you sleep, Third?" Inga chirped, when the boy came into the dining room. "Was the mattress too soft? I've thought for a while I should replace that thing, but there's been no one here to sleep on it, so there wasn't any need until now."

Her welcoming smile was as sweet as her lyrical voice.

"I slept fine, Grams. I'd like a shower, though."

"Sure, oh, sure. I guess I need to pull out an alarm clock so you can wake up in time for a shower. I didn't think . . ." she trailed off.

"That's okay, Grams," he continued. "Liz says you grew up in Germany."

"Yes, that's true," she affirmed, stepping up into the kitchen.

"Maybe you could tell me about it sometime."

"Sure. Anytime."

Her voice was so lilting and high, so like birds singing, that the thought occurred to him that hearing her tell him about Germany would be pleasant on more than one level.

"What would you like to know?" Grams asked as he followed her into the kitchen.

"Um, I don't know. Liz said you grew up with Nazis. What was that like?"

"Oh, no, not exactly with Nazis, but certainly there were some around. I had to put my hand in the air and say, 'Heil, Hitler' whenever I met someone on the street. And there was a Nazi flag hanging from our house, but we weren't alone. Here, wait a minute. Put these on the table, please."

Grams gave Joe a handful of forks and knives and three plates and then opened a kitchen drawer. "It's not here anymore," she remarked, half to herself as she sorted through papers and photographs. Then she followed Joe into the green room. She rummaged through a drawer in a corner bureau for a minute and pulled out a black and white photo of a two-story house. The house looked ominous and dark, with black shingles. A swastika hung from the front second story window. Grams handed the photo to Joe.

"Here is the house where I lived for a time. We had to hang that flag. Everybody did. At night, we would pull down all the blinds in the windows and turn the lights down low so no light could be seen from the outside. If anyone could see light coming out our windows, we would get a visit from the authorities."

"Why?"

"The black-outs were to protect the town from air raids."

"Where was this house?"

"A little town outside of Berlin called Korbach. I lived in that house until a bomb dropped on a neighbor's house down the street. The concussion knocked the windows out and the shingles off. The roof partially came down, and we couldn't live there anymore. The town was a railroad hub, so we were targeted all the time.

"My mother used to make us go to bed with our clothes on so if the bombs started, we could go to the basement dressed. It was that way for a long time. My brother and sister and I spent a lot of nights in the basement. One morning we came back upstairs and there wasn't much house left."

Inga turned back into the kitchen and resumed preparing breakfast. Joe followed her. Gramps came out of the bathroom and touched her arm with affection as he went by.

"Ready?" he said, gesturing toward a plate of fried potatoes she had set on a counter. Inga nodded, and her husband picked the dish up and carried it to the table.

Joe returned to the dining room gazing at the photo Grams had offered.

"Come sit, son," his grandfather invited. "You drink coffee?"

"Yeah, that would be great, thanks," Joe replied, still looking at the photo, but moving toward what had already become his chair. He sat down and propped the photo up against the centerpiece so he could examine it.

His grandfather returned to the table with three mugs of black coffee and sat at the head chair. Inga joined them a moment later with a pitcher of orange juice. She noticed the photo propped up on the table in front of the boy, and her mind returned to a distant time and place.

As the three ate, Grandpa Joe told Third many of the features of the farm and farm life.

Inga daydreamed, remembering her troubled childhood. Thoughts of Germany flitted about randomly, forwards and backwards in time. She recalled moments of great joy as she tried to block out times of great sorrow.

At eleven years old, Inga Wentzel was already a war veteran. As the conflict between the Third Reich's powerful military force and the U.S.- led allies escalated, the bombings in Inga's rural neighborhood in Waldeck County also escalated. But the bombings were far from the first sign of conflict. The German economy, ravaged by the first World War, rendered poverty a universal condition. Inga and her siblings had never known another way. It was all they knew of life. The family had little money, but had a prodigious vegetable garden in the back of the house. Their mother was masterful at managing with very little, and knew more than her fair share about growing a garden and living off of it, so they didn't go hungry.

Inga's mother taught her children to knit at early ages. They made their own garments from raw sheep wool, sheared and spun by hand. When the children walked a half hour to and from the local school building, and arrived with wet feet if the weather was bad, it wasn't for lack of wool socks.

Inga and her siblings, as well as the neighbors and friends, were not driven by envy because they couldn't buy the finery in the local markets. There was no finery or much else to buy in the stores. The kids didn't know they were poor. They were no different than anyone else.

Inga's mother, Hedda Wentzel, widowed before baby Konstanze was born, was also unremarkable in her station. She managed in a matriarchal society bereft of men, owing to the war. She was among many single mothers distinguished only by the abject certainty that her husband would not return with the other soldiers. It made little difference during the harrowing, uncertain times.

Inga had many memories of nights spent in the basement, dressed, but chilly, wearing the only shoes she had, and a school dress. Huddled together with her mother, her sister, Konstanze, and her brother, Christoph, as the concussion of bombs both near and far away assailed their ears, Inga had trembled with fear on each occasion, and the terror of loud noises would follow her to adulthood.

If her mother was fearful, she never showed it. She wrapped her arms around the waists of two children while the third child hugged her neck. They stayed that way until it was deemed safe to go back upstairs.

Inga returned to the present as her husband rose from the breakfast table and started out the back door. He turned to Joe and said, "You'll help your grandmother clear the table and load the dishwasher. Then join me in the hen house."

The two Joes worked until noon, and then stopped for dinner. Inga had ham sandwiches ready. She dolloped a delicious scratch-made sauce on the ham.

"You've got a good appetite, Third," Grams observed. "I like to see a man eat well."

Joe considered the nickname "Third." It was stuck on when he was small. At that time, it was fine. By the time he had started school, the kids changed it to "Turd," and the shine was gone. But here, in isolated Sylvia, Missouri, the name sounded different. Not like vulnerability. More like a badge of family honor.

After dinner, the old man turned the boy loose to assist Inga. Once it was ascertained that the youngster had a valid driver's license, Inga gave him the keys to her blue Ford Taurus, and sent him to town to explore, meet people, learn the lay of the land, and bring home a pound of butter, a pound of brown sugar, and a bag of pecan halves.

Joe smiled to himself on the way to the car. There would be a pecan pie in his near future! As Joe parked the sedan in the town square, he struggled to recall his vague memories of a visit to this town when he was young.

It was close to the time his mother died. At the age of only twenty-eight, his mother was swept away by a flash flood on the way to Joe's day care . The only clear memory he had of her was the visit to downtown Sylvia — a great adventure for a small child. All the other memories of his mother were shadowy and nonspecific — the mere idea of a mother with no tangible substance.

Downtown Sylvia, when Joe was small, consisted of a four-block-long strip of ma and pa shops. There were the requisite stores –

hardware, variety, grocery – along with a post office, barbershop, florist, and a drugstore. His memories of the drugstore were the most distinct. His mother had taken him there for a cherry Coke.

It was the first place he looked for as he got to Sylvia's town square.

When Joe was a mere five years old, the little shops did a fair trade. Sylvia was never a bustling metropolis, but the merchants survived. As the economy declined and big business agriculture pounded the family farmer, each family-owned store felt the strain. They began to close, one after another, and in time there was no point in coming to town. There was barely any town to come to. A Walmart opened twelve miles away in Macon, and the death rattle of downtown Sylvia began to sound.

On this visit, Joe found it tough to reconcile his vague memories of a busy street filled with shoppers who stopped and chatted with each neighbor or friend they encountered, with the Sylvia of today. Twelve years after his first visit, downtown Sylvia was changed. A near-ghost town supplanted the town he remembered, as he walked up and down the four-block stretch past one dark door after another, and countless soap-opaqued windows. One or two shops remained, including a sizable grocery store that looked new. But there was no sign of the drugstore with the cherry Coke- -only empty, dark buildings.

Joe stepped into the grocery store, itself an enigma. One cashier stood on duty. She was the only person in the building, it appeared, until Joe arrived. Deserted aisles sported a full line of grocery items, but no one was inside buying them. Another small business on the threshold of evaporation, Joe told himself.

Joe's interest in the vanished drug store piqued as he drove the groceries home to Inga. As he unpacked the shopping bag, he said to her, "Grams, do you remember that drugstore in town where you used to be able to get fountain Cokes and ice cream sodas? I couldn't find it. I wanted to stop in and, I don't know, see if the cherry Cokes were as good as I remember them."

"Oh, yes," Inga replied. "My cousin, Bert, used to run that drugstore. It's gone now. It was on the corner between West Street and Claiborne Avenue. It's been gone at least five years."

"What happened to it?"
Inga told him the troubling story.

For decades it had been a gathering place for neighbors in the town. Each Saturday morning, farmers would converge there to exchange news, notes about their crops, and gossip. Tobacco was chewed and liquor sipped. Farm wives picked up whatever they needed that wasn't growing in their fields at home.

The drugstore was among the last establishments to fall to the economic woes that ate so many businesses. The store was vintage Norman Rockwell, with ceiling fans, white hexagonal ceramic tiles on the floor, and stools where you could sit at the counter and order fountain soda pops, sundaes, and ice cream cones. Through the previous forty years of its life, it changed little, but farm failure, unemployment, and the mass exodus to the city had rendered the community a skeleton of its former self. With its itinerant part-time pharmacist, the drugstore continued to do a fair trade owing to an aging population whose prescription needs flourished in an otherwise inert economy.

Bert had a routine she had held for decades in the drugstore, revolving around her crowd of regulars who kept her company and drank coffee. Her regulars were like family.

They would arrive early in the morning and their faces changed throughout the day as one farmer left and another arrived, but the coffee was poured continuously, and at six p.m., the door was locked and Bert went home.

One day, about five years before Joe's summertime visit, one of her regulars remarked to Bert that the ceiling was sagging. Bert said yes, she needed to have that looked at. Then she kicked them out, locked the door and went home. At six-twenty, the entire roof collapsed in on the building and within moments it was reduced to a pile of dust and rubble. One of the last in a long strip of hollowed-out, musty storefront shells — the dark and yawning symbols of decaying rural America— died in this poignant way.

Inga told Joe of the roof collapse over cookies and ice tea, and the image stuck with him. It was tragic and bittersweet — and also funny in a macabre sort of way. When he got back home, he would tell the tale to his friends, and he would be laughing. He wondered if he would have felt his mother's spirit, or at least triggered a memory of her, if he could have stepped inside the store one last time. Now he'd never know.

One thing was for sure: a person couldn't take a snapshot and thereby stop the ravages of time. Buildings age, people age, times change. A community that once flourished on soybeans and corn was now barely surviving on crystal meth. And the old timers were dinosaurs – out-of-date, stale, and irrelevant. They looked back wistfully on an old and archaic heyday, a simpler time. At least it seemed so to a seventeen-year-old from the big city.

His grandfather Joe might be the exception to the rule. As wise as his years, and as sophisticated as his son's college degree, Gramps seemed out of place in his own hometown. "Seemed" was the operative word to Joe. It was early. He was new to this place. There was much left to see and learn about old Joe and Inga. But whatever the discoveries turned out to be, there was joy and anticipation in the knowledge that part of them was inside of him. Theirs was his legacy, too.

CHAPTER 3

It was under the slow awakening of his legacy, and the burgeoning understanding of this small-town culture, that Joe settled into his summer routine. Up early in the morning to follow Gramps around and lift and move things the eldest Joe no longer could, check on the livestock, or go into town for Inga, if needed, the work schedule soon became predictable, but most afternoons he was left to explore and play with the animals or rent videos .

"Third!" his grandmother hollered from downstairs early one morning. Joe's eyes opened and he focused on the clock radio she had put in his room. It read five-forty-five. Fifteen more minutes. He turned over and dozed off, barely aware of her voice.

Then Inga appeared at the bedroom door. "Third? Joe needs you in the barn. Better get up."

He sat up and headed to the bathroom. Farm people, he mused drowsily, believe six a.m. is sleeping in.

Joe went out to the barn to find old Joe. His grandfather was dragging a tall extension ladder out of the barn, and Joe hastened to pick up the far end and carry it.

"What are we doing today, Grandpa ?"

"Repairing shutters on the house."

"It's still dark."

"It won't be by the time we're ready to get up the ladder."

"What shutters are broken?"

"I'm going to nail the shutters closed over the rooms we don't use much — or, rather, you are — and fix the others so they can close good and tight from the inside."

"Why?"

"It's just that time of year, boy."

"You do this every summer?"

"I at least give them a good look. While we're at it, we'll replace the door on the storm cellar. I bought a new piece of wood for the door and a 2 x 4 to brace it on the inside."

Joe was not going to have the afternoon to loaf. Just as well. The time passed faster when he was busy.

"Gramps, we don't do any of this at my house. I don't get it."

Gramps, smiling to himself, stopped in place and surveyed the vista. "Look around, Third. What do you see as far as you can see?"

"Corn and soybean fields."

"Right. And what don't you see much of?"

"Huh? I don't know. There isn't much else to see."

"Yep, this isn't the city. There are no skyscrapers, hardly any trees, and the land is flat as a hotcake. When it storms here, there ain't nothing to break the wind. When a storm comes, it comes in hard."

"So, you go to the storm cellar."

"Right."

"I guess I never connected that the storm cellar was actually for storms."

His grandfather chuckled. "Yeah, it's for storing supplies, too. We keep a few bottles of water down there, candles, rope, a transistor radio, and your grandma puts up some corn relish and tomatoes in the fall, and some other things, and stores the jars down there."

"I've been down there. I thought it was just like, you know, another closet, only outdoors."

"I dug that cellar out not long after Inga and I bought this property. It's pretty solid. See, your grandma doesn't like storms.

"Truth to tell, Third, these shutters and doors have needed a good going-over for a few years, but I just can't do it by myself anymore, and I hate to call on neighbors. But while you're here for the summer, well, Inga and I are mighty glad to have you. We've been real lucky with the weather. The whole county has."

"I live to serve," the boy remarked, amused, but the words rested on him for a few minutes. He couldn't remember his father ever telling him anything like that — a confession that he was needed, or even wanted. Joe II was always with a client, at a dinner, or in a meeting. Nothing he needed a son for. Third had felt for as long as he could remember, that he was an unnecessary burden to his father.

The boy didn't say anything to old Joe, but he thought he would keep his granddad's words for a long time.

Gramps continued his explanation as the boy followed him into a tool shed and helped the older man collect supplies. "I've seen some amazing storms in my lifetime, Third. Ones out of horror movies. I've seen rolling black clouds two miles high come through a county carrying dust so thick, a body couldn't breathe. I've seen animals run away by the thousands from these storms. I've seen storms like this bury a tractor in dirt. And that was before I saw my first tornado.

"What the hell are you talking about, Gramps?"

Old Joe smiled at the boy and chuckled. "Look, Third, you have to forgive me. You look and act so much like your father, I forget sometimes that we don't know each other very well yet. There's a lot of history in our family I guess your dad didn't share with you, and a lot of interesting things have gone into my life and your Gram's life. You know how the Chinese say, 'May you live in interesting times'? It's a curse. Your Grams and I have lived in some very interesting times."

After the third upstairs window shutter was nailed, the boy asked, "Are you going to leave these shut all the time now, Gramps? It seems a shame."

"I guess so, boy. I won't have anyone to get them back open for us."

Something else to think about.

After a moment, the older man continued, "You reach an age and you have to scale everything back, ease the load."

Joe learned during the day that he was nervous about standing high on a ladder. The first few windows were scary, and his knees shook. Then he got used to it, and told himself that if he didn't look down, it wouldn't bother him. He had to do this for the old man, so he would.

His resolve shook when he lost his footing late in the day. Too cocky, a little tired, and he almost fell. He caught himself, and the old man on the ground saw him falter and braced the ladder, averting an accident. The younger Joe mentally catalogued all the things he had learned that day.

As the sun set lower in the sky, and the two began picking up tools and the ladder, Inga appeared holding an orange tabby kitten. She rubbed it against her face.

"Are you men ready to eat?"

"Yes, ma'am," they said in unison. Third, now on the ground, took the kitten from Inga and kissed the top of the kitten's head.

"Be in shortly," the older man said.

Over a dinner rich in home-grown vegetables and fresh chicken, the boy had a lot to say, which delighted his grandparents. He had been there almost two weeks and had been somewhat distant and laconic. Today, he started to come out of himself and talk about his life at home, his friends, interests, and aspirations. And he had questions.

"Gramps, what's the worst tornado you've seen here?"

Old Joe thought for a minute, his eyes distant with memories.

"Tornado? There was a twister that came through the county about fifteen years ago that was really something. I exchanged three head of cattle with Wade Turner down the road."

"What? What do you mean?"

"Well, when we came out the cellar, the property was torn up. Spent six months puttin' it right, 'cause the strangest thing was what these twisters do. They can pick something up, travel it a few miles, and set it down in the strangest places and in the strangest way.

"I was picking up the yard and I found a cow under a piece of aluminum sheeting. The sheeting came off the top of Turner's shed, and the cow came out of his yard. I rang him up, and he said he had two of my calves."

"Were they okay?"

"Oh, no. They were all dead. Dead of their injuries, but it just tells you how strange those twisters are. One year, one of 'em sent a cyclone fence pole clear through the barbershop window in town and speared the barber chair. Dead center. If a man had been in that chair he would have been stabbed through the heart."

"Wow," Joe said, deadpan. Then, after a moment, "My mom died in a storm."

"Yes, she did," Inga interjected, passing potatoes. "You stayed here for two weeks after while your pa straightened things out."

"I don't remember that."

"You were real little. Don't you remember me taking you to Bertie's drugstore and buying you a pop?"

"That was my mom who took me."

"No, Third. It was your Grams. I don't believe your mama ever came to Sylvia. Not even once that I recall," old Joe remarked.

Joe was silent, bewildered how he could have remembered something so wrong. He could see his mom in his mind. He could see himself look at her on the counter stool. How could he have made that up?

"You were just about five, Third. You've had twelve years to mix that up in your head. I guess you just wanted it to be your mom," Inga said .

"Then I don't have any," he said, shaking his head.

"Any what?" Inga asked.

"I don't have any memories of my mother. I have pictures, so I know what she looked like, but the only thing I thought I knew, I had it wrong. I don't have anything of her in my mind."

His grandparents remained silent.

Then the old man said, "I guess that storm that took your ma from us was a trickster all right. As I heard the tale, she was on the way to get you from the day school when it happened."

"Yeah, it was kind of a freak accident. If it hadn't been for picking me up . . ."

"Oh, mercy, don't blame yourself, boy!" Inga burst.

"I don't, Grams. Not at all. But do you ever think about fate? What if you had turned left instead of right, or gone up a side street instead of the main road, or any number of tiny decisions we all make every day? Any one of them could change your whole life. What if you drop off the dry cleaning first and then go to the bank instead of the other way around? Then you learn that the other way around would have walked you into an armed robbery, and maybe you'd have died.

"Or you could meet someone you'd marry someday at the bank, but only if you go there first. We have no idea.

"If she had decided to leave me at the school, I would have been safe from the storm, my dad said. And she would still be here."

"I've thought of that dozens of times, Third," Inga said, "but you can drive yourself crazy with that. I know it's hard, but it's best to just accept that what's done is done. Now, are you going to want pie?"

"You're making me fat, Grams," the boy returned, smiling.

"Not to worry, Third. I'm gonna work that fat right off you," his grandfather said, also smiling .

"What else is a good slave for? At least you don't beat me," he said.

The smile disappeared from each of his grandparents' faces, and they were quiet a minute.

"Third, do you think your daddy sent you to us as punishment?" his grandfather asked.

Joe flushed, feeling caught. He didn't know how to answer, so he improvised, hoping to take the sting out.

"Well, at first I did. I mean, I wanted to have my summer to myself and hang out. I didn't expect to be sent off. But nothing I ever do or plan is the way my dad wants it. Most of the time I feel like I'm just another chore for him to attend to.

"But now I think it was a combination of getting rid of me for a few months and also that, well, you can use the help, Gramps. So, I don't mind. Not at all."

Joe realized he should have started and stopped with the acknowledgment that Gramps needed help. No one believed otherwise. The rest was overkill. Trying too hard to convince. It was lame. He would have to find a way to make it up to them.

Gramps, sensing the kid's discomfort, shifted the topic. "You know, Third, tornados aren't the only storms I've seen," he stated. "I told you about the black clouds of dirt I saw in my childhood."

"Yeah, but you didn't explain, and I really can't picture it. When did that happen, and why?"

"'Where' is a better question," Gramps said. "I came up during the Depression in the panhandle of Oklahoma. My dad and mom had a wheat farm there, and when the drought of the 30's set in, we were living during what they called 'the dirty thirties.'"

"How did the drought make it dirty?" Joe asked, relieved that the topic changed.

"It was all a combination of Mother Nature at her ugliest, and human error at its most foolish, I guess," Gramps began.

Inga picked up dishes and began moving them to the kitchen. She waved young Joe off when he tried to help. She was glad to see her two men talking and getting to know each other. She knew of the dirty thirties, having lived with her husband for many decades. She remembered that the thirties she had known in Germany were plenty dirty in their own way.

Gramps continued, "You see, about that time, farming and other technology began to improve, and new, advanced farming equipment was made available to farmers. I was just a kid but I remember that many of them, including my dad, bought the machinery on time. It was a booming era for farming. Europe was decimated after the first big war, and there was nearly no limit to the amount of wheat a farmer could plant and harvest and find buyers for overseas.

"The farmers plowed every inch they could, but they did it with the wrong rules. A lot of the farmers had migrated from the east to farm in the Plains without really knowing that rain in that part of the world isn't guaranteed. So, they took out the grasses that kept the soil moist, and planted grains. Lots and lots of grains. When the sky dried up, there were no grasses left to hold the moisture in the ground, and the wheat largely died without enough water. The soil became airborne."

"Airborne?" Joe asked, scooting his chair closer.

"Yep. Strong winds came in. Fierce ones, and they picked up the dry, dusty soil and moved it, sometimes hundreds of miles. One dust storm went all the way to Chicago and dropped tons of dirt on the city. Some of the dirt was black and some of it was red, so the authorities could tell from the color where it came from. Some came from as far as Colorado."

"Wow," Joe said in a flat voice.

A six-year-old Joe MacDonald didn't know any way to live other than to be dirty and hungry. He lived in a broken-down shack in northeastern Oklahoma, a hundred miles west of Tulsa. His earliest memories were of filth covering everything in his home, and of his little brother, Obadiah, coughing through the night with the dust pneumonia that had crippled so many families and had killed so many children. It was 1937, and the drought had gone on for years. Most of the community was starving, or malnourished, and the children were dying from that as well as from pneumonia. Times were desperate, and the only hope articulated by anyone followed the phrase, "If it rains . . . ."

The visits from an officer of the bank became weekly. When did Liam MacDonald think he'd be able to pay on his loan? The bank had been very generous and very understanding, the bank officer assured Liam, but the patience of everyone in the county was wearing thin.

When the bank eventually repossessed the tractor, Liam asked the officer how he expected payment when there was no longer any way to plow a field. The bank man responded by asking Liam how he expected to plow a field with no soil on it.

Liam spent that evening at the kitchen table in the darkness with his head in his hands. The weight of fear and desperation weighed him down like a boulder. He watched his wife, Amy, in a chair holding Obadiah, wiping the stream of snot-soaked mud from his nostrils. "Is he any better tonight?" he asked his wife.

"What do you think?" she replied.

The following day, a rumor circulated that a tractor was available on the far side of the next county. The owner would give it away for free to the first comer. Liam packed Joe, Amy, and the baby up in the truck and headed to the neighboring county, hoping and praying to be the first there to get the free tractor that would be the difference between life and starvation.

But only if it rained.

The plan was for Liam to drive the tractor home while Amy drove the truck and Joe held onto the baby. It was a family affair, and everyone had a job.

The job turned out to be more daunting than the MacDonalds counted on. When they got to the Miller farm and interviewed Mr. Miller, he told them that yes, he would give them his tractor. He was giving up and moving west to California where there were jobs and opportunities picking fruit. The tractor was Liam's for the digging.

What did Mr. Miller mean, "for the digging?" Liam asked. Mr. Miller gestured Liam to follow him out back. There the tractor stood under a mountain of dust with barely the top of its steering wheel visible. It was parked near a fence that was also covered with dirt. It stood to take Liam, Amy and Joe most of a week to dig out the tractor, because they had to stop frequently to cough the dust from their lungs.

Amy put her foot down. She took her husband aside and told him, "I'm likely to lose this baby from the dust in his chest and there ain't a thing I can do for him. I'll be damned if I lose my other son, and you too, to this dirt. No. We're leaving it alone. Let's go home."

Joe didn't remember his father's reply;', only that his mother wanted no part of the buried tractor. As they piled back into the truck, Mr. Miller admitted that the MacDonalds had been the fourth family to come for the tractor, and leave without it.

Third listened to the tractor story in silence. His grandfather fell silent as well, after the tale and young Joe considered, then dismissed, dozens of questions. At last, he asked, "Your father, Liam – is that his picture in the living room?"

"Yes, it is. How did you know that?" his gramps replied evenly.

"Lucky guess. Did your mother lose the baby ?"

"Yes, she did," the old man replied. "It took another month. The doctor came out to the farm and gave her some medicine to try on him, but the doc told my mom that for one this young, whose lungs were so small, the dust takes over. There isn't enough lung left for the child. After he died, my momma was never the same. I think it led to her early death, too."

CHAPTER 4

Sarah Dednum walked the streets of Sylvia to get out of the house. She called it "getting her exercise," or "taking a walk," or "getting some air." But these were all euphemisms. She was escaping.

Her boyfriend, Jack, had rented a house in Sylvia, and she had moved in with him. It was an old frame, dirty yellow in color, nearly falling down, but cheap as hell and more than enough space.

The mold in the rotting floor boards and roof eaves drove her allergies crazy, and the smells downstairs were also maddening . Jack supported them making crystal meth in the basement.

Typically, Sarah took their baby on these walks, but today she left the child in Jack's care. He was on the sofa with a ballgame on the TV. Jack was a good father. He changed diapers and played with the baby, but Sarah hadn't thought very far ahead when she hooked up with him. What would the future hold? What would become of her and baby Dustin when the inevitable ramifications of Jack's line of work became a reality?

Having enough to eat and a roof was enough for Sarah right now . Expecting much more than that was for people whose station was higher than hers.

Sarah left the meth alone. Jack had tried to share it with but, she had learned she was in the family way. She considered what meth was made with: drain opener and charcoal starter, and thought better of it.

Sarah had seen some of Jack's customers become violent on meth. She didn't want the baby around it, but couldn't support herself or little Dustin without Jack's cottage industry, so she continued to tread a thin line, abstaining from the meth, but tolerating Jack's fondness for it.

Jack was quite fond of it. It made money and provided a good time.

In every ashtray and several drawers in the home lay little glass tubes and cigarette lighters –tools for the user to fill the glass tube with a shard of the meth, light it until smoke appears, and then inhale it. Jack Sample was happy to demonstrate for his new customers several ways to ingest the chemical.

Routinely, Sarah purchased calamine lotion and anti-itch cream. Jack felt bugs crawling on him, and would claw himself raw. His teeth had grown dark brown and rotted. The winning smile Jack had when she met him was preserved only in the photo album. The bottom incisors had fallen out, and his breath was bad. She had noticed that Jack's twitch was worsening, too. Uncontrolled movements of his head and hands evidenced that the legacy of his meth jones had taken over his body–another of the symptoms known to beset many meth lovers . Sarah walked along the barren streets of Sylvia toward the post office. She told Jack she needed to buy a money order and pay something on the electric bill. It was as good an excuse as any to get out of the house, and she was in no hurry to get back home.

As Sarah neared the post office, a pickup truck pulled in front and parked. White but dusty, she gathered it was off one of the farms outside of town. When the driver stepped out, she didn't recognize him, but surmised the young man was about her age.

They reached the door at the same time and the young man smiled at her as he held the door for her. She smiled back. She wondered who he was. Did Jack know him? Where was he from?

"Ah ain't seen you in these here parts, stranger," the young man said, doing a very bad John Wayne impersonation.

"I haven't seen you either, stranger. What brings you to our town?" Sarah replied.

"I'm staying with my grandparents for the summer since my old man got rid of me. They're outside of town. The MacDonald farm."

"Okay, I don't know the MacDonalds."

"Well, you're in luck. You just met your first MacDonald, Joe. My family calls me Third. You can call me either one." He stuck out his hand to shake hers. He was too friendly, too eager. She cautiously returned the handshake, revealing her first name only.

"Third?" she questioned.

"Yeah, I am the third Joe in a row. My grandfather, father, and me."

"Oh, I see. Joe the third."

"So, Sarah the first, tell me something. What does an average garden-variety Sylvian do to have fun around here?"

"Around here? Leave town and go somewhere else."

"That, I believe," he said, laughing. "Where do you go?"

"Oh, we get together with friends and hang out. Have a few drinks or whatever. There's some stuff to do in Macon. Depends on what you like."

"Almost anything beats hanging around the farm."

"Understandable. Where do you come from?"

"St. Louis. I'm a city boy. I like action, the fast lane. Bright lights, the bustle of a booming metropolis. You know, an occasional bowling alley or movie house—something—anything."

Sarah laughed, sympathizing , and found herself warming to the big-city stranger with the ebullient charm. His wide smile was as engaging as Jack's used to be. It brought back a vague, pleasant memory of an ancient flirtation with a handsome man before the baby and the meth came into her life.

She stepped to the counter and bought a money order.

"Where do you live?" Joe asked.

"On Broad Street, a few blocks over. The yellow house with the sagging porch."

"All of the houses around here are yellow with sagging porches."

"No, they aren't," she replied, with feigned defensiveness. "Some of them have sagging roofs."

Laughing, Joe stepped to the counter and presented a slip to the clerk who retrieved a rather large box and gave it to him.

"Maybe you could take me on a tour some time."

Joe regretted the come-on line as soon as it was out of his mouth. He only wanted a friend his age, someone to talk to. But his words sounded like a decision. It might be one of those little decisions, like turning left or right, that changes the future. He wished he could take the words back.

Sarah, however, sensing a flirtation, demurred. "I have a boy-friend at home, and a baby, so I guess I shouldn't take strange men on tours. What did you get in the mail?"

"I don't know yet. It's from my stepmom. Clothes, probably. Nothing interesting."

"Any nice dress-up duds in there, you think?"

"I haven't had much need for those."

"I'm thinking there is a dance at the VFW hall in Macon every Saturday night. I usually go. I could introduce you to people. You could wear nice jeans."

"What about your boyfriend?"

"He'll have to work."

"I see. Where does he work?"

"He has a business in the home."

"Gotcha. What does he manufacture?"

The girl bristled, and Joe felt a wall go up.

"He's in entertainment, sort of. You might say he manufactures a good time for people. "Smells bad, though." She said the last sentence softly, as if to herself, as though she didn't intend him to hear her, but he did.

So, thought Joe, this cute girl has a boyfriend who runs a meth factory in their house and entertains customers on Saturday nights. And she has a baby.

This girl is in trouble, no doubt. As cute as this girl is, he told himself to leave it alone. Leave it alone. Even if she was easy and needy, he wanted no part of this mess.

Once after coming home stoned, his punishment had been a Saturday-long class on the dangers of drugs, what's in them, what happens to users, and so on. He knew more about meth than he ever wanted to know.

Leave it.

Still, he reminded himself, if he kept it friendly, well, he sure could use a friend, and this might be better than nothing for now.

"Okay, well, I could pick you up and drive you. . . .."

"Oh, no. I'll just see you there. I'll go alone, or with a girlfriend. It's on the main drag through Macon, right off the highway. It ought to get rocking' about nine."

The pair walked out of the post office, and Joe strode toward the truck. "Can I give you a ride home at least?"

"I have another stop to make."

"I don't mind taking you. Where to?" he said, opening the passenger door.

"I guess I'll just go to Hocks. I need lotion."

"Hocks? The convenience store by the highway? Won't that be expensive?"

"Insanely. I usually get the large bottle at Walmart, but I don't have a car today—it broke down—and can't get to Macon."

"Macon, it is, then. Hop in."

The pair rode twelve miles to Macon, which served as the region's shopper's mecca. Joe followed the girl around the Walmart and watched with interest as she placed a bottle of charcoal lighter and two pints of peroxide in the shopping cart.

"What's your boyfriend's name?"

"Jack."

"How long has Jack been using glass?"

Sarah spun around and stared at him, shocked and threatened .

"How do you think you know so much?"

"Doesn't take a rocket scientist. Meth is the only in-home business around here, I believe, and certainly the only one likely to do business on Saturday night. Plus, charcoal starter and peroxide are a dead giveaway."

"I'd like to go home now, please. You're too smart for your own good."

"So I'm told. Your boyfriend is deep in his jones. He has the itch, and you buy calamine lotion all the time, don't you? And it doesn't do much, does it? And he's never going to stop, is he? And you're raising a kid with this guy?"

"You're way over the line."

"Certainly. And I wouldn't say a word, and I'm not judging, I'm really not. But he'll never give up the meth. You should know that.

"One other thing. I am not getting busted with you. Take the cold pills out of your purse and put them back on the shelf."

Sarah stared—caught, angry, embarrassed . She turned and headed back to the cold pill aisle.

"I don't think about Jack's jones, as you call it. And it's none of your business. I think I'll call a friend to pick me up. Thanks anyway."

"Okay. Topic dropped. I won't mention it again. Let's get your stuff, and I'll take you back. Lips sealed. Won't bring it up."

"Fine."

"Except for one thing . . ."

Sarah looked at him, sullen, eyes narrowed.

"Sarah, if I can make you that easily, I wouldn't kid myself if I were you, that the sheriff isn't hip to your boyfriend's factory. You may want to change addresses before the ax falls."

Sarah was silent.

The ride home wasn't as much fun as the ride to Macon. Sarah didn't talk, and Joe's attempt at witty banter was unreciprocated. He had given her a lot to think about, exacerbating her fear of the house being raided She would lose custody of Dusty, and it would be the end of everything.

Sarah often used her imagination to make the world look prettier. She didn't think about bad things, so they weren't real. Now, Joe's words forced her to focus on the real threat Jack's lab posed. She now realized she was on borrowed time, and so was Dusty.

When Joe dropped her in front of her house, she thanked him coolly for the ride and shut the car door behind her.

"Hey, I'll see you some Saturday," Joe offered through the open passenger window as she turned away.

"Yeah, okay. See ya."

Joe made a mental note to ask Gramps where the VFW was in Macon. He felt a little apprehensive about showing up at such an event, but it was the first time in weeks he would have a chance to meet people his own age, get out, do something.

A voice in his head whispered that he had turned Sarah off by making her boyfriend as a meth chemist. But at the time, the impulse to show her his sophistication overwhelmed his social graces. Bad planning, he told himself. Shortsightedness.

He realized she wouldn't want to see him there, but he would go anyway, if not this Saturday, then a Saturday very soon. Maybe he could make it up to her. And if not, at least he would be out of the house on a Saturday night. While he didn't fancy befriending glass-heads, he did look forward to making friends with someone near to his age who might have some common interests.

When he got back to the farm, Joe got out the phone directory and called the VFW in Macon. The elderly-sounding woman who answered the phone didn't know much about the band that was scheduled for Saturday night. She gave directions to the hall, and she found a promotional blurb on the bands.

"Warthog plays covers from The Red Hot Chili Peppers, Mari-ah Carey, and The Backstreet Boys among other current favorites," the woman read from the press release. "I hope that helps you. It doesn't mean much to me."

"Warthog is the name of the band?" Joe asked.

"That's what it says. Usually we have country western bands on Saturday night. Very popular. One group, The Dolbys, does a lot of Garth Brooks. At least I know who he is. This'll be the first time this group is in. We'll see how they do," the woman said.

"Thanks," Joe said. "It's a great band name."

As it happened, Joe was a huge fan of the Backstreet Boys, so if nothing else came of his evening out, he might enjoy the music. This plan was shaping up.

CHAPTER 5

Sheriff Mitch Ollman had just returned from a DEA seminar in Columbia, Missouri. Meth had recently shown up for the first time in the college town, so the venue was as appropriate as the sense of urgency. Ollman was fired up about putting meth labs out of business in Shelby County.

He knew of two in Sylvia—where they were, how much they produced, and who traded there. It had been an on-going investigation for months, and he was close to pulling the trigger.

The investigation had been time-consuming and difficult. No one wanted to talk to the authorities about the burgeoning meth epidemic in the region. Clearly, money was changing hands — a lot of it — and that always buttoned up lips.

Ollman had sent two deputies to Paris, Missouri on weekends for two months to watch a couple of suspected drug houses there. The sheriff in the slightly larger Missouri town had sent two men to Sylvia to watch houses. With plain clothes and changing unmarked cars, the subterfuge seemed successful. The suspects didn't seem to know they were being watched and photographed.

It was a double-edged sword, the small town, Ollman reminded himself. The same familiarity that lent itself to identifying a drug house by its flow of out-of-town traffic also alerted the drug dealers because strange surveillance cars—strangers in general—were sources of suspicion.

The deputies from Paris had seen plenty, however. Ollman had a thick file of photos, license plate numbers, and complaints from neighbors demanding the drug houses be shut down.

The department identified the frequent patrons, mostly kids, but also one or two out-of-towners, suspected of buying in quantity and distributing. Those were the most wanted. This, Sheriff Ollman believed, could be a big pay-off. He planned to bust the distributors in the act of a big buy .

Ollman's training called for a detached, business-like air toward police operations of this kind. One could see from a distance the harm done, the lives ruined, the ugly avarice created by these in-home labs. But Ollman wasn't entirely detached. His teenaged daughter, Emily, had been targeted by one of these dealers. Two years before, the then eleven-year-old had been sitting at a middle school tailgate party on the school's parking lot when a man she later described as Phil Collins with bad teeth approached her and invited her to try some glass. "You'll feel great," he had told her, and the girl, aching from menstrual cramps , wanted to feel great.

The moment she ingested the chemical, Emily knew she'd done something stupid. Her father regaled the family with dinner table tales of the destructiveness of the meth. She left, walked home, and went straight to her father with the tale. Dizzy and hyper, she confessed what she'd done, and cried in his arms, pleading with him to fix it so she wouldn't be an addict.

Ollman kept an eye peeled for a guy like Phil Collins with bad teeth on every street tour he'd gone on since. Though two years had passed, his outrage had not quelled, and he intended to find this dealer and take him down within or without the confines of the law.

Ollman's sole hiccup in his plan to drive out the labs was the circuit judge in Shelby County. Sheriff Ollman didn't know whether Judge Harlem Bennett was stubborn, stupid, or a meth addict himself, but his criteria for issuing a warrant were exceedingly unreasonable, and while the sheriff was close to making arrests in the case, and had a compilation of evidence that would immediately convince most judges, Bennett was soft on criminals. The frequent buyers that Ollman had identified on Broad Street were expected to show up Saturday night, according to the pattern established by the surveillance, and when they did, he would be poised to strike if Bennett would let him.

When that Saturday night arrived, however, Sheriff Ollman was cursing, full of piss and vinegar. He'd planned this raid for months, called in police from the next county, coddled the state's attorney with promises of rounding up a number of dealers, and, by way of a deluge of phone calls, had finally gotten the judge to put the grease on the wheels.

Now it was all going to be derailed by this damned storm that was set to blow in. The usual traffic he expected on a Saturday night on Broad Street wasn't going to show up with a twister and pounding rain coming. There would be no one there to bust other than Jack Sample, and he could get Sample anytime. There were bigger fish to fry and now they were going to be swimming away in rainwater.

"Mitch, we'll just set it for next week, is all," said Under-sheriff Bill Fast. "No harm, no foul."

"Plenty of harm, plenty of foul, Bill," Ollman countered. "You know how big this is. I've got law enforcement coming from the state capital. I've alerted everyone but the press about this bust. I have a time-sensitive search warrant, and a certainty that if I hold this for another week, word will leak about the raid, and this investigation will come to nothing."

"That's a problem. We're sure we've got deputies on the take. We don't know that it isn't these very meth labs paying the moles in the department," Fast agreed. "But the weather report is awful. Law enforcement will be happy to stay where they are tonight."

"If we don't do this tonight, there's no point in doing it at all. I say we be ready in case. I say we park around the corner in unmarked cars in case the storm breaks," Ollman said, disregarding Fast's words.

"I say we stay here so we can go to the basement when a twister shows up," Fast returned.

"You that scared of a storm?"

"I've lived here all my life, Sheriff. You can't take a warning like this lightly. A twister can pick up a car, marked or unmarked, and toss it a hundred feet in a second without breathing hard."

"I guess you're right. Damn!" Ollman thought Fast was being overly cautious, but he realized that this had to be done right, not half-baked, which it would be if he attempted it now. He might as well settle in for the night. At least, he mused, if word did get out, it would scare the users away from Broad Street, if only for a while. It was a small comfort.

CHAPTER 6

Joe got permission from old Joe to have the truck Saturday night. His grandparents were glad the boy found something to do. They knew he was bored and friendless, and this dance was a good opportunity to make some new friends.

As it happened, the box from Joe's stepmother contained CDs, a CD player, some videos, and a money order. Liz was all right, Joe thought. Thinking about him all the time. He would use the money to buy some clothes. Sarah said the party at the VFW called for nice jeans. He wondered what that meant in Macon. It might mean a sports coat, but was more likely to mean a tee shirt without holes in it. Whatever it meant, the last thing he wanted to do was look like an outsider.

In the end, a khaki sports jacket would match his khaki Dockers, more or less, along with a black tee shirt, would be good enough.

It turned out, he needn't have worried. As Joe entered the VFW, the fashions ranged from grunge to business casual, so he didn't stand out. The dark, smoky room was filling up, and the band was setting up to play. Joe anticipated ten minutes of being able to start a conversation with someone before the music made it impossible.

Most of the people he saw were a few years older than he was. No sign of Sarah, and most people looked paired off. Disappointing. The beer was running out the taps in force, so Joe figured he'd give it a shot. He walked up to the bar and ordered a beer. The bartender smirked as if reading his age, but served him anyway. He drank the beer slowly, making a mental note to get Tic-Tacs at Huck's before going home. He didn't need a scolding. He'd nurse the beer and be okay by time to drive home. If Sarah never showed up, well, hell and damnation! He'd drive home early with one beer in his gut and call it a lesson learned.

A man stood next to him at the bar, a youngish fellow, and friendly. "Hey, how's it going? John Taylor. I don't think I've seen you around." John stuck out his hand and Joe shook it.

"No, you haven't. I'm just here for the summer, working on a farm in Sylvia. Joe MacDonald."

"You here alone?"

"Yeah, I planned to meet up with somebody, but she's not here yet."

"Well, come sit with my crowd till she gets here. This way," John offered, pointing across the room. He picked up his two beers and headed off with Joe behind him.

Joe made chit chat with John, his girlfriend, and two other couples. They were introduced, but their names didn't stick with him. His main interest was in watching the door from his seat. He entertained questions about his life in St. Louis, what movies he'd seen, and how he got the gig on the farm. He couldn't complain that these people weren't friendly, he thought, just a little dull.

He'd been there an hour before he saw Sarah at the door. She was spruced up and kind of pretty, he thought. He cautioned himself to curb his impulses. He reminded himself of the meth lab and the baby, and reiterated how important it was to leave the girl be. He just wanted someone to talk to.

When Sarah saw him, she didn't seem surprised. He noted with relief that she didn't seem annoyed either.

"So, you came," she said flatly.

"I came. How've you been?" he asked, berating himself mentally for such a lame start, but he recovered with, "Can I get you a beer?"

"I don't drink beer," she answered in the same disinterested monotone. "I'll take a wine cooler. They usually have 'em. I'm going to sit down." And she did, at an empty table that would seat six people. He guessed she expected more friends and didn't intend to give him much attention, but he should have expected that. This wasn't a date.

He returned with the wine cooler and set it down in front of her. Just as he did, the band started the second set and he raised his voice over the music. "Do you wanna dance with me? It's a fast song. No touching, since you're hooked up and everything."

Joe winced and wondered if he was going to say lame, embarrassing things all evening.

"No, not yet," she yelled back. "My feet are killing me. I had to walk."

"You walked from Sylvia?" he yelled, unbelieving.

"No, the car quit again about a mile and a half out. It's on the side of the highway. It breaks down all the time. Jack will get to it tomorrow. But I sure wore the wrong shoes for all that walking."

"Oh, man   , I'm sorry," Joe said. "Let me know when you're ready and I'll take you home, and I'll stay as long as you want."

"Thanks. You're a nice guy, for a nosy, know-it-all jerk."

"Gee, thanks. And I don't smell bad for a fat guy, I guess."

Sarah laughed. "You aren't fat!"

"No, I'm skinny, but I think we should use all of the back-handed compliments possible, don't you?"

"Definitely. I'm just glad I got here before the rain started."

"It's raining? It wasn't when I came in."

"Not yet, but a storm is blowing in. The sky started to look bad—kind of creepy. I thought I'd get here soaking wet by the time I walked, or get struck by lightning, or something."

Joe was only able to pick up bits and pieces of her explanation because of the loud music, but something else was distracting him. The windows were open, and he could feel the change in air pressure just as he heard thunder. It was loud and nearby. And the humidity had intensified. It was sultry and hot, but the breeze was blowing in cool.

"I see what you mean about the lightning. I just saw some. Did you?"

"Yeah. Glad we're inside."

Without warning, Sarah slipped her foot out of her sandal and plopped it in Joe's lap under the table.

"That appears to be your foot."

"Yes. Rub it for a minute, will ya?"

Joe complied tentatively, a little embarrassed. Her foot was tiny and soft. He didn't speak again until the song ended.

"Don't you want to look at the storm?" he asked. "I used to love to watch storms from my front porch when I was a kid."

"Not really. They make me nervous. Plus, all I can think about is how it is probably leaking water into the baby's room."

"Where is the baby, by the way?"

"I left him with Jack. It's my night out."

"I thought Jack was working."

"Oh, yes, very busy. But I want to remind him that he's a father twenty-four-seven. It's his turn to sit with Dustin."

Joe didn't respond, reasoning anything he could say would offend her. He was still on the more fundamental question of why she would stay with a glass-head and have a baby in a meth house. Best to shut up. Presently, he said, "Give me the other foot."

Just as he did, a member of the band stepped to the microphone and said, "Folks, there's a tornado warning just issued. Seems that several tornados have been sighted to the north and west and we may all have to go to the basement ."

A collective groan went through the crowd. Several people stood and began closing windows just as hail pelted the window screens.

"I wanna go check it out," Joe announced. "I'll be right back." He half-ran to the door and stood under the awning outside. The storm was violent, with blinding rain. The sudden change in air pressure exhilarated him. Cold rain sprayed his face, and he was pelted with hail, but Joe didn't care. He didn't remain outside long, though.

The air turned cold, and the rain surged as the wind blew it horizontally . Joe got a bad feeling. He returned to the table and sat next to Sarah instead of across the table, to avoid foot-rubbing.

"It's getting really wild outside." The tail end of his sentence was drowned out by a crack of thunder that sounded like it was right on top of the building.

Sarah's demeanor changed. Joe noted that her hands were shaking. "I need to go home," she blurted. "I have to see to Dusty."

Joe did not know the baby's name, but he remembered his promise. His baser nature wished to show her his heroic side, strong and capable—in case it mattered someday. The conditions outside became an afterthought. "C'mon. I'll drive you."

At the edge of the parking lot, Joe took off his jacket and draped it over Sarah's head against the rain. He spoke close to her ear to be heard over the storm.

"My truck is two rows to the left of the door. Ready to run?"

She nodded, and the two took off in the pouring rain. They were soaked within seconds because Sarah lost a sandal on the gravel parking lot and was hopping most of the way. She couldn't retrieve the shoe in the dark, but Joe came to the side of her and supported her as they hobbled.

This is useless, he thought. It's going to take forever to get to the truck like this. Joe stopped her on the gravel, and as she stood there with her shoeless leg lifted off the ground, he bent, picked her up, and carried her to the truck. He set her down on one foot and opened the door for her. She scooted across the seat and nodded thanks as he got in behind her and closed the door. Water was running down his face as he smiled back.

"I'm glad you were here," she confessed. "I would have had to sit there all night. Jack would have been furious if he'd had to leave the house, get a ride with somebody and come get me. Thanks for taking me home."

"Not a big deal. Glad I could help." Joe wondered how a guy could be furious with a pretty girl like this when she's stranded in a storm. Sheesh.

CHAPTER 7

The MacDonalds attended services most Sunday mornings at Good Shepherd Lutheran Church in Shelbina. It was about as staid and conservative as young Joe could stand, but he went along as a dutiful grandson.

His affection for his grandparents was growing as theirs was for him, and he wished, on some level, to please them, although religion in any form was not his cup of tea.

It actually was easy. You go in, sit for an hour, think of Marissa Barth, the blonde beauty from last semester's trigonometry class, and what fun you could be having with her on a Saturday night in your house, while Liz and your dad were at a cocktail party at his brokerage firm. You wait for the minister to utter the dismissive, "Go in peace," at the end of the service, then you smile disingenuously at everyone who greets you and pretend you actually want to be there.

The Sunday morning following the storm, Joe began to understand that his grandparents were extraordinary. He woke up with the alarm, showered and dressed for church. He dug through the closet for something nice, since his sport coat was still wet from the night before. If he hurried, he'd have time to throw a small load in the washer—something Inga had taught him to do with the admonition that he was a grown man and should learn to do his own laundry. While he piled his wet khaki pants and jacket in the washer with his black tee shirt, Inga listened to the radio in the kitchen.

When he joined his grandmother, she was toasting bagels. "Hi, Third. I'm glad you made it home okay. The VFW hall was damaged in the storm."

"Damaged? How?" he asked, squeezing her shoulders.

"It took the roof off that place! Four people were hurt and are in the hospital. They stayed upstairs, the news said, while the rest went to the basement. They said it wasn't a tornado, but I have my doubts. Anyway, thank the Lord you got home before all that happened."

"Wow. Who knew? Well, I would have been in the basement with everyone if it weren't for that girl I met who was afraid of the storm and wanted to go home. If I hadn't been driving her back to Sylvia . . ."

Inga nodded at him, and he saw the unflappable look flash in her eyes. His grandmother had seen a lot of things. "I was scared, too," she said. "I don't like storms. I don't like them one bit. It wasn't nearly as violent around here, but I went to the cellar anyway, and took Joe and Lady with me."

"Oh, wow, Grams. I would have stayed home if I'd known. I wouldn't have left you alone. It's like I keep thinking. The tiniest decisions can change your whole destiny," he said.

She nodded. "I wasn't alone. But thank you for caring." She smiled at him.

He hugged her hard. "I care in spades, Grams," he assured her.

Shortly after breakfast, Joe put on clean, dry khakis, and the three piled into the Taurus and drove to church, where an incident occurred, causing Joe to rethink the naïve and sophomoric assumptions he'd made about his grandparents and the gentle, peaceful lives he believed they lived. Perhaps he had rushed to judgment about the simple, reasoned folks they appeared to be.

Inga wore a blue flowered dress that morning, with a straw hat decorated with the blue and pink flowers. The colors looked pretty, Joe thought, accentuating her blonde hair and piercing blue eyes. The senior Joe wore a navy polo shirt with gray pants. Joe had never seen his gramps so dressed up.

Before the service, Joe stood with his grandparents in the narthex as it filled with worshipers. Inga held her husband's elbow, and he covered her hand with his.

"Hey, Okie Joe," a voice came from behind young Joe. The three turned toward the voice. His grandfather reached out with a broad smile, and clasped the hand of a man about his own age.

"Hey, Jim Bob," Gramps bellowed, "Great to see you. How's the family?"

Jim Bob replied, "We're all good, Okie Joe, all managin.' June's parkin' the car. She'll be in to see you in a minute. Who's your young friend?"

Young Joe immediately noticed that the stranger's speech bore the same dialect that his Gramps' speech bore.

"Jim, this is my grandson, Joe the third. He's here stayin' with us for the summer."

"Oh, surely," Jim said, shaking young Joe's hand. "I've heard a lot about you, Joe. Jim Bob Cutter, pleased to meet you. Or should I call you Third, like your grandma does? Great to put a face with the name. Your granddad and I go back a long lotta years. We grew up in the same area in northern Oklahoma. Our dads were both farmers a few miles apart from each other."

"Nice to meet you, Mr. Cutter," Joe replied politely. He wondered what his grandfather had said about him. He chided himself for continuing to greet every stranger with a lame, irrelevant cliché. Jim's smile was so warm that Joe thought this would be as good a place to start as any. He continued, "So you knew Gramps in the Oklahoma days. I'll have to pick your brain some time. I'm betting he was a real troublemaker when he was young, and you might just have a story or two to tell me." Joe returned the friendly smile as he did his best to emulate the local speech patterns.

Jim Bob seemed to Joe to be the first adult he had met since he got to Sylvia who didn't put Joe on his guard. Sure, he was growing to love his grandparents, and he enjoyed their affection, but they were MacDonalds. They had spawned his father, the bane of his life, and were therefore in that same category of people to be guarded around. It's amazing about blood, he thought. As soon as you know you're a blood relative of another person, the relationship changes. The power to hurt or be hurt increases when blood is involved. It matters more. He wondered why blood was so powerful. Joe refocused on the conversation at hand.

Joe's grandfather took Jim Bob by the arm, patted his elbow, and excused himself to greet another parishioner.

Jim Bob turned to young Joe and spoke. "A story? Oh, yeah, I have a tale or two. Okie Joe and I go back fifty years or so. He's a man of courage. I saw him jump a train once that must 'a been goin' twenty miles an hour. Not long after his momma died, I heard he jumped another train with his daddy. It took some stones to jump another train after one killed your momma, all right."

Joe stared at Jim Bob. He was afraid to say anything because he was embarrassed to reveal that he had no idea what the man was talking about. Where on earth, did Gramps jump trains? And why? And what about Gramps' mother dying? This was news to Joe, and he realized he didn't know much about his family. Now, he'd have questions to ask at the dinner table. Wow.

The two chatted for a few minutes more until Joe and Inga gathered Third to enter the sanctuary.

The church bulletin that day announced the arrival of Joshua Caleb Armstead, six weeks old , whose parents, Don and Lynae, had asked for his baptism to take place this Sunday. The service would include the baptism, and the sermon would be truncated to make room for the ceremony.

Joe secretly appreciated the dedication of Pastor Roy in keeping these Sunday services under an hour so that the whole day wasn't wasted.

Pastor Roy began the service by making announcements. The I Am the Bread of Life committee was collecting canned goods and non-perishables for the food bank in town.

Flowers would be sent from the church to the funeral homes servicing those who were killed in the tornados the night before. Church representatives would visit the bereaved this week, and members were invited to bring covered dishes.

The Habitat for Humanity team would be building a home for a single mother and her two little ones in neighboring Elsa, down the road ten miles.

Adult Education classes would be suspended for the summer, and Vacation Bible School would begin the following Sunday at nine thirty. Children ages four to twelve were invited.

"Now please welcome Don and Lynae Armstead and their son, Joshua," the pastor said.

The couple rose from their pew and approached the front. Lynae was carrying the baby in her arms, wrapped in a pretty orchid blanket, and Joe could see a tuft of fuzzy black hair in the crook of Lynae's elbow. The child was asleep and peaceful.

"Because Don and Lynae have consented to raise Joshua in the nurture and admonition of the Lord," Pastor Roy intoned, "and because they have dedicated their child to the faith of the Lord Jesus Christ, and have called upon the Holy Spirit to bring this child to a saving knowledge of Jesus Christ . . ." Roy continued as he raised a cup of water over the child, "I now baptize you, Joshua Caleb Armstead, in the name of the Father, Son, and Holy Spirit." As he spoke these words, he dribbled water on the child's head.

The sleeping child awoke and squalled like it had been slapped and Lynae pressed the baby to her shoulder, in an attempt to comfort the screaming child. Pastor Roy invited both Don and Lynae to state their faith in Jesus Christ and to affirm their desire to see their child grow in the Christian faith. But that part of the ceremony was lost on the witnesses. The child's loud wailing rendered the words of the pastor and the parents unintelligible, and neither Don nor Lynae could comfort their son. Joe had never heard such a small infant cry as loudly as Joshua.

Gramps began to fidget, uneasy with the crying, and Joe could sympathize. The noise was annoying, even painful to listen to.

Gramps rose from the pew, and scooted past Joe, Inga, and another family, before reaching the aisle. He hastily exited out the back to the narthex, letting the sanctuary door close behind him with a dull thud.

Joe watched him, curious and a bit embarrassed when he saw several people turn to watch his grandfather exit the sanctuary.

He looked at his grandmother next to him. Her eyes were closed as if in prayer. She shook her head briefly, as if fighting off an unpleasant thought.

Surely, she must be embarrassed by her husband's behavior. Hell, Joe thought, the shrieking was truly irritating. He, himself, fantasized about stuffing a sock in that kid's mouth. Still, the upset his grandfather displayed was exceptional. He didn't know the senior Joe that well, but whatever was troubling him, drove him out the door, making a scene that embarrassed Inga.

The senior Joe never returned to the service. He sat for a few minutes on the concrete steps outside the church. The memories that sparked the outburst were from an age long past, but the old man was still haunted. Here in 1992, that awful sound, was as troubling and fearsome as it had been six decades ago. He breathed deeply until his hands stopped shaking.

Inga and Joe found him in the Taurus on the parking lot following the service. Joe was uneasy about asking what happened, but could not remain silent. *You're part of this family, or you're not. Ask him.* Joe slid into the back seat and opened his mouth to speak.

Before he could say anything, Inga slid into the front seat beside her husband and looked at her husband with the shrewd, alert look for which she was famous in Joe's eyes. "Are you all right?" she asked.

"Yeah, sorry," Gramps said. He stared out the window, but didn't appear to be looking at anything. "It wasn't just the crying this time. I always hear rabbits, but that child—I guess 'cause he's so little—well, the sound was just exactly like a rabbit."

"Gramps, what are you talking about? You hear rabbits? If I am in this family, I think I should know some things. What happened in there?"

"Aw, Third. Of course, you're part of this family. You're all the family we got, I guess." When Gramps said that, Inga's expression darkened from understanding to anger. She looked down in her lap, her lips pursed.

"I grew up in Oklahoma during the Depression," Gramps began. "That's why Jim Bob calls me Okie Joe. When I was there as a child, and everyone was called an Okie, it was an insult. It was kinda like calling a black man a nigger. Same level of hatred from some folk. But now, folks don't look down on us anymore. If a man came through that time and in that place, and survived, it showed he had some stones. I feel proud now when someone calls me an Okie. It means I'm a survivor."

Inga glanced up at him and nodded.

"But what's with the rabbits?" Joe pressed.

Joe MacDonald was only seven years old when he saw his first dust storm roll across the Great Plains. There had been plenty of them, but Joe's mother had kept him inside with thick sheets of cloth pulled tightly over the windows in a fruitless effort to keep the filth out of the house. It was as dark as night in the house, and the loud hiss that rose from the large dust cloud battering the small shack made the house as noisy as it was dark. The family huddled in fear, much the way Joe would one day learn that his future wife had done in a German basement across the ocean.

Typically, following one of these storms, the family would emerge from the shack to find everything covered in a thick pile of red or brown dust. Days would be spent uncovering tools, fences, and vehicles.

When Joe was seven, another threat joined the dust storms: jackrabbits. That year there had been just a tiny bit of rain, and Liam MacDonald and some of the other farmers had high hopes that something would grow in the nearly dead earth. The drought had gone on for a while, and the topsoil was nearly gone, but the brief, inadequate rain had brought a teaspoon of hope to the farmers. Crops had sprouted. Not much, but there was hope. The tiny snippets of green pushing through the earth must be protected at all costs. Jackrabbits would certainly eat anything green they could find, so when a storm was on the horizon, the jackrabbits feared it as much as the people did. The rabbits were as unpredictable and unwanted as the storm.

Joe was told what to do. He was given a plank of wood, two feet long, with a carved handle small enough for a boy to get his fist around. He was told to hit the rabbits in the head as hard as he could until they were dead.

The prospect horrified the young boy. He loved animals, and it had always distressed him to see the animals just as hungry as he was. He had never, in his life, killed anything.

When hundreds of jackrabbits came from over the hill, chased by a dust cloud, onto the MacDonald's land, the boy's parents were as ready as they could be. Liam and two men from town ran alongside the rabbits, steering them away from the fields of crops and alongside the house where a makeshift enclosure had been built. Joe waited in there with two men from down the road, and his mother, all with weapons of wood.

Joe's alarm mounted swiftly when the first jackrabbit was hit in the head by the neighbor. The rabbit screamed in pain and terror as the man pounded the life out of it. He then moved on to the next rabbit.

Joe watched, frozen and helpless. He knew how important it was to stop these rabbits. Yet he couldn't do it. It wasn't in him to kill an animal, especially an animal seeking to survive. As each rabbit screamed, the child's horror grew. The rabbit screams sounded very much like the sound of a baby crying. The cry was familiar, reminding him of his own baby brother, Obadiah, who had died recently.

Maybe his mother thought so, too. As she broke the skulls of rabbits, their cries were joined by hers. She sobbed with each swing of her wood, and when the rabbits were mostly dead, she went to her boy, knelt beside him, hugged him, and the two sobbed together. She led him by the hand into the house as the blowing dust pelted their faces.

There would be jackrabbit to eat for several nights to come, and his belly would be full for once, but the cost was high. The traumatic memory would stay with Joe MacDonald the rest of his days and jumped to life whenever he heard a baby do the thing that babies do.

"I learned about the Dust Bowl in school," Joe said quietly from the back seat when Gramps had finished his story. "I didn't know it was like that."

"It was much worse than that, but you learn to get along. Someone said to me once, there's no limit to what a person can do—if he ain't got a choice. It hurt me, Third, to watch those rabbits get killed, but it's what my parents had to do, and it's what they expected outta me. Sure, I was too young to be put on that kind of duty, but that didn't matter as much as the need to get it done.

"I never let my parents down again after that. I did what they asked, and I didn't complain about it."

"It was very courageous of your grandfather," Inga added, "to make himself be strong. It's a lot of why I grew to love him so much. He was like my mother was in that way. Backbones of steel, both of them. But your grandfather still can't stand the crying of an infant. Joe would jump up and run out the house whenever your daddy would cry as a baby. He helped out with the baby a lot, but he couldn't stay in the room if there was crying."

"Does it bother you to talk about this, Gramps? 'Cause, I'd like to know more about your life. I think it's important I know stuff."

CHAPTER 8

Early Monday morning, Inga got a phone call from the church office.

"The church is pitching in for the Armsteads. Don is in the hospital. He's got smoke inhalation from a fire he was battling Sunday night," explained Madelyn Scott, the church secretary. "Don has only minimal hospitalization coverage anymore, because of cutbacks in the county. He'll get Workman's Comp, but it may be weeks before he sees money. The medicine he's on will be expensive after he's out, so the church is trying to dig in to help the family with expenses. Can we count on your help?"

"And on the same day as his baby was baptized," Inga said. "I'll be happy to help. What would you like me to do?"

"Inga, since you raise chickens, well, could you see your way clear to bring the family some eggs?"

"Eggs?" Inga said. "Sure, I'll bring over some eggs this afternoon."

She disconnected the call after exchanging amenities, and went out back to where the men were giving fresh water to the livestock.

"Hello?" her voice rang out as she stepped to the fence.

Her husband looked at her and broke out in a smile to greet her. She smiled back before turning to her grandson.

"Third, I have to go to the other side of town this afternoon and take some eggs to the Armsteads. Don was injured in a fire yesterday, and the church is helping out. Can I ask you to drive me over?"

"Don got hurt?" the older man interrupted. "How bad? Is he going to be all right? What should we do?"

The urgency in his voice was a message to Third. This man was important to Gramps, whoever he was.

"Uh, sure, Grams. Do I know this person?"

"Yes," she replied. "He's the father of the baby who was baptized yesterday."

"He gonna come out okay?" the older Joe repeated. His brow was knit with concern.

"Yes, he will, but the medical bills will be a burden, so we're pitching in to cut household expenses."

"What time are we leaving, Grams? I'll get cleaned up."

"About one o'clock will be fine."

"Okay."

When Inga turned, and went back in the house, Third, remembering the events around the baptism, turned to Gramps. "Gramps, have you always been repelled by babies crying since that rabbit thing?"

"Well, sure, son. Your grams told you that, but that whole era was a terrible time for the farmers, and babies aren't the only things that remind me of those times."

"What was the worst part?"

"The bigotry."

"The bigotry? I don't understand."

"I told you that being an Okie was like being black and being called that one word. I don't generally use that word, and I don't have much use for folks who do. I guess I did when I was a kid, but you learn fast how to treat people when you walk in their shoes. The Okies, at least, could clean up, get haircuts, put on nice clothes, and then few people could tell them apart from other whites. Blacks are black all the time, so the bigotry they face is unstoppable."

"Why were the Okies so hated?"

"Well, we were filthy and hungry and poor, and when we got to California, the Californians made us unwelcome. They could tell by lookin' where we'd come from and who we were. The politics and the economics of it all were very ugly."

"How?"

"Well, when our farm was failin', when we were starvin', and most miserable, the bank came and tore apart our home to force us off our land, and then they took control of it. See, my daddy couldn't pay his farm loan when the drought hit, but he heard there was plenty of work pickin' crops in California. Enough to keep us in clover for a long while until we could build up. So, the three of us set out in the truck. This wasn't long after the jackrabbit slaughter. My baby brother had died by that time. Momma and Daddy packed the truck with everythin' we had, which wasn't much after the bank took the house, and we headed west."

Okie Joe paused and turned off the water that had been filling the trough before he continued. He looked at the ground, not his grandson, as though the memories swimming in his head were taking all his attention, and hard to endure.

"We got as far as Arizona, and the truck broke down. I don't remember what was wrong with it, but it couldn't be fixed and we were stranded.

"My folks set up camp on the side of the road, and we slept in the truck for four or five nights. We had nothing to eat unless my daddy could kill something.' One night he killed a rattlesnake and we ate that. It was a bad time."

"I read about a lot of this in school. We did one week in American History class about the Depression and the Dust Bowl, but they never mentioned the bigotry. What do you mean?"

Gramps paused for a minute thinking and remembering.

"I'm gettin' to it." He paused again, picking his words. "Folks can be awful mean to each other, especially when they feel threatened. This time, though, the meanness of some people went way past feelin' threatened. It was meanness to get money."

Joe watched his grandfather rub one foot on the ground as if to scrape off some ugliness. He thought the older man's face seemed to age before his eyes, and imagined his memories were kept in a shallow area of his mind, quick to access, but unwanted and reviled. For several seconds, Gramps seemed to forget where he was. His body jerked slightly when he returned to the present, as if he was seeing his grandson for the first time that afternoon.

"Anyway, no one came along to buy the truck, so we had to leave it in the road. Daddy had so wanted to get a little money for it, but he couldn't. We were just stuck there in the middle of no place. There was no water until he found a little pond about two miles away, and he would go there in the mornings and bring back drinkin' water in an old tin can. It was terrible, tasted like duck shit — probably for a good reason. Mom boiled it, but it still tasted bad.

"Finally, an Okie family came along and offered us a ride to California. The Weavers. They had a daughter I took a liking to, and we played together for a couple weeks. Daddy fed the whole outfit with squirrels and rabbits he shot as we all camped out together every night. I have vivid memories of the stars in the blackened skies at night on that trip.

"Well, anyway, both my daddy and Mr. Weaver had come up on ads from fruit farmers in Kern County, California, wantin' workers to pick fruit. But when we got to Kern, we started seein' signs on the side of the road that told a different tale.

"'Okies, Go Home,' and 'No Work for Okies,' and the like. Now, remember it wasn't just folks from Oklahoma. Once you got all the way out there to California, the hatred was for every farmer that had been run off his land by the dust. Kansas, Texas, New Mexico, Nebraska and Colorado farmers all came to be lumped together as Okies.

"Then it got worse. Daddy and Mama came to find out that there was some fruit-pickin' work after all. Problem was, there were so many folks out there wantin' to pick it, that the price of labor dropped quite for pennies. Ridiculous low wages.

"Mr. Weaver one time took a job pickin' peaches for a guy, Henry. I still remember the name and to this day I dislike the name Henry. Anyway, Mr. Weaver picked 2 tons of peaches himself. That's 4,000 pounds of fruit, and Mr. Henry paid 'im a dollar and a half for his trouble."

"What?" Young Joe cried out. "How could he get away with that? That's slavery, almost."

"Yep, it sure was. He could get away with it because if Mr. Weaver hadn't agreed to a dollar and a half, there would a' been somebody else willin' to do it for even less. That's how desperate folks were.

"That's where the economics came in. Sure, the Okies were hated by the folks who lived there 'cause we were dirty and hungry and unpleasant to be around, but while the people were hatin' us, they also loved the cheap labor . . ."

"Slave labor," Joe corrected.

"Yeah. It's a shame how folks treat each other."

Gramps beckoned Joe with his hand, and the two walked together into the barn.

"It's just human nature," Gramps continued, "that people with money want to keep it, and people without money want to get it. My daddy figured out real quick that the ads they'd seen calling people to California were planted deliberately to bring too many people in to up the competition for work and lower the wages. Basic economics. says that too much supply of somethin' drops its price. Labor, in this case. And it was done deliberately to hurt people who were already hurtin.'

"Eventually, it got so's that the government started to help the Okies. They set up low-cost camps where they could live, and brought in food and even built bathrooms and showers and laundry facilities. I believe the first hot shower I ever remember havin' in my life was at a place like that.

"I don't remember how long we stayed in that camp. It could've been weeks or months, but before too long, my daddy'd had enough of California. One day, he saw me running in a field with Wendy Weaver, the little girl I played with, and he saw that I could run real fast. Faster'n he ever thought a boy my age could go. That give him an idea that if I was fast enough to jump a train, then we could jump one east outta California."

"Oh, yeah. I heard about this story from Mr. Cutter. You lost your mother. That had to be bad. How old were you?"

"Eight or so. Then it was just my daddy and me. It was a bad time," Gramps said. "A lot of folks lost their legs or arms or lives tryin' to jump trains. And those train bosses had some goons on the trains, so if you did jump on one of 'em, you'd just as likely as not get your head beat in anyway.

"I still see it in my mind—my mother torn up by a train. There was a lot of blood. Dad took a chance and we paid dearly. He blamed himself the rest of his life, but I never blamed him."

"Tell me about my great-gramps. What was he like?"

At Gramps' beckoning, the two began hanging tools on the wall hooks in the barn.

"Oh, my dad–Liam–was like a lot of the Okies, but I think the fire in him took longer to die than it did with some. I mean, he got very angry in California because of the terrible injustice that happened, and he wanted to strike back. He went to meetings with other like-minded farmers and workers. My mother disapproved, and they argued. She thought it was dangerous. I guess it probably was. I remember at one point, he was part of a group that wanted to organize a fruit pickers' strike for wages. He wanted every worker he met to sign on, and a few did, but a lot of the organizers like my daddy got their heads bashed in."

"Did he get hurt?"

"No, he was one of the lucky ones. Irony was, my mother was afraid of losing her husband to the struggle, but she was the one who died. She was too young to die."

Joe was mesmerized by the life his grandfather had led. Listening to him was like reading a history book—and Joe liked history—but Gramps' talk was far less dry and removed from reality than schoolbooks.

"Well, about that time, we found out that the plantation holders knew they had all the labor they'd ever use, but kept the Okies coming anyway so's they could pick and choose what they wanted to pay a worker."

Joe stayed quiet, absorbing the story.

"My daddy taught me back then that anywhere there's conflict in the world, it's always, always rich against poor. The working class is always forced to fight like hell for just enough to survive, while rich folks . . .."

Joe was quiet . His grandfather's tone became suspicious. He remembered studying socialism in school, and the lesson concluded that it was a bad system, that it didn't work, and that anywhere it had been tried, it led to the destruction of human rights.

"Gramps, you sound a little like a communist."

His grandfather cracked a smile. "Yeah, son, I suppose I do. Is that so bad?"

"My dad would have kittens if he heard you talk like that."

Gramps chuckled. "Yes, he would. He's heard me talk like that most of his upbringing, and he did, from time to time have kittens, like you say. It caused a lot of trouble, the disagreement, and it broke your grandmother's heart, the way it all happened. But it was years ago."

"I think it broke your heart a little bit, too, Gramps. My dad has spent most of his life not talking to me about anything. But he especially didn't talk to me about you. All the talking, I think, has been between Liz and Grams."

"Joe, I want you to understand one thing and take it with you. Do you hear me?" Gramps said.

"What, Gramps?" It was not lost on the boy that his grandfather called him "Joe." He hadn't ever done that before, and Joe felt validated by it.

"Son, remember this always. If a person is hurt, if a person is being mistreated by others who are more powerful or more numerous or more wealthy or more selfish . . . if one person is made smaller by others for a reason that's wrong . . . I want you to do what you can to stand against it. Speak up. Take action. Whatever it takes. I don't want to see you turn a blind eye to someone suffering. Sometimes it takes courage, more than you think you have. But without people standing against that kind of thing, this isn't a civilization."

"What does that have to do with my father, Gramps?

The old man looked at the ground and took a deep breath. "It's a failure of mine, Third. I didn't teach your dad right about my belief. Or else I taught him too well and he rebelled and went the other way.

"Do you understand?"

"Hey, I've got to go. It's almost one and Gram will want to leave in a few minutes."

"Do you understand, Joseph?"

It was clear then that Joe needed to acknowledge the importance of this to his grandfather and promise to give his words serious thought. "I understand, Gramps. I just don't know if that's in me. I've never tested it. Thanks for the great history lesson, though. I feel like I know you a lot better."

"We'll get there, son. Go on, then. I'll see you two when you get back."

CHAPTER 9

Inga took her seat in the Taurus as Joe piled boxes of eggs in her lap. She had donned a colorful pantsuit with pink flowers and her prettiest smile.

"What are you thinking about, Third?" Inga asked as the two pulled off the property onto the two-lane highway that led into downtown Sylvia. ""You seem a little distracted."

"A talk I had with Gramps earlier. I was thinking of how his views are the opposite of my dad's, and I wonder how they got so far apart."

"They're not really so far apart, I don't think," Inga mused. "They both are good, and they both want the best for everybody. It's only the method where they differ. What did Joe say to you today?"

"He talks like a communist. My dad has preached against communism all my life, so that's what I mean about how far apart they are."

"It's true that Joe leans to the left in his politics quite a bit, but look where he came from. He grew up listening to Woody Guthrie singing folk songs about the plight of the working man and the inhumanity of the wealthy," she explained.

"I have no idea who you're talking about. Who's Woody Guthrie?"

"Oh, I see. Woody Guthrie was an Okie. He was a songwriter and singer in the 30s, and he was a socialist. You know his work. He wrote . . ."

Inga launched into a lilting rendition of "This Land is Your Land."

"Oh, I've heard that song," Joe said when she concluded. "I had no clue it was written by a socialist. My dad would be surprised if he knew that."

"I'm sure he knows it."

"I'm not. My dad always insisted that everything about socialism or communism was anti-American, so a song that raves about the wonder of America would be the opposite of socialism."

"I guess it's understandable how your father got to be that way," Inga remarked. "He has spent his entire career helping very rich people get richer with investments in companies they don't even work for themselves. He's built his own fortune helping rich people get money without working for it. That's capitalism at its best. And it's the opposite of what socialism is about."

"What exactly *is* socialism about, Grams? I guess I don't know enough to have an opinion. Do you understand it?"

"Partially, but not entirely. I think you need a college degree in economics to understand completely, but boiled down, socialists want a more even distribution of wealth in a society.

"As far as the difference between father and son goes, it didn't help that the two of them fell out quite a few years ago, so that naturally anything your grandfather believes will send your father to the extreme opposite position."

Joe looked at his grandmother for a full second before turning his eyes back to the road. "I do that, too," Third admitted.

Inga raised her eyebrow with curiosity.

"I mean, I took a liking to Gramps right away just because he's so different from my dad. I mean, I liked him at first, and I love him now, but he's the complete opposite of my father, and that sped up the process of getting to know him. Sorry, I interrupted you, Grams. Go on."

Inga looked at her grandson for a few moments before continuing. "Businessmen have a long history in this country of fighting a decent wage for their workers while raking in tons of profits for themselves," she continued.

"Now, you sound like a communist, too, Grams," Joe accused.

"It's just a different way of thinking. One side emphasizes profit as the driving force in an economy. The other side emphasizes what is the best for the most people."

"Grams, somebody has to make money to get everything to flow. Where does anything come from if nobody wants to make money selling it?"

"I'm just telling you about the spiritual environment where your grandfather grew up. There was a constant struggle. I think this may have been what went wrong between your dad and Joe."

"II don't understand."

"I think that the struggle was in my Joe all his life, but by the time your daddy got here, we were fairly comfortable. My Joe tried to teach about his experiences, but your daddy got the idea somehow that making money was the best and only way to get comfortable."

"Gramps told me about a guy he knew growing up who picked 4,000 pounds of peaches for a dollar and a half."

"Yes, exactly," Inga said. "But your father never grasped that level of desperation because he never saw it. He never saw the virtue of standing up for everyone, not just himself."

The Taurus fell silent, as Joe's grandmother sorted through her memories. Finally, she broke the silence, "Woody Guthrie's son went on to write and sing folk songs in the 60's with the same sort of flavor, I think."

"You don't mean Arlo Guthrie, do you?" Joe asked after a moment.

"Might be. I don't know. I don't remember the son very well. It's not the kind of music I like the best."

The two were quiet for a few more minutes. Then Joe asked, "What kind of music do you like, Grams?"

In this isolated corner of rural America, Joe had come to expect the twangiest of country western singers to spew forth from any piped-in music at any retail store—a genre that did not appeal to him at all. The shed at the edge of town whose red walls announced it as the home of "Cow Pie Radio—AM 915" reinforced his presumption. He immediately dreaded the answer to his own question, but his grandmother surprised him.

"I probably don't like much of the music you listen to, but I try to be open to things. I think that Whitney Houston has quite a voice, don't you?"

"You're kidding."

"No, I like her music. But my favorite music of all time is classical music. The nearest symphony orchestra to Sylvia is all the way to Quincy, and it's really not very good. "

Inga rolled down her passenger window and turned off the air conditioner. The breeze coming through the window was unexpectedly cool.

"When I was growing up in Germany, there were classical composers whose music was very popular because they were Germans, so I got a taste for that. Hitler was all about touting everything German, so the German classical composers were played everywhere."

"Have you heard the St. Louis Symphony Orchestra?" Joe asked.

"I have, but not for many years. I'd love to go again someday."

"How about I call Liz and find out what concerts are coming up? Maybe we could go to my house and I could take you to one of them. Spend the night and come home the next day. Would you like to do that?" Joe suggested.

"Ooh, that would be very nice, Third. I hope we can do that."

This could work, Joe told himself as a plan began to form in his mind.

The conversation lapsed into silence again as Inga mused on the growing closeness she was building with her grandson, and the reciprocity she felt from him. She considered that his growing openness might have many causes: resentment about his father, a genuine desire to help the elderly couple, and improving self-esteem as he came to feel needed and wanted. She thought about her son, Joe II, and she wondered where his parenting had taken a wrong turn. Surely, it is harder to parent a child by yourself with no mother to pitch in, but lots of people do, she thought. This level of animosity was extraordinary, even considering the boy's age. She wondered how she might help.

"Third," she asked, "what does your father say or do that upsets you so much? You have such anger toward him, and it seems odd to me."

"Nothing." Joe snapped. Then after a moment, more gently, "It's not really nothing. But what he does is not as upsetting as what he doesn't do."

"What doesn't he do?"

"Anything with me. For my whole life, he has been in meetings, scheduling conferences, on the phone—he's worked. Like I said before, he's never been to a basketball game I played in or taken me to a game of any kind. Liz does, but that's different. There's never been a camping trip or a vacation, or an outing. He's never done anything I want to do. I'm just in his way.

"For my birthdays, he gives me cash. He doesn't know enough about what I like to buy me a real present. He gives money as a bribe to soothe his conscience and get me to go away.

"Third, now really…"

"It's true. And on the rare occasions that he does talk to me, there's a tone. He gets this superior tone in his voice, like he's talking down to me. Like he's always trying to teach me something. He never wants to know what I know or what I think. He's always talking at me, not to me. He doesn't act like he wants to be around me at all. Every time I'm with him, he reminds me of what a chore I am."

"Third, I know your father loves you. The first time I ever saw you, you were a tiny baby, days old, and you and your mama were in the hospital. Joe and I came to see you, and your daddy was holding you, and the love in his eyes was crystal clear," Inga said.

"A lot changed since I was days old, Grams. And you may remember all that, but I sure don't."

As she rode, Inga occasionally pointed out the window, guiding Joe where to turn to get to the Armstead's house on the north side of town until they pulled into the driveway of a tidy two-story home a block off of Baker Street. Flowers in hanging baskets decorated the porch, and a barbecue pit stood nearby.

Joe carried the eggs to the porch, and Inga pressed the doorbell.

Joe recognized Lynae when she opened the door. The frustrated mother with the fussy child at the front of the church looked quite a lot different up close. She had fifteen years on him, he guessed, but her dark mahogany skin was beautiful. Her eyes were lovely. They were round and prominent, but they turned up on the outsides into a shape that reminded him of a cat.

She carried too much weight, he thought. Maybe it was from the baby, he reasoned, but he suspected otherwise . It was too much extra weight.

Lynae invited the MacDonalds in. "Hello, Inga," she said. "How nice to see you. Hi," she acknowledged Joe. "Can I help you with your things?" She reached out her hands to take the boxes of eggs from him and set them on a kitchen counter behind her.

"Yes," Inga chirped. "These are for you. Fresh eggs. I hope you can use them."

"Oh, thank you so much. We shall surely have omelets for dinner, Jamal and me. Madelyn Scott came by earlier with red bell peppers from her garden, so those will be great slivered in omelets, don't you think? Would you like coffee?"

Joe cut in. "I'm Joe. I'd love a cup of coffee. I'm still not used to these early, early mornings on a farm."

Lynae laughed politely. "I'm Lynae. How do you know Mrs. MacDonald?"

"She's my gram," Joe answered, pride evident in his tone.

"I have a son close to your age," Lynae revealed. "I think he's upstairs. Please make yourselves at home."

Lynae stepped to the foot of the stairs and bellowed, "Jamal! Come down here. We've got company."

She rested her substantial weight on one leg and jutted her hip out, resting her hand on it. Shortly, Joe heard footsteps on the stairs. Jamal descended the steps, stopping on the third step from the bottom when he saw Joe. He looked at his mother with a raised eyebrow. Jamal was, in fact, close to Joe's age. He was rail thin, wore a dark brown tee shirt and sported the start of a thin, inadequate beard. His jeans were baggy and ill-fitting. His skin was not as dark nor as even as Lynae's. His skin tone was more cafe au lait, Joe thought. Jamal suffered from acne, and the dots and scars were more than noticeable . The mother and son bore little resemblance to each other.

He descended the last two or three stairs slowly, having seen the guests. His posture, when he got to the foot of the stairs, was pure alpha-male. Another guy was on his turf, his body language suggested, and he would be clear on his standing in the home.

"Hi," Joe said. "I'm Joe MacDonald. We heard your dad was sick, and we brought over some fresh eggs." Joe stepped forward and extended his hand, but he quickly curled his outstretched hand into a fist as Jamal made a fist and fist-bumped him.

"Jamal," is all he said.

Awkward silence ensued. Lynae retreated to the kitchen and came back with a cup of coffee. She handed it to Joe. While Joe would have preferred cream and sugar, he thanked Lynae and resigned to drink it black. It was pretty good. Like the kind Liz made at home in St. Louis.

"What do you do in this town for fun?" He addressed his query to the other teen.

"I got my music. What do you wanna hear?" the young man said.

Joe, trusting his first impression, said, "You got any Boyz II Men?"

"Sure do," Jamal replied easily. How did this kid know, Jamal was thinking, that Boyz II Men was his favorite act? "I got the new one, just out. Wanna listen?"

"Oh, yeah, man. Has that got 'End of the Road' on it?"

"Yeah, man. C'mon upstairs."

On the way, Jamal asked, "You're not from around here, are you?"

"No. Neither are you, huh?"

"Why do you say that?" Jamal turned to ask.

"'Cause you don't talk like the folks around here," Joe answered. "People in this town have a rural accent. I'm from a city, and I can tell you are, too."

"Detroit," Jamal acknowledged. "My dad moved us here a few years ago. He worked there for a fire district. He moved here to be closer to my aunt who was sick. She's dead, now, but then the town wanted my dad to be the fire chief." The two young men reached the top of the stairs. Joe, balancing his coffee cup, followed Jamal into a modest bedroom with green painted bead board walls exactly like the ones in his gram's dining room. A picture of Jesus hung on the wall right next to a picture of MC Hammer. Joe smiled to himself at the incongruity.

"My dad didn't move me here. He dumped me here," Joe told Jamal. "Like a sack of shit."

"I take it your dad and you aren't close. That's too bad. My dad and me are real tight." Jamal put the CD in to play.

"Yeah, it's bad," Joe replied. "It's been like that since my mom died, and that was when I was real little."

"I'm sorry about your mom," Jamal offered.

"Thanks. Hey, I'm sorry about your aunt."

"It's okay," Jamal said. "Happens."

"I'm serious about what you do around here for fun. I know about a VFW in Macon that has a band on weekends, but other than that, I don't know of anything."

"There's nothing to know. Those bands are usually country rock, and I can live without 'em," Jamal said.

"I heard that. So, you . . . what? Sit home and listen to music?"

"Ah, no. My dad and I hang out and go all kinds of places. He's real cool. I hope he's not in the hospital long."

"Yeah, what happened to him?"

"He ran in a burning house again chasing after some kid, and he breathed too much smoke. He told me his mask got knocked off, cause it was dark and he hit a wall. So, he breathed some smoke while he was rescuing some kid. Then the kid was in a high chair and my dad tried to get him out and burned his hands."

"He does this a lot, does he?" Joe asked.

Jamal cracked up laughing. "No, man. 'Course not. But it's his job to save people in fires."

"Then he's a hero. I'm envious, man. I am."

CHAPTER 10

"Hey, Liz, it's Joey ," Joe said on the phone when he and Inga returned home.

"Hi, Joe. How are things in Sylvia?" Her voice was warm and loving. He pictured his sweet step-mother, her pretty face and perfect smile.

"Things are all right, I guess. I'm helping Gramps and Grams, so that's good. It's kind of boring here, but I just met a kid my age and he's cool. Likes music and he's pretty nice. Name's Jamal."

"Great, Joe. It's great you have someone to hang out with."

"I don't know yet if he wants to hang out with me. He probably has lots of friends. Anyway, I called to ask you for a favor. Could you check the schedule for the St. Louis Symphony? Grams would like to see a concert, and I want to drive her down and take her to one, spend the night, and come home the next day. What do you think of that?"

"Oh, wow. That would be great," Liz said. "Hold on a sec. I'll get the paper."

Joe could hear Liz set the handset down. He heard her speak to his father in the background to tell him it was Joe on the phone. A moment later, his father picked up the handset.

"Hey, Joey, how are things going?

"Fine."

"You a redneck yet?"

"What do you mean by that?" he asked defensively .

"I'm asking if you're a redneck. All the farmers have red necks from the sun on their backs. It's a point of pride for folks who work outdoors."

"I know what a redneck is. I just don't know why you would ask me that."

His father said nothing. He let his arm fall, holding the phone, and let it hang at his side a full ten seconds.

His father got out of the tension by changing the topic, lightening his voice. "Hey, did you get the box Liz sent?"

"Yeah, I thanked her two phone calls ago. Where's Liz? Has she found the paper, yet?"

"She's coming. What are you doing on the farm? Anything interesting or fun? Tried out for any rodeos? Ridden a bucking bronco?"

Joe interpreted the questions as an invitation for him to absolve his father's decision to send him to Sylvia. He ignored his father's attempt to engage him. He didn't bite down. "Grams wants to see a symphony concert, so I called to ask Liz to look into it. That's all. She can call me when she finds it out."

"Liz brought me the paper," his father assured him. "It says there's a concert featuring music by Richard Strauss and J. S. Bach in two weeks. It's the symphony's last show of the season. It's on Saturday night, the twentieth."

"Fine," Joe said. "I'll ask Grams if that's a good date. I'll call back when I know something. Bye." He hung up the phone without waiting for a reply.

Joe II hung up the phone when he realized he was disconnected. He lamented about his inability to reach his son. The kid had a thin skin. He had tried, for years to narrow the distance, but the disconnect came early and at this point, he feared it might be irreparable. He wondered where he had gone wrong.

Anne's death at so young an age changed everything, and it still stung after all this time. Of course, he loved Liz. He had since he met her. But Anne was a treasure, and as a wife and young mother, her death was ill-timed and decimating for those she left behind. The once-close relationship between dad and son fell apart after that, and Joe figured it was his own fault. He thought back over the years, re-tracing the steps.

Joe II was just starting with Jansen Evers in downtown St. Louis. A novice at twenty-six, not long out of college and with an ambition and purposefulness he hoped would trump his peers, he started at entry level, building a client base and devoting himself to his career. He seldom took a day off, but he was home for dinner every night to eat with his wife, the lovely Anne, and their young son. Little Joey was a bright, inquisitive boy, and his father adored him, lavishing the child with attention and gifts. He also lavished attention on the beautiful brunette who had married him and given him this child. He brought her gifts and apologies for his daunting work schedule. He gave her flowers and jewelry, and hoped she could accept that his career, while time-consuming, would make a solid way for their future.

At ten twenty-seven, the morning of March 12, 1980, the phone rang. A violent storm was battering the city. Warning sirens had gone off two or three times that morning, and the floor manager at the brokerage had threatened to send everyone to the basement twice. Joe's son was in school, and his wife was at work, or so he thought.

The phone on his desk rang. It was Officer Drake from the St. Louis Police Department. There had been an accident involving a beige 1979 Buick LaSabre registered to him. The car was inundated with water while crossing a railroad track in Lemay. The woman driver was taken to the hospital. Would Mr. MacDonald please come to the hospital?

Joe rose and grabbed his jacket. In the parking garage, he entered the car and dumped the content of his pockets on the floor in search of his employee badge to get him out of the garage. He'd left it in his desk. Cursing, he floored the accelerator around and around the spiral slopes of the garage. When he pulled to a halt at the cashier, he threw a ten dollar bill at her and yelled, "Open it!"

He would later wonder if those few moments of delay had cost him the chance to say good-bye to Anne while she was alive.

When he marched into the emergency room and identified himself, Joe was taken to a waiting room lined with beige chairs designed to calm him. A doctor entered in a few moments and sat down, expecting Joe to do the same.

"Mr. MacDonald, a levy burst in Lemay, and a railroad track was flooded. The water swept your wife's car off the track and carried it for a space. The water submerged the car, and she never even got her seat belt off. I am very sorry. She drowned.

The words were meaningless gibberish. This could not possibly be his wife, and what did this man in burgundy scrubs mean by dragging him all the way down here? His wife was eternally alive. She was the definition of normality in his life. A constant. An icon of reality. She was life itself, unwavering and forever enduring.

Twelve years later, Joe II could still see in his mind's eye the doctor in the burgundy scrubs, his lips pursed, bracing for Joe's reaction. The memory of it was still seared in his mind as he relived that day in his nightmares. As the cotor explained what had happened, a pounding sense of urgency welled within the stockbroker. He had to see her. Surely the dead woman was not Anne. Surely there was some mistake. His sense of foreboding was urgent, or was it? Did Joe remember he prescient sense of doom, or had the last twelve years planted that in his memories. Did some part of his subconscious think he didn't deserve Anne, and accept that she was gone? Or was he remembering wrong, remembering with a jaded hindsight. His urge, on that day, was to immediately straighten out this whole terrible mistake.He asked to see his wife.

She lay on a gurney in an empty hospital room, covered in a sheet. The doctor revealed her face, her hair sopping wet. Joe had touched her flesh. It was cold. He leaned down and kissed her lips. They were unresponsive, also cold, empty. There was no Anne there.

An hour and a half later, he was driving home with his son in the back seat. His mind was racing. The windshield wipers echoed his pounding heart as the storm itself mirrored the turmoil inside him. What to do. What to do. There was so much to do. There were dozens of people to call, and a mountain of details to take care of.

Joe's temperament called for activity at a time like this. He was in denial; the death of his wife wasn't real to him yet. At this moment, he could only process the need for action. At the same time, he could not fathom how to break the news to his son.

He called Joe and Inga in Sylvia first. Inga cried on the phone. He talked to his father just long enough to ask if he could bring the grandson up there to stay for a time while arrangements were made. Inga had offered to come to St. Louis, but Joe had said no, it's better his way.

Then Joe called Anne's family and told them the news.

There were many more calls to make. The funeral home, his boss, his co-workers and Anne's friends and co-workers. Each phone call, each repetition of the story, each expression of sympathy, made it more real and less abstract, but he couldn't make very many of those calls at one time. A hollow, aching sense of being kicked in the gut by an angry mule disoriented him. The young father sank into a chair and sobbed while his little boy sat alone in his room wondering what was going on.

Joe II emerged from his reverie. His hands were shaking as they always did when he retreated into those dark memories. Now, he realized, the day of Anne's death was where the disconnect had started. Joe had been so overcome with grief, he'd not considered the needs of his five-year-old son who was too young to understand such a devastating loss. Anne's death was the beginning of unintentional neglect, as Joe withdrew to mourn alone, while his little boy was left to find his own way.

The disconnect deepened in the following weeks when he took his son to Sylvia, abandoned him there, and left it to his parents to deal with a lost child.

CHAPTER 11

Joe II called his mother early in the morning from Jansen Evers. He was beginning to realize that having sent Joey to Sylvia could present a secondary benefit besides building the boy's character. It might just be a chance to narrow the chasm he had allowed to form between himself and his parents. He had resisted Liz's efforts to be the blessed peacemaker because he had feared his father's rejection, but if he approached indirectly, from the standpoint of his son's visit, maybe he could reconnect and mend some fences.

"Hi, Mom," he said lightly when he heard Inga's lilting German accent. "How're things going up there? Is Joey behaving?"

Inga hesitated for a second before answering. She was signaling the boy in the room with her that his father was on the phone, but the pause of only one or two seconds was interpreted by the man in St. Louis as rejection. Or disappointment. Or at least judgment. He asked himself why he was so nervous.

"Oh, hi, yes, of course," she said. "How are you?" She didn't say his name, he noticed. He wondered if his father was in the room and she was trying to conceal his identity from Dad.

"Uh, fine, Mom. Say, Joe said you might like to see the symphony here, so I took the liberty of buying five tickets for the concert. Is that okay? Bach and Strauss." He couldn't believe his hands were so clammy and moist, waiting for her answer.

"What was the date again?"

"The twentieth."

"Oh, that's right. That should be fine. I asked because I bought a booth at the farmers' market for this coming Saturday. Third and I are going to sell eggs."

"I see. Well, I'm pleased to know my son hasn't eaten all your eggs already. I know how he eats, and I know how you cook."

"No," she said, amused. "He's eaten only a normal number of eggs. There's plenty left to feed Shelby County. I'm worried about the cow population, though."

Joe chuckled on the phone. "How are you doing, Momma?"

"I'm fine. Still in one piece. Your father's having some trouble, though. His eyesight is failing, and I'm afraid he won't be driving too much longer. He has an eye appointment coming up."

"Okay, well I hope he checks out." Joe's words sounded hollow, even to him. He wanted to exit the call and escape the discomfort. He started to tell his mother that Liz would be calling with details about the visit and timing and everything, but then he thought it through, and changed his mind.

"I'll call you again closer to time and give you details on everything. How about if I take us all out to dinner ahead of time? It's an eight o'clock performance."

"That would work out well," Inga replied.

When Inga hung up the phone, Third, who had been listening, appeared to have no interest in what his father had said on the phone.

Instead, he said, "I'm selling eggs Saturday?"

CHAPTER 12

"Inga, you know I can't leave the farm for a weekend. Who would feed the livestock?" Those were the first words out of Joe's mouth when Inga told him of the plan to visit their son in St. Louis.

"Can't you get one of the neighbors to come in and feed them?"

"Feed them, water them, shovel their droppings? It's too much to ask. No. I can't go. You and Third go. I'll hold down the fort here."

"I don't believe you really want to go," Inga accused.

"No, I really don't care about symphony music, ," Joe said.

"Going to the concert is not the point," Inga reminded him. "The point would be to visit your son. Joe, I can think of at least four people who could come over here and do your chores for one simple day. Bryce and Sarah Conrad's son is fresh back from college and looking for work. Angelynn Sumner's husband was laid off at the factory and could use a little cash —"

"Inga, my presence would change the event," he stated.

"What?"

"If I went, the way I am with Joe, the way he is with you, the way Joe is with Third, all of it would be difficult and unsettled if I were there. You'll have the best time without me."

"I can't believe you're saying this."

"I just don't want to create a problem."

"You're creating one by not going."

"I don't agree."

"Joe, it could be the chance for reconciliation I've prayed for."

Her husband looked at her for ten full seconds. "Well, it doesn't matter. I can't go. Leave it at that," he said with finality.

CHAPTER 13

Saturday arrived, and Third was out at the pickup truck before sunrise, loading boxes of eggs into cushioned slotted holders which he and Gramps had hoisted into the truck bed the night before and secured to minimize damage on the trip.

When the eggs were loaded, Inga walked to the truck wearing dark blue jeans, a blue plaid shirt, and her pretty straw hat with blue flowers. The intent was clear. She sought to look like a gentlewoman farmer. She smiled at her grandson and pinched his elbow.

"Thank you for helping with this, Third."

"Happy to help, Grams."

"Are you hungry?"

"I just ate a huge breakfast an hour ago. One of your best, in fact."

"Sorry," Inga replied. "It's a habit for me to ask."

Joe opened the passenger door of the truck and held it for Inga. "Your carriage awaits," he said with a smile.

The farmer's market in Monroe City was an open-air affair with plywood booths set up for farmers who came from Shelby and surrounding counties to vend their produce and other goods. The booths rented at a reasonable rate, and local merchants also took advantage with homeopathic remedies and herbal supplements, inexpensive belts, jewelry, hats, and hair ornaments. Some sold oriental-style throw rugs, wall hangings, and there was a wide assortment of home-made jams, preserves and salsas.. If you needed an acrylic-paint rendering of Elvis on black velvet, the Monroe City farmers' market was the place to go. There was even an enclosed butcher shop, spice shop, and pet shop. But mostly there was every variety of home- grown fruits and vegetables, mostly organic, and all at good prices.

"Grams, there's a market similar to this in St. Louis. It's called Soulard," Joe volunteered as they arrived. "I've been there plenty of times with Liz, but I was always the shopper, not the farmer. It feels weird being on the other side."

"I bet it does, Third. It's also quite a lot more work being on the other side."

Inga's booth was inside the north gate of the market. Joe unloaded the fresh-laid eggs while Inga stacked and arranged the booth to make it attractive to the buyers, who would be arriving shortly.

As the two were working, another family began unpacking their wares in the booth next to theirs.

Joe noticed the girl immediately. About his own age or a little younger, he guessed, she was riveting. Her long hair was ebony black and cut around her face to highlight her large sapphire eyes. He stopped what he was doing and watched her.

"Third?" Inga said lightly.

"Oh, yeah." Back to work.

But the young woman noticed him, too, and smiled before he turned away.

Shoppers were flowing into the market.

To Joe's amusement, Inga began calling, "Fresh eggs! Fresh eggs!" in that high-pitched Julia-Child voice, knowing full well it would attract attention from the shoppers.

It caught the ear of the raven-haired beauty in the booth next door as well. She had been setting out colorful scarves, costume jewelry, socks, shoelaces, and assorted goods. She stopped and walked straight up to Joe.

"Is that your grandmother? She has a lovely voice for this kind of work. Does she hire herself out?"

Joe inhaled, but couldn't feel his breath. Her beauty was suffocating. He stammered at her.

"I apologize," she offered. "I caught you off guard. I don't really want to hire her. We couldn't afford her anyway. I just wanted to say hi, since we're neighbors. Chelsea. Nice to meet you." Her demeanor was friendly, but her body language suggested a shy-awkwardness with which Joe was unfamiliar, coming from a female of this extraordinary beauty.

She put out her hand and Joe shook it. He looked down at the ground, gathered himself and said, "Joe MacDonald the third. You can call me Joe or Third. Nice to make your acquaintance. And yes, that is my grandmother."

Inga, nearby, made her first sale. She made change for a red-haired woman with too much lipstick, and a green scarf around her head. She thanked the woman for shopping at the MacDonald farm, and then glanced over at Joe and Chelsea and waved. It was both a greeting and a summons.

Joe saw the glance and realized Inga wanted help.

"Hey, we'll talk more, but I gotta peddle eggs right now."

"Yeah, me too, except I gotta peddle Chinese-made crap."

"Your stuff is beautiful," Joe said, hating to end the conversation. "Do you sell it in any stores?"

"Yeah, it's in town. You should stop by and purchase a barrette with dolphins on it for your girlfriend."

"My girlfriend doesn't like dolphins. Oh, wait, I don't have a girlfriend. But, if I did, she wouldn't like dolphins."

Chelsea, cracked up, laughing. Her loud, raucous, unexpected laughter drowned out Inga's calls of "Fresh eggs!"

The older man—her father, Joe guessed—who was with her, rolled his eyes. The laughter continued for long past its natural end.

"It wasn't that funny," Joe stated.

"It was to me." The girl's eyes were watering. She wiped her face with her hands and looked up at Joe. She began to giggle again.

"Chelsea, c'mon," her father interrupted. "We don't have time for that now." His words were polite, but something about his body language disturbed Joe. He couldn't put a finger on it.

As the morning progressed, Joe was busy taking money and making change, while Inga bagged the purchases. Joe was glad he had worked the previous summer at a roast beef sandwich stand and had learned how to make change. With no phone lines accessible in the market booths, credit cards were useless, so transactions were cash-only. His mind wandered often to the girl in the booth next door.

Early in the afternoon, the rush died down, and Joe and Inga breathed a sigh of relief. Inga sat on a folding chair she had brought. She stretched her legs out and wiggled her toes in her sandals.

Joe sauntered over to Chelsea, looking as cool and casual as he possibly could. He smiled at her suavely, he hoped.

"Chelsea's a pretty name," he began. "Do you have another one?"

"Another what . . . name? Oh, sure. Christmas. Chelsea Christmas." She returned his friendly smile.

"Wow. What a cool sounding name," Joe said.

"Why, thank you very much. I picked it out myself when I was naked and wriggly out my momma's belly," she said, still smiling.

"Okay," he replied cautiously. "Thanks for that visual."

Her laughter began again. It went on a full half a minute. Joe considered that perhaps she was nervous talking to him. How could she be shy with a face and body like that? Made no sense. He noticed that her father didn't look at her, but rather straightened merchandise and counted money in his cash box. Joe got the sense he was embarrassed by her laughter. Okay, Joe reasoned, it was weird, but it was way too early in what he hoped would become a relationship, to judge her.

When the laughter subsided, Joe asked as lightly as he could, "Done?"

"Hey, if you don't want me to laugh, don't say hilariously funny things."

He took her hand, held it and gazed into her eyes. "Chelsea, I am being very serious." He looked at her somberly for three or four seconds. He opened his mouth as if to say something, but instead crossed his eyes and wiggled his ears.

She dissolved into laughter once again.

"Chelsea, let's get this mess cleaned up," her father interrupted. He was tossing unsold merchandise into a box.

"I'm sorry to distract her, Mr. Christmas," Joe said, raising his voice to be heard by her father who was on the other side of the booth. Then, to Chelsea, "Can I call you sometime?"

Wordlessly, the young woman picked up a piece of scrap paper out of a box and scribbled on it. She handed him her number and resumed her tasks.

Joe folded the paper evenly and tucked it into the empty cash sleeve of his wallet. Better than money, he thought.

CHAPTER 14

Sheriff Ollman's drug bust plans continued to be thwarted by factors he could not control. Though he had abandoned his idea to raid the meth factory on Broad Street, the surveillance continued, and the latest reports from his officers in the field were putting a disturbing spin on the project.

New buyers were visiting the Broad Street house, and they looked like they meant business.

Well-dressed and moneyed, at least two newcomers had visited the Sample residence and left with large parcels. They drove a late model van capable of transporting a good deal of merchandise. Surveillance officers in plain clothes told Sheriff Ollman that it looked like the two men might be checking product quality and turn-around time for future large-quantity purchases. The license plates on the van were from Missouri, but from a county in the south-central part of the state. The newcomers had come a long way for this buy, and if Ollman handled the matter properly, this bust could lead to some much bigger fish to fry.

Still, there was pressure to act. Bill Fast was quietly asking questions within the county, trying to get a lead on who on the force was selling or giving away information about the drug investigations. He was worried about the window of opportunity closing if the meth maker caught on that he was being surveilled. The baby living in the house needed to be removed for his own safety, but there were more lives to be saved by not sending Social Services to get the child, thus effectively telling Jack Sample to flee Ollman's jurisdiction before the sheriff could act.

"What does your gut tell you, Bill?" Ollman asked his chief deputy.

"Get that kid out of there." Bill replied flatly and without hesitation.

"But if we tip Sample off and don't bust him with his new-found dealer friends, it could cost far more lives than the life of that baby. Far more to let this joker get gone without busting him."

"I know that, Sheriff, but if word got out that you left a baby in that kind of danger knowingly just to score a couple of well-heeled drug tycoons, that would be the end of your career with the county. You'd never get re-elected," Bill pointed out.

"I don't care about a re-election. I am aware of what standard protocol is. And the public can vote me out. I care about cleaning up Sylvia and the whole of Shelby County. That's what I care about."

"So, you don't care about that baby, I guess."

Sheriff Ollman was silent.

CHAPTER 15

Jack said it was a good thing, so Sarah supposed that it was. She wasn't much of a deep thinker when it came to long-term eventualities. Sarah concerned herself with the here and now.

Here and now, Jack had hooked up with a couple of dudes from southern Missouri who, Jack said, could bring a level of demand for his concoctions that would put the three of them—himself, Sarah, and Dustin—in gravy for a long time.

Dix Simpson, the one with the mouth, told Jack that he could buy as much as four-large worth of product a month. Could Jack cook that much?

Why, yes, he could.

Truth be told, Sarah knew there was no way Jack could fill an order like that unless he cooked around the clock and had Sarah's help with it. But she'd been with Jack long enough to know that he thought it was more important to seal the deal first and work out the kinks later.

Dix's friend, Ernesto Soto, was the strong, silent type. More like menacing, Sarah thought. She was uncomfortable enough to go for one of her walks when the two were around, but Jack only saw dollar signs.

This was do-able, Jack had told Sarah. He might have to get outside help. He might even have to train a local user or two to cook. But it'd be worth it. It would mean breaking into the big time. And that meant a profitable future.

Sarah supposed that would be good, but her inner voice whispered to her. It was a worrisome trade to be in. So much could go wrong. She remembered what that guy Joe, from St. Louis, had told her, and thought he might be onto something. The big secret might already be out. Jack may already be on the sheriff's radar.

"So, are you going to help me or not?" Jack had asked after much discussion.

"I don't know, Jack," she had answered. "I'm so tired after last night, I can't think straight. Give me a little time."

"What about last night?"

"Oh, I had a nightmare and it woke me up. I never got back to sleep."

"Oh." Jack turned back to his cooking, but Sarah felt the need to share.

"I was a space alien, and I landed on a watery planet. This dream was really real, Jack. And it was kind of upsetting," Sarah explained.

"Uh huh," Jack said, measuring and stirring.

"So, anyway, I got in this water and started to swim. It was really dark blue and kind of pretty and serene, but a message came into my head. I somehow knew that something was going to happen, something important, and what I did next would determine if I lived or died."

Jack looked at her for a second, shrugged, and then returned to his stove.

"Suddenly, I looked down in the water, and I saw a little boy about ten. He could have been Dustin in my mind, but much older than Dustin is now. He had on bright pink swim trunks."

"I panicked. This was it, I thought. This was the thing that's going to happen. I reached down and grabbed the boy by the waistband of his trunks, pulled him up, and pushed him toward the side at the surface. Just as I did, a flight of concrete stairs appeared in the water. He landed on the stairs. I screamed at him to run, but he looked at me hatefully and stayed right where he was."

"I got on the stairs behind him and pushed him forward, screaming at him to go."

"We both ran, and I turned around to look as this fish, this enormous fish came up out of the water and set its mouth on the side of the pool. Jack. Its mouth must have been twelve feet across, and it had a ferocious roar. It was angry that it didn't catch the boy or me. It was trying to kill us, and we barely escaped, but because I had gotten that message in my mind, I acted, and saved us both. That's when I woke up," Sarah concluded.

Jack paused and stared at her when she concluded.

"My God, Sarah," he said. "Why on earth are you afraid of me?"

Sarah stared at her boyfriend. It hit her. The dream was about Jack. He was the big fish that she feared would consume her. At the same time, it also hit her that Jack was straight. He hadn't smoked that morning, so he'd be sober when Simpson and Soto came to meet with him.

Sarah's felt conflicted. Jack's reaction to her dream was insightful, right on the money. It was a rare taste of the old Jack she had known before meth was in the equation . Yet, somehow, he was right in warning her to fear him. He was the huge, roaring fish, the imminent threat—to herself and Dusty. He wasn't the smart, lucid Jack she had once loved. Not anymore.

CHAPTER 16

Inga sat quietly in the truck on the way home from Monroe City, and let her grandson talk. This was the most animated, interested, and happy she had seen the boy since he had arrived in Sylvia. Naturally, he talked about the girl.

"Did you get a good look at her, Grams? She's beautiful. Just gorgeous. Her eyes are clear and blue, and she has just the kind of body I like. She is tiny, tiny, but she has a big chest." Joe glanced sideways at his grandmother and blushed.

"I guess I'm not supposed to talk to my grandmother about girls with big chests, huh?"

Inga smiled at him, glad to see her grandson take an interest in something.

"And she laughs so much. So much. Everything is funny to her. I can't believe everything I say is so amusing to her." He looked to Inga for a response, but she remained silent.

"I hope she likes me. I'm gonna ask her out. Liz sent me a little money, and I'm going to use it to take Chelsea out for a good time," Joe rambled.

"Oh, that reminds me," Inga interrupted. "You have money coming from me for today. You did a good job, and I'll pay you for your labor. I'll give it to you when we get home."

"Really? Wow, thanks. I wonder where I can take her that'll be fun and nice. I wish there was something to do around here. I wonder what she likes to eat. It doesn't look like she eats anything, she's so thin. She's just beautiful, and smart, and she likes my humor."

Inga's mind wandered. Something Joe said about the girl reminded her of her own first crush. There was a boy in Germany. A handsome boy that made Inga's heart beat fast and her hands grow sweaty.

Inga was fourteen, and in high school when she first laid eyes on Gunther Wolf. Tall, with a square jaw and penetrating brown eyes, Gunther reminded her of a movie star, but she didn't know which one.

He was very sophisticated and at least three years older than she. He was smart and articulate, and he talked of a better world and a better life for everyone. He spoke of the danger of Adolf Hitler and how the war could not possibly come to a good end for the German people.

He stated that Hitler was a madman, and that the rumors of prison camps and experiments on Jews were no doubt a thin whisper of a far uglier reality.

Inga did not know at first that Gunther was repeating the words of his father, a pastor of a small church in the town, whose preaching against der Fuhrer was going to cause big trouble. The only thing Inga knew was that she was simply mesmerized by Gunther Wolf.

One day, Gunther invited Inga for a walk. Her inner voice cautioned her against being alone with a man. The memory of the last time she had been alone with an older man would haunt her forever. But as she got to know Gunther, she was convinced of the goodness of his heart and the guilelessness of his soul.

She accepted the invitation.

The talk was of moonlight and war, the beauty of Aryan Inga's blue eyes and the smell of gunpowder, the taste of warm strudel and of the disappearance of a Jewish family in town, whose furniture store was abruptly boarded up.

Gunther told Inga that he opposed Hitler's insistence that the Aryans were a super race. He pontificated that viewing all people as equals, no matter what their race, nationality, or religion, was the only way to have a fair and just society.

"Anytime a society has one group of people that's regarded as intrinsically better than another group of people, it can't call itself a civilization because that belief is simply uncivilized," he told her.

While Inga agreed, she later realized that Gunther's words were a direct quote from his father's most recent sermon.

Decades later, in 1992, and with her teenage naiveté long gone, Inga knew she should have questioned Gunther. There were other, larger questions to ask at that time. Had she known what was to come? Perhaps not or perhaps she did not want to know.

Pastor Wolf's church was closed two months later, when Gestapo officers came to collect Pastor Wolf. Three weeks after that, Mrs. Wolf received a letter stating that her husband had contracted pneumonia and had died in Konzentrationslager, Dachau. The letter was signed by Heinrich Himmler. Most likely, the signature was that of a low-level flunkie. Surely the task was too trivial for Himmler himself, yet it was important to keep community leaders terrorized.

Gunther didn't talk much about politics after that. The intense young man was tenderized by the loss —as though pounded with a meat mallet.

Inga, by that time, deeply in love—or as in love as a girl can be at that age—was convinced of the trouble one could borrow speaking out against the Reich, even if it was the right thing to do.

"My God," her mother complained when the news reached her. "That poor preacher didn't do anything but talk to a tiny congregation of twenty Christians on a Sunday morning, give them a cracker and a sip of wine, and send them home."

She said it in private to her children, but not to anyone else. By that time, the home in Korbach was destroyed, and the family stayed in a crowded house on her grandfather's farmland. He had taken in two other homeless families and was housing a group of soldiers as well, but not by choice. There was one German soldier who was particularly kind to the nine children in the house, but that was not to say you should speak ill of the authorities while within earshot. The Wolfs were an example from which a terrible lesson had been learned.

The truck braked hard as a deer trotted across the road, shattering Inga's reverie about her once-beloved Gunther, and jolting her back to the present. If she learned nothing from Gunther, she had learned that a man who knows how to be civilized, who knows the value of seeing everyone equally as God's creation — that's the kind of man she would want, and would marry, the kind she had adored for decades.

Her musings ceased and she reached for the dashboard to steady herself.

"Sorry about that, Grams. I'm still not used to deer appearing in the road like that." He grinned at her. "Hey, what did you think about Chelsea? Did you like her?"

"I have no idea," she replied after a moment. "I know nothing about her. If you like her that much after you get to know her, invite her home for dinner one night and I'll get to know her. Then I'll have an opinion."

Joe was floored by the suggestion. Not only was it a great idea, given his Grams' cooking, but it was unheard of in his life. At no time in seventeen years had Joe's father ever expressed an interest in getting to know Joe's friends—male or female.

"Wow, Grams, that would be fantastic. Just fantastic. Will you make white spargel?"

"If it's still in season by that time, sure," she told him.

"Oh, it will be. I'll ask her soon. Really soon."

"Did you know that I had a love once in Germany before I came to this country and met your grandfather?"

"You did? Why didn't you marry him instead of Gramps?"

"His name was Gunther, and he was very smart and very political. We never married because I was too young, and not long after that, my mother got remarried and we came to Missouri. But Gunther was quite a young man. We used to go on long walks."

Inga may have exaggerated. She honestly only remembered one long walk, a number of meals at the Wolfs' home, and some visits to their church.

"Did Gunther live in Korbach?" Joe probed.

"Yes, he did, but by that time, I was living with my grandfather and several other families on a farm in the country."

She briefly told the story of her house in Korbach being all but demolished when the home down the street was hit by Allied bombs. The family had to find other accommodations, and so became tenants of her grandfather.

"At one point, about the time we moved in, some authority in the area came to my grandfather's house and told him that the house was to be used to house French prisoners captured in the war. The upstairs bedrooms were turned into prison cells with doors that locked on the outside. A guard was sent to watch after the four Frenchmen who were imprisoned."

It was all he could do to keep his eye on the road with this surprising disclosure.

"You lived with prisoners of war?" he asked, aghast.

"Yes, and the guard. They were mostly very nice and we weren't afraid of them. Well, I kind of was after something happened, but mostly they were just sent for work release in town every day. The guard slept while they were gone. Then at night, they all sat up together, played cards, and drank."

Joe grinned. "They're supposed to be mortal enemies and they sat up playing cards and drinking?"

Inga shrugged her soldiers. "Listen, after sitting in the basement so many times while bombs dropped all around me, an enemy who just plays cards was fine.

"Besides," she continued, "people start wars for many reasons, but usually it has little to do with the actual warriors. I've seldom seen that the people embroiled in a war—the soldiers on the ground risking their lives—really want to be at war. "

"What was the thing that happened that made you more afraid of the prisoners?"

"We'll talk about that some other time," Inga said. "We're home, and I need to start dinner."

"What are we having, omelets?" Joe smiled.

"Aren't you sick of eggs by now?" she winked. "I am."

CHAPTER 17

Joe expected church on Sunday to be typically tedious, but it took an upward turn when he got there. He had barely walked in when he saw Lynae Armstead in the narthex. She was holding the baby, but freed a hand to wave to him. He waved back.

He took the corner hurriedly on his way to the restroom, and when he pushed on the men's room door, he nearly hit Jamal in the face with it.

"Oh, hey, man. How you doing?" Jamal spoke in the phlegmatic, understated tone which Joe had come to expect.

The two fist-bumped, and Joe could feel his mood lift at once.

"Good, good. How's your dad coming along? Is he out of the hospital?"

"Yeah, he came home Saturday morning, plopped on the couch and hasn't budged since. His butt is the only part of him that isn't sore!" Jamal's jovial remark did little to conceal his underlying concern.

"He okay?"

"More or less. The doctor, the pulmon . . . pulmo . . . some specialist wanted him to stay another night, but the insurance wouldn't cover it."

Joe objected. "Really? If he was injured while at work — he was, right? — then the city should pick up the whole tab."

"'Should' ain't always what happens, man," Jamal stated. "The town of Sylvia is running out of money, and there's no tax money coming in. Lynae thinks Workman's Comp will send a check eventually, but she doesn't want to get in more debt if it doesn't. It's complicated, but, anyway, he came home."

"I heard that," Joe agreed. "Gettin' to know this town makes it pretty clear that the only businesses that seem to do well here are the glass labs, and I'm guessing they don't pay their fair share of taxes."

Jamal cracked a smile. "No, probably not. A lot of folks use that shit around here, so money's changing hands, for sure."

"A lot of kids use it in the Lou, too," Joe said.

"In the what?"

"What?" Joe asked, not following.

"You said kids use meth in the something. What you mean?"

"Oh. In the Lou. St. Louis. That's where I come from."

"Oh, yeah, right. I guess the kids who get on that mess have their reasons or whatever. My dad would murder me."

Joe didn't respond.

"You ever try it?" Jamal asked.

"Wait a minute, will ya? I gotta take a wiz."

"Oh yeah, sorry." Jamal stood in the hallway until Joe came out.

"Hey, Jamal, you wanna ditch this service and do something else for an hour?"

"Oh, man, I can't. The preacher is going to name my family, thank everyone for helping out with food and stuff, and ask us all to stand up during the service. I have to be there."

"It'll be your fifteen seconds of fame," Joe teased.

"Yeah, well."

"Let me sit with you, then. Maybe some of that recognition will rub off on me."

Jamal smiled as the two walked back up the hallway toward the narthex.

"Hey, I got a question," Joe ventured after a few steps. "I met this girl–"

"Famous last words," Jamal interrupted.

"Yeah," Joe said, smiling. "Anyway, I want to ask her out, but where is there to take her that isn't two hours away that would be fun and make an impression?"

"She white?" Jamal asked.

"Don't know. I didn't ask," Joe joked.

"You met her and you don't know if she's white?" Jamal asked, not getting the gag.

"Yeah, man, she's white."

"Then I don't know. I know a place or two in Macon and Columbia where the *brothahs* hang out with the *sistahs* but those places wouldn't be your kind of place." He affected a dialect from some hood, and Joe was amused.

"You sayin' I have to sit in the back of the bus?"

"Yeah, exactly. Let me think on this for a minute — Dad!"

As the two young men turned the corner into the narthex, Jamal noticed his father standing with Lynae, Gramps, and Inga. The four were chatting. Jamal's father was dressed in a suit and tie. His hands were bandaged in white gauze.

"Dad, I didn't know you were coming. Why didn't you come with Mom and me?"

"'Cause I didn't know I was either until a few minutes ago. I just want to say thanks to everyone who helped out. Let's go do that." He put his arm around his son's shoulder, hugged him, and pulled him toward the sanctuary door.

The man was tall, like Grandpa Joe, very dark-skinned and portly. His gut hung over his belly, but there was no doubt about his musculature. He was a strong man, accustomed to physical tests. He had a winning smile set into fat, dimpled cheeks, and brown eyes so dark it was hard to tell where the irises stopped and the pupils began. When he smiled, his dark eyes crinkled and gave him a jovial look.

"Dad, this is Joe. I just met him at our house. He's the one who brought us the eggs."

"Pleased to make your acquaintance. Don Armstead. Thanks for the omelets." Don winked at Inga to acknowledge the true source of the eggs.

Don led his family into the sanctuary. The MacDonalds followed and Joe whispered to Inga, "I'm gonna sit over with Jamal, okay?"

"Let's all sit with the Armsteads," she replied.

CHAPTER 18

"So, what do you know about this girl?" Jamal asked. The Mac-Donalds and the Armsteads were in Dylan's Eats in Shelbina having lunch. The young men sat at the end of the long table, across from each other, while the adults talked among themselves.

"Well, let's see. Her name is Chelsea, she's from Monroe City, and she's beautiful. And she laughs a lot."

"That's all you know? What does she like, man? Sports? Movies? There's a movie theater in Macon, you know. Sometimes there're concerts in Hannibal with big-name acts, but I don't think anyone good is coming up too soon. Help me out here. What does she like? Else, I can't tell you where to take her."

Joe thought for a moment, thinking over the scant information he had about Chelsea. "Oh, uh, her dad owns a boutique in Monroe City. I met her at a farmers' market in Monroe City—"

"I know the place."

"And she was selling, you know, scarves and hand-made jewelry, hair barrettes, and stuff like that. Did I mention she laughs a lot?"

"Twice."

The two fell silent and thought for a minute or two.

"Word up," Jamal said finally. "There's a crafts fair in Hannibal a week from Saturday. I think my mom wants to go. They have all kinds of things there. Paintings, and home-made shit like purses and hair stuff, little wreaths and signs and decorations to hang on your walls, jewelry and all like that. She might like it.

"You got any money, you could buy her something nice, and that would make an impression."

"A week from Saturday? Cause I'm going to St. Louis this coming Saturday, but I could call her this week and at least try to talk her into it. I'd like to see her before then, though." The last sentence he spoke more to himself than Jamal.

"What's in St. Louis Saturday?" Jamal asked.

"I'm taking Grams to the symphony."

"You're kiddin' me."

"No, she really wants to go, so we're going. Gramps is staying here, though, so it's just her and me. She wants me to drive. She drives, and all, but doesn't really like to."

"Well, let me know how it all goes. I think I'm going to Hannibal, too, that day with my dad to look for a new stereo for our house. He's cool like that."

Joe noticed that Jamal and his dad were tight, and he was stricken with a pang of envy.

Jamal's dad's voice could be heard in the ensuing silence, and the boys turned their attention to the other end of the table, as the adults' conversation piqued their interest.

"Okie Joe, did you hear about the shooting in town last night? It was horrible," Don lamented.

"God, no. What happened?"

"I talked to Bill Fast at the sheriff's office late last night. He and Ollman have been watching a drug house in town with undercover cops. It's been under investigation for a while now."

"Should you be telling me this?" Gramps asked.

"No point in not telling you now," Don explained. "When a cop gets shot, all bets are off when it comes to security. It'll be on the Quincy news station. Bank on it."

"What! What cop got shot?"

"Mark Newstead got shot in his car," Don explained. "I heard it on the police scanner in my office and called Bill Fast."

"I don't know Mark Newstead," Gramps replied.

"Of course, you don't. But I did, and he was a good guy. Young guy in his 30s. He left behind a wife and baby girl, Jill."

"He died?"

"Right there in his car. The perp walked up and opened fire. Shot him clean through the head," Don continued.

"Oh, that's just terrible!" Inga cried.

Lynae looked in her lap. The baby was in a carrier next to her, and she touched his stomach lovingly as if trying not to think about it.

"Wow. Awful," Gramps remarked. Any motive?"

"I don't know. That's all Bill told me. Sheriff Ollman is real upset. Newstead was on the force ten years. Even worse, his widow is Ollman's daughter."

The two young men at the end of the table eavesdropped quietly. When the conversation shifted to another topic, Jamal looked across the table at Joe and stated flatly, "It's about meth. No doubt. Gotta be."

Joe considered his new friend for a moment before he turned to Jamal's father. He said, "Mr. Armstead —"

"Call me Don."

"Uh, okay. Where did the shooting happen? Do you know?"

"It was in Sylvia. The corner of Broad and Beamer. Why?"

"I had a feeling," the young man stated.

"You had what feeling, Third?" Inga asked.

"Remember that girl I took home from the dance a while back?" He turned to Jamal and said, "Not Chelsea. A different girl I met." He turned to Grams, "The night the storm hit Macon? I took her home to a house on Broad. I'm pretty sure it's a meth lab."

"What makes you think that?" Don interrupted.

"That girl, Sarah, as good as told me. She said her boyfriend runs a business in their house. What else could that be in this town? And she was buying all the stuff that goes with it."

"Could very well be that Bill Fast or Sheriff Ollman may want to talk to you," Don suggested.

Joe said, "Sure. Happy to help." But he was thinking something else: Why did I open my big mouth?

CHAPTER 19

"Darius Simpson, aka, Dix Simpson, is wanted in five counties in Georgia, two in Texas, and seven in Arizona," reported Bill Fast to the sheriff on Monday. "He's a pretty bad guy, according to this FBI report. He traffics in crack cocaine and opiates, especially black tar heroin. It looks like he may be hooking up with Jack Sample so he can dabble in meth."

Ollman was uncharacteristically quiet. He was taking the day off — in fact, several days off — to help his daughter, Dottie, with her husband's funeral arrangements. But Mitch had a job to do, closing down meth labs in the county, and now he had a personal score to settle.

"There's more," Fast said, when Mitch didn't say anything.

"Of course, there is," the sheriff said with fatigue.

"Simpson is wanted by the DEA. They suspect he works for the Mexican organization known as the Hal'cons, and would, if we allow it, bring all that violence to our little county."

"Shit!" Ollman lamented. "What else?"

"Ernesto Rodriguez Garcia Soto is his second-in-command. Ernesto is reported to have murdered fifteen Mexican nationals, including a child. He's Simpson's enforcer, but he's got leadership chops of his own, and a terrific thirst for blood. The smart money bets he was the one who murdered Mark."

"Bill, I don't want to play this one like an easy win. I want proof that Soto is our guy. But I want the sewage who did this to my Dottie — left her widowed with a youngster. Nothing can go wrong on this. I want the guy, whoever he is, nailed to a wall.

"If it isn't Soto, I wanna know who it is, and I want him real bad. We square?"

"Square, Sheriff. Now, what about Sample?"

"We know for an iron-clad certainty that he's cooking. I want him real bad, too ," Ollman said with conviction.

"And what about that baby in the house?" Bill asked.

"I'm biding my time, Bill. I don't care if it does cost me my career. I want him caught in cahoots with this Simpson and Soto syndicate. Interstate trafficking will get them all gone forever. I want Mark's killer the most, though. We'll do what we have to."

Fast kept his lip buttoned. He had a much different view, a view more centered on the life of a child. But if he said a word, law enforcement in Shelby County could easily lose any victory in this.

CHAPTER 20

"Hello. Is this Chelsea?"

"Yes. Who's calling?"

"Hi, Chelsea. This is Joe."

Uncertain silence. Two or three long seconds passed during which Joe MacDonald's hands became clammy.

"I met you Saturday at the farmers' market in Monroe City," Joe continued.

More uncertain silence.

"I was at the booth next to yours selling eggs."

Maddening silence. Finally, Chelsea spoke. "Of course, I remember you, Joe. I was just waiting for a little privacy to talk . How has your week been?"

"My week has been great. Is this a bad time to talk?"

"I never know what kind of mood my dad is in until the screaming starts," Chelsea explained.

"Ouch! Do I want to know any more about that?"

"Probably not at this point. Hell, I don't want to know any more about it either, but I'm stuck."

"He screams a lot, does he? I wish my dad would scream once in a while. If he screamed at me, that would probably be the most attention I ever got from him," Joe revealed.

"Is it all fathers, you think? Or just the ones who drink?" Chelsea lamented.

"Okay, see, that's the exact kind of detail I'm not sure I want to know any more about," Joe demurred.

"Oh, sorry. New topic. What can I do for you this fine summer day?"

"I was just calling you," Joe said. Then he thought, "Here we go again with the lame, idiotic remarks. Why can't I talk to girls other than Grams and sound like something besides an imbecile?"

"You're calling me?" Chelsea teased. "I was entirely misled. I thought this was a fax coming in."

"What?"

"A fax. A facsimile."

This time, it was Joe who responded with awkward silence.

"I'm just kidding you, Joe. Just making a bad joke. Sorry."

"Chelsea," Joe said seriously, "I'm calling you about a very important problem."

"Really? What's the problem?" she said, curiosity piqued.

"It's your weight problem. I'm concerned for you and your weight problem."

"What? You've got a lot of nerve, jackass, if you're saying I'm fat. I am not, and what's your problem anyway?" she stammered.

"No, you're way too thin," Joe interrupted. "And I'm here to help."

"What are you talking about?"

"It just so happens that my grams, whom you met, is the best cook in any twelve counties, and I would like to invite you for dinner so that you can experience her cooking. How's Friday?"

Yet another silence.

"Chelsea, I was just kidding about you having a weight problem. You don't. I was just saying I want to invite you for dinner," Joe explained. "Grams is a great, great cook, and though you don't have a weight problem now, you just may after you come to dinner. I've put on five pounds."

"Since you've been where?"

"Sylvia. I live in Sylvia, or just outside of it," he answered.

"And how long have you been here?"

"Just a few weeks. My dad and stepmom left me here to help my grandparents on their farm for the summer."

"Is this the same dad who doesn't scream enough?"

"That's the one. How about dinner?"

"Um, okay, I guess. I won't have a car, and I can't count on my dad to drive me . . ." Chelsea said with some embarrassment.

Joe guessed that her dad would be too drunk to drive her. "No worries," he said. "I'll come get you, okay?"

The conversation continued for some time. The two discussed fathers and their foibles, German cuisine, basketball, the Shelby County high school, and the raccoon that Chelsea said was living under her house.

"I love animals," Joe told her, "but I don't think I've ever seen a raccoon up close and personal."

"Oh, they're very nice people," she assured him. "But you shouldn't say what you said."

"What did I say wrong? I was completely serious. I'm a point guard for my high school team, and my average is twenty-three points a game. What's wrong with saying that?"

"No, no. I mean before, about my weight problem. You have no idea what girls go through in this country about their weight."

"Since I've never been a girl so far, I would have to agree," Joe acknowledged.

"So far," she repeated, and she began to laugh. The laughter lasted a long while, and Joe waited with thinning patience for her to wind it down.

She was breathing hard by the time she finished laughing. Joe was silent. He feared getting her started again.

To change the subject, Joe said, "I hope you like spargel. Grams' spargel is fantastic."

"I have no idea what that is," Chelsea confessed.

"I didn't either until I got to Sylvia. It's a kind of asparagus and it's not fattening at all until you put on the hollandaise sauce."

"Ooh, that does sound delicious. I think you could put hollandaise sauce on golf balls and they'd be yummy."

"So, dinner Friday, okay?"

After a moment she replied with finality, "Sure. Dinner sounds great. You driving?"

"Count on it."

"What time should I be ready?"

CHAPTER 21

"Jack, that guy who got shot outside, who was he?" Sarah demanded to know. "Do you know who killed him or why? It was just around the corner. It could have been me walking home with Dustin. Do we need to pack up and move?"

"I don't think that would help," Jack said.

"Why not? I don't want to live somewhere bullets are flying all around. We have a baby! I thought Sylvia was safe. And what in hell are you doing?"

"I'm getting high," Jack replied.

"You're sticking a needle in your neck. I've never seen that before with you. When did that start?"

"It's a better high, is all. And I thought we were safe here, too. Oh, God, that feels so good."

Knowing Jack as she did, Sarah could tell he was hiding something from her. For one thing, the mainlining meth was new, so something must have happened to change Jack's ways. In keeping with her own nature, though, she didn't ask. Ignorance was bliss— or so she wished to believe.

Still, something spurred her to keep the pressure on. She said, "Who was the guy who got shot? I think you know."

Jack took a breath. "He was a cop spying on us, okay?" Jack raised his voice. "They're onto us, and it's happening at the worst possible time." Jack's body was already beginning to reflect the hyperactivity brought on by the stimulant. He slammed his fist down on a counter next to a batch of meth. "Whew, that feels great," he repeated.

"I disagree," Sarah answered in a quiet voice. "The worst possible time would be when one of us gets shot and killed. Did you shoot this cop?"

"Me? Hell, no. What with? We don't have any guns. You know I wouldn't keep guns around Dustin."

The hypocrisy of the remark was plain to Sarah. "So, you're saying it's okay to cook crystals in a house with our baby, invite all kinds of strangers from God knows where doing God knows what, allow a shooting to go on yards from our front door, but I shouldn't worry about my son because you don't keep guns in the house? Jeez."

"Hey, I didn't tell anybody to shoot anybody. I didn't tell the cops to stake out our house. I didn't shoot anybody!" Jack was yelling now.

"Who did, Jack?"

"I dunno. I was in the basement when it happened. I didn't see it."

"Who was it, Jack? I know you know. It was one of your people. Which one?" Sarah yelled back. This level of assertiveness was unlike Sarah, but the murder around the corner had her unnerved.

"Ernesto — Okay? Ernesto did it."

"I knew it. That guy creeps me out. Do we have to have him around?"

"Yes, we do, Sarah. He and his partner Dix are going to bring us enough business to make anything worthwhile. We've just got to get away from these cops, now that they know we're here."

"I guess you're right. I'll call the landlord and tell him we're moving. We'll find another house in another town."

"I can't cook here anymore. The next house, you sign the lease. It'll be easier to hide."

"It costs money to move, Jack."

"We got plenty of money. Dix is seeing to that," Jack assured her.

"Good. Then maybe we can get a place that isn't such a dump," she complained.

Sarah went up the basement stairs feeling stuck. An inner voice agreed that the thing to do would be to move—but without Jack. Pack up Dustin and get going. But with no job, no marketable skills, no money of her own, no reliable car or other resources, where could she go and how could she survive? She was a prisoner, and so was her baby boy.

CHAPTER 22

"Hi, this is Joe," Joe said to Lynae over the phone. "Is Jamal around?"

"Jamal! Telephone!" Lynae bellowed.

Joe waited an uncomfortable number of moments before he heard movement on the other end of the call. Then Jamal answered the phone.

"Hey, whaddup?" Jamal asked after Joe identified himself.

"Hey, it's all good," Joe replied. "I talked to Chelsea. She said she'd see me."

"Who? Who's Chelsea?"

"That girl I told you I met in Monroe—"

"Oh, yeah, right, right. What you got planned with her?"

"She's coming for dinner Friday night."

"Family dinner? Real sexy, man. What then? A slide projector showing pictures of your vacation?" Jamal kidded.

Joe paused, thinking through Jamal's take on the planned evening. "Wow, man, why do you always make me feel like such a loser dweeb?"

"It's not me, Joe. Maybe it's 'cause you *are* a loser dweeb," Jamal teased. "Hey, man, 's okay. Maybe she's the kind who goes for the homespun type. Maybe she'll fall over for the family cat."

"We do have a great cat," Joe agreed.

"No, I mean you. You're the cat and you like family dinners, see? Family cat. Never mind. Forget it."

"Did you ever eat my grams' cooking?"

"Your grandmother's cooking is legendary, though I haven't eaten any of it myself."

"So maybe you can understand that a family dinner is a great idea as long as she's doing the cooking."

"Okay. So, why are you calling me?" Jamal laughed.

"Just to show off, I guess. What's new with you?"

"Me and my dad are going golfing this afternoon. He thinks the walking and fresh air will do him good."

A second twinge of envy hit Joe. "I didn't know you play golf," he said.

"I didn't say I did. I don't. I know Dad will give me some great tips. He's off on sick leave, still, but he has to go back to work to-morrow, so this is our last chance for a while. Weekends get too busy. You wanna go with us?" Jamal invited.

"Really? Uh, sure. Where do you want me to meet you?"

"We'll pick you up."

"Okay. Let me ask Grams real quick if she needs me this after-noon. I'll call you right back, okay?"

"Square," Jamal said, and hung up.

CHAPTER 23

"Joe," said Inga when she walked to the shed to find her husband, "Third went golfing with Don and Jamal. I guess he'll be home before dark."

"That's great, Inga. I like to see the boy make a friend."

"Me, too," Inga agreed, "I think he's been lonely since he's been with us. Two hundred miles from his friends, and only old people to talk to."

"That Armstead kid is all right. A lot less of a trouble maker than a lot of kids his age."

"He seems nice. Poor kid, he has terrible skin," Inga protested gently.

"So, is that a reason Third shouldn't be friends with him?"

"No, of course not. It's just that I feel for him at that age," Inga said.

"Agreed. But while lots of kids have clear skin and are better looking, a lot of them don't have the kind of parenting that kid does. Don is real involved in the kid. They do a lot together and the kid means the world to him. And now, a new baby.

"By the way, Inga, you look beautiful today."

"I do?"

"You do."

Joe took his wife of many years and laid a kiss on her that any teenage boy would admire.

Breaking the kiss, Inga looked her husband square in the eyes and said, "We have the house to ourselves for a while, you know."

CHAPTER 24

Jack and Sarah found new digs in Elsa, a town even smaller than Sylvia, Elsa was referred to as the poor stepchild of Shelby County.

Jack put down first and last months' rent on a small house with a basement. It was well off the main drag and was suitably nondescript from the outside. One could drive by it five times without noticing it, which is what Jack sought. It was a funny color , but all the houses in Elsa were funny colors, so this one blended right in.

He paid cash to the eager landlord, and Sarah Dednum signed the lease knowing she'd never pay a dime of the rent.

The landlord, also named Jack , was unaware he was renting out his property to a meth cook and his girlfriend. Indeed, Jack Carson had no idea what was coming. He doted on the baby, held him and kissed him, and told his wife later what a fine young couple the new tenants were.

Jack and Sarah began packing as soon as they got back to Sylvia. They moved things to the car on the down low, staying circumspect about any possible observers. The surveillance team had temporarily evacuated after Mark was killed, so it was important to Jack to move quickly, get out of that house, and not be followed to the new one.

A quick phone call to Hannibal secured Jack's reservation of a U-Haul truck for the next day. With any luck, they'd be out and gone before the cops knew any different. Fortunately, the couple had few belongings. They had moved into the furnished house with little more than their clothes, a few baby toys, some kitchen utensils, a mattress and box springs, an overstuffed chair, and the equipment from the basement. There was a medicine chest stocked with calamine, but little else of importance.

Sarah packed five cans of tuna fish, three boxes of mac and cheese, a frozen pizza and a quart of milk—the entire contents of the cabinets and fridge. She didn't bother to clean the refrigerator, or anything else. If the landlord kept their hundred-dollar security deposit, so be it. Haste was the operative word.

If Sarah's nature had been more given to introspection, she might have realized sooner that life with Jack was bound to be a series of fast, abrupt moves from one community to the next as escaping law enforcement became the primary consideration. But it wasn't. Even as a mother with a baby, the young woman seldom looked backward or forward. She was in the moment.

CHAPTER 25

"Have you played golf before, Joe?" Don Armstead asked the young man as he drove the golf cart across the first green.

"Never, Mr., um, Don. My dad and I don't do things like this."

"What do you do together?" Don wanted to know.

"We remain separate together," Joe answered with an ironic tone. "He goes to work and I go to my job when I have one. We do it at the same time, but there isn't anything together about it," Joe answered with thinly-veiled acrimony.

"I see," Don replied.

Jamal spoke up. "Hey, Dad, Tim Flynn is having a pool party at his house Thursday. He invited me. Can I go?"

"Depends. Drugs and drinking?"

"No, I don't think he's into that. Just pool."

"Swimming pool or billiards?"

"Billiards, I guess. A swimming pool didn't come up."

"Will there be adults in attendance?"

"As far as I know, yeah."

Joe, listening, recognized the vernacular. Jamal was lying—at least in part—to this father he was so devoted to. Joe felt let down, but he wasn't sure why.

"Can I bring Joe with me?"

Startled, Don hesitated to answer. "Uh, that's entirely up to Joe and Inga. And Tim Flynn. I can't speak for them.

"You know, don't you, that Elsa isn't the safest place to be. Will you be indoors playing pool and not wandering around town?"

"Indoors, I guess. Why, Dad?"

"It's just not the best place to hang around outside, but if you go in the house and stay in the house, I have no problem with it," Don relented.

"What am I invited to?" Joe put in. "Who is Tim Flynn?"

"A guy I met at the gym. Dad and I go work out at a gym in Macon. This guy's not much older than you and me," Jamal explained, "but he owns his home and works a good job. He's real straight. Nice guy. He gets me."

"He doesn't get you, Jamal," his father intoned. "White people don't get black people."

Joe was uncomfortable, and looked away, staring out from the golf cart as it sat at the edge of the course.

"No offense, Joe," Don offered with little tone of apology. "It just is what it is."

"What exactly is it, then, Mr. Armstead?" Joe asked. "I don't think I'm prejudiced. I don't think my family is. Why shouldn't I be offended when you say that?"

"Joe, I've known your granddad for ten years. If there's a white guy I have ever met that gets black folks, he might be it. His view of society is, shall we say, enlightened. But he doesn't really understand me or the life I've had to live. He can't. It isn't possible. He doesn't have what's known in the trade as continuity."

Joe's discomfort ratcheted up, and he felt disinclined to continue with this line of preaching. But he kept his feelings to himself, rather than risk his new friendship with Jamal.

"See, black people are black all the time," Don continued. "There is never any time when we can go home and take off our black skin and be just like you. You may be able to understand and sympathize about the discrimination that has never let up since this country began. You might stand against it, and you might look inside yourself and resist the poison within yourself, but you can't really understand it until you've lived it every day.

"Case in point, I was at Walmart in Macon. A lady was in there demonstrating the air fresheners, so I went over to her to smell the stuff. White girl. Very nice. There was a white guy behind me who didn't know I could hear him. He turned to his wife and said, 'This guy's probably just trying to get the stink out of his house.'"

"Oh, my God!" Joe cried out.

"Yeah, it gets bad at times. Black guys like me who have some prestige in a town have it real, real easy by comparison."

Joe was silent. Don realized his preaching was embarrassing the young man, and he relented, but not in time to stop Jamal from speaking up.

"Dad," Jamal countered, embarrassed by the diatribe and desperate to change the topic, "can you explain what a mulligan is?"

"Your grandfather understands more than most 'cause he's lived a lot of it," Don continued as though he hadn't been interrupted.

"He told me about that once," Joe said.

"Why are you bringing this up now, Dad?" Jamal asked.

"Because you want to go to a party in Elsa. There's a well-known Klan enclave there, and I want you safe. You and Joe, if you take him."

"I'll be okay. I'll hide behind my white skin," Joe promised.

"Yeah, you will," Don agreed. "And that's my whole point. A guy can come down the street toward me, and he can be two blocks away. He has formed an opinion of me based on my skin before I ever have the chance to say hello, or smile at him, or tell him to have a great day. My skin goes before me everywhere. There is no escaping it."

Don and the boys sat in silence for a few moments. "Joe could be in danger, as well, just for hangin' with you – white skin or not. Look, I don't want any son of mine to be afraid to live his life, but I also want you safe. So, I guess you two can go to the party if you promise to stay where you know people. But be careful, for heaven's sake!"

CHAPTER 26

Joe showered in the middle of the afternoon on Friday. He had carefully calculated travel times to and from Monroe City. It was forty-five minutes each way, almost all the way to Hannibal. Joe wished he could get a beer to help him calm down. Sure, he'd met and dated beautiful young women before. Well, no, not really. Not this beautiful. Not like Chelsea.

He expressed his nervousness to Inga who smiled, saying, "No, you can't have a beer, especially if you're driving to Monroe City. But how about some chamomile tea?"

Not his first choice, Joe thought with some dissatisfaction, but he drank it—with lots of sugar.

He followed the directions from Chelsea and got to her house within ten minutes of his planned arrival time. Her home was in a trailer park, and the double-wide was dilapidated and awful. It was mud-brown and many shingles were gone or hanging by one nail, holding on for dear life.

A sizable sycamore tree stood near the trailer, and branches hung over the trailer roof, to crush it if a windstorm descended. The roof was decorated with fallen branches, and more branches peeked over the sides of the gutters. The place was neglected, Joe assessed, but it wasn't his business.

He knocked on the screen door, and Chelsea answered immediately. She must have been waiting just inside. She was just as beautiful as he remembered.

Rather than inviting him in, she stepped outside with her purse on her shoulder and said, "Hi. Are you ready to go? I am." There was a very slight edge, almost unnoticeable, of disgust in her voice. She glanced back with just a tiny curl to her lip.

Joe didn't ask.

"I sure am. The menu tonight has changed. It will be Asian. Shrimp stir fry with home-made crab rangoon. There will be hot sauce and plum sauce — both made from scratch, and for dessert, strawberry shortcake.

"Sounds terrific. I'm hungry. And I'd sure rather be at your house than mine."

"Oh?" Joe coaxed, "Care to explain?"

Chelsea smiled. "I'm looking forward to your grandmother's cooking."

Joe loved the Asian restaurants he'd eaten at in St. Louis. He was confident that his grandmother's adept hand could match or exceed his tastiest memory.

"Mrs. MacDonald, this is fantastic!" Chelsea said, as they dug into Gram's cooking at the dining room table. She spooned extra plum sauce over her crab rangoon. "If I ate here all the time, I'd look like Jabba the Hutt. Thanks for inviting me."

"You're welcome," Inga said, and smiled. "It's all healthy, too, because I use low fat ingredients."

"Low fat is always good," Chelsea stated. "Well, actually, no, it's not always good. But it's always preferable to us girls since we have to watch every calorie or pay the price. But guys can be heavy and they don't get ridiculed. "

"I agree there's certainly a double standard," Inga nodded. "But to be fair, at least the female gender is making strides every day for an equal share. Only last week, a friend of mine from church got a job changing oil at a mechanic shop, and they never even asked if she was a girl."

Chelsea started to laugh, and Joe rolled his eyes with embarrassment, not unlike the way her father had done at the farmers' market. While he normally enjoyed her laughter, on this occasion, he wanted to make a favorable impression on his grandparents, and he feared Chelsea's near-hysteria was bound to have the opposite effect.

Her laughter continued for a good five minutes. Gramps watched her with a big smile on his face. Inga giggled twice, but was as bewildered as she had been at the market.

When Chelsea's laughter subsided, she wiped her melted mascara with her napkin and then asked to use the bathroom.

Inga guided her to it and returned alone.

"Third," she began quietly, "Why is your friend so unhappy?"

"Unhappy?" Joe asked quizzically. "If anything, she is a little bit too happy. I don't know why she laughs like that. It's never all that funny, the things she laughs at."

"Usually when someone laughs that loud and long at things that aren't very funny, it means he or she is quite sad and trying to make themselves happier—"cause they really aren't," Gramps suggested. "Let's try to get to know her and maybe we'll get some clues."

"So, tell us, Chelsea," Gramps asked when she returned to the table, "What do your parents do for a living?"

The elderly man noticed that Chelsea's eyes were red and her face was puffy. He suspected that she had laughed at the dinner table, but cried in the bathroom.

"Well, my father was laid off from the Butler plant in Hannibal. So, he's been out of work for a while now. My mom owns Sugar 'n Spice. It's a boutique in Monroe City. Sometimes he pitches in and helps her. Most of the time, though, he stays home." Chelsea picked at her napkin and licked her lips.

"Neither one of them cooks, though, Mrs. MacDonald," she continued, turning to Inga, "so I really appreciate a good home-made meal. They are far and few between for me. This is a great meal, and I thank you for having me. Please excuse my laughter, though. I don't know why some things just strike me as much funnier that most people find them to be." She smiled sweetly.

"I reckon it's kind of a struggle with only one parent working," Gramps probed.

Chelsea looked at the old man for several seconds before she took a deep, resigned breath. "Maybe my father's reputation is the problem. He was fired from the Butler plant for drinking on the job. He was drunk while supervising the machinery, and a lady lost her hand because of it. It was all over the paper. Since then, all he does is drink. Well, that's not right. He does other things besides drink, but the drinking might be the least awful thing he does."

The cryptic remark hung in the air while all the MacDonalds digested the words of the troubled young woman. No one dared to ask for an explanation.

"Anyone for strawberry shortcake?" Inga segued.

"Real whipped cream?" Chelsea asked in a quiet voice.

"I wouldn't have it any other way," Inga assured her, smiling.

CHAPTER 27

Inga and Third woke up Saturday morning ready for their big travel weekend. They timed their expected arrival in St. Louis for the middle of the afternoon so they could change, go out to dinner with Joe II and Liz, and then to the symphony. They left mid-morning after Gramps kissed Grams and hugged Joe.

As they pulled onto the highway, Joe was reminded of his trip to Monroe City earlier to bring Chelsea to the house. He rambled on to his grandmother about how pretty and smart she was, but glossed over the awkwardness and discomfort of the apparent crying jag in the bathroom.

"Yes, she is certainly pretty, and seems nice," Inga said. She sought to gently ease into the questions she had about the young lady. "But don't you wonder about her . . . I don't know . . . ways?"

"What do you mean?"

"I got the sense that she is really dissatisfied with her situation. How much do you know about her family life? She seemed to have been crying in the bathroom, and I wonder what was wrong," Inga continued.

"Wait a minute, Grams. We don't know for sure she was crying in the bathroom."

"Her eyes were red, and her makeup was mostly off."

"Maybe she was laughing in the bathroom. Some people cry when they laugh," Joe ventured.

"So, do you believe that everything is a-okay with the young woman?" Inga challenged. "Did you see or hear anything else that might make a person wonder what's going on in her life? Because I'm uneasy about her. I think there's something real wrong at home or somewhere. She might just need some help," Inga cautioned him.

Joe thought about his evening with Chelsea. He remembered odd remarks and behaviors he could report, but he had second thoughts about confiding in Inga. He mulled it over a moment before speaking.

"No, I'm not saying nothing's wrong. It's pretty clear that her father drinks too much, and there may be something else. When I got to her trailer —"

"She lives in a trailer?"

"Yep, a double-wide. Why?"

"Because trailers are inexpensive housing. Makes me think the family really is struggling," Inga explained.

Joe shrugged. "Anyway," he continued, "it was pretty run down and in need of some repairs and maintenance that would be easy and inexpensive to do. If her dad is off work, I wonder why he doesn't do some of those things."

"What kind of things?" Inga wanted to know.

"Simple stuff like cleaning the gutters and getting the tree branches off the roof—something I could do in a half hour.

"Plus, when I picked her up, she wouldn't let me in. She came right out the door and didn't suggest I come inside. I assumed it was because the house was a mess and she didn't want me to see it. Or maybe her dad was passed out drunk or something."

"How old is Chelsea?" Inga asked.

Joe raised his eyebrows and glanced at his grandmother. "She's sixteen. Why?"

"Just wondering. Here's my idea. Why don't you call her up and ask her if you could come by and clean off the roof and clean out the gutters Sunday? Joe and I will drop you off in Monroe City before we turn back to Shelbina. We'll pick you up after church. Maybe you can find out more, or at least meet the mother. This is all very suspicious to me."

"We can't go to church this Sunday because we'll be in St. Louis. But next week sounds good—if the gutters hold up that long." Joe realized that this was what Gramps was talking about. When someone needs help, a MacDonald pitches in. Even if it's hard, even if it's dangerous, a MacDonald pitches in. It's his family duty. While Joe wasn't comfortable interfering in another family, he put his discomfort aside.

Inga fell quiet and looked out the window. The two rode in silence for a long while, as memories from a distant time and place began to haunt Inga. Presently, she said, "There is something very familiar about this young woman's ways. When I was young, I went through some bad things, and I wonder if she might be, too."

"You're gonna have to explain that, Grams," Joe said..

Inga sat quietly for several minutes, gathering her thoughts. Joe let her be, but he was curious as to what she might say.

Inga inhaled. "Do you remember how I told you that four French prisoners of war lived in our house in Germany?"

"Sure. It's hard to forget."

Inga was about thirteen when it happened. One of the French prisoners was named Hugo. He was a short man with dark hair, and a stocky build. His beard was untrimmed and ugly —they were all unkempt – and he smelled like sweat and cigarettes. Inga never liked him, although most of the prisoners were nice to the children.

The guard's name was Abel Hess. The kids called him Uncle Abe. Uncle Abe was not very good at watching prisoners. One night when Abe had had some ale, he failed to lock Hugo's door.

Inga got up to go to the bathroom and get some milk. The house was quiet as the families slept. Hugo surprised Inga in the kitchen.

She was a frail child at thirteen, and timid—a perfect hostage.

Hugo clamped his smelly hand over Inga's mouth and told her she would be leaving with him. If she uttered one sound, he would kill her entire family. She complied, even though if she screamed and awakened the household, several men, all larger and stronger than Hugo, would outman him. Hugo would be no match for any one of them. While Inga as an adult, understood the predicament, Inga as a small, terrified teenager, was overcome by fear, and it quieted her reason.

Hugo took Inga by the hand and led her outside, dragging her down the road with him. The night was black as tar, and the two of them kept tripping over things in the road which was unlit for fear of Allied bombs. The sky was moonless and overcast.

Hugo realized after he stumbled the first time that doing so provided the young girl the chance to get away. He compensated by repeating the threats against her family, describing the horrible and sadistic ways he would kill them should she run off.

Inga did not struggle, certain that Hugo would make good on his threats.

Captor and captive arrived at a farm. It was barely visible, but Hugo identified the barn and took the girl inside. It was pointless to run off without any direction in the darkness, so he told Inga they would stay there until there was more light in the sky.

Inga cried, begging him to let her go. She recognized he was supposed to be the enemy, but she had gotten to know the prisoners over many weeks, and she felt just as betrayed as if a member of her own family had kidnapped her.

Inga took a seat in a corner of the barn and prayed for release. They were an hour and a half out of the house but only about a half mile away. Hugo was far from safe, but the night was too black to venture further. With three or four hours till dawn, the fugitive had time on his hands.

"What does this have to do with Chelsea?" Joe asked. After the most recent tale of Inga's early life, the extraordinary nature of her upbringing fascinated Joe, but the tale he was hearing now had the flavor of a horror movie, and he wasn't sure he could stand it.

"I'm getting to that, Third," Inga promised. "I'm just not sure you want to hear the rest. I am counting on you to be the strong young man you have shown me you are."

Joe stared into his grandmother's inscrutable face for several seconds before looking back at the road.

It might have been Hugo's fear of dozing off. It might have been his familiarity with the young girl, or the time he had spent without a woman. It might have been pure meanness, or the drive to feel control over something in his life.

His abuse of her was brutal. He began by wrapping his large strong hand around her neck and squeezing until she fainted. She came to after several moments to the ripping of her dress, this horrible man forcing himself into her. She screamed at the moment of violation, and he covered her mouth with one hand.

"Your mother will get much worse than this if you make another sound," he told her in German she could barely make out, but his violence and ugliness were articulate.

She remained still, praying for it to be over. Suddenly, Inga thought she heard something. Her eyes followed the sound to the barn door. Someone was coming in with a lantern.

Hugo, intent on his task, his eyes closed in pleasure, didn't notice. There was, abruptly, a loud, hollow crack, and he collapsed on top of Inga. She heard a woman gasp with terror and sadness as the unconscious man was pushed off of her.

Inga was blinded by the bright lantern that was now next to her. When her eyes adjusted, she saw her mother holding a shovel in one hand. She had clobbered Hugo with it, and was now collapsed not far from her, overcome with grief and anger.

Inga rolled away from the brute and went to her mother. Hedda dropped the shovel and grabbed her girl up in her arms, sobbing and cursing. She let Inga sob for a time, too, then gathered herself and stoically lead Inga outside, her reassuring hands on the girl's shoulders.

Hedda Wentzel sat her daughter down on a tractor and told her not to move. She would be back in a few minutes. Don't move, she admonished. She was safe here. Don't come back into the barn, no matter what, okay?

Inga nodded mutely and started crying again.

Hedda went in the barn, Inga assumed, to retrieve her lantern.

The unconscious Hugo began to stir as Hedda approached him. Her lantern provided the light she needed, and the shovel did the rest. She beat the man in the head with the metal edge of the shovel. The blood splashed her dress, but she kept beating and beating, blow after blow, until Hedda was sure he had breathed his last. Then she kept it up for ten more blows until his skull was cracked open and his brains looked like raw sausage.

Outside, Inga could hear her mother's sobs and shrieks punctuating each blow. She sobbed again herself, and buried her face in her hands, wiping her running nose and trying desperately to will away the pain from the violation.

Inga could feel blood running out of her. As she did, her fear took a leap forward.

When the blows stopped, Hedda came out of the barn, lantern in hand. The shovel was left behind, but proof of her actions was splashed liberally over her dress and shoes.

She took her daughter in her arms again, and the two hugged and cried for a long time.

At last, Hedda broke the hug, took Inga's pure young face in her hands, and spoke.

"Inga, this is a terrible thing that has happened to you, and I'm very sorry. But for now, we must keep it just between us. You are not to speak of this to anyone. Not Christoph or Konstanze or anyone else at all. Do you understand?"

Inga nodded.

"Things in Germany are bad right now for everyone. When something like this befalls a young one like you, or any woman, well, you would be looked down upon. You would be tainted and sullied, even though it wasn't your fault. So, we will keep you from that further hurt by keeping this a solemn secret. Just you and me, right?"

Inga nodded again. "Momma, you killed that man, didn't you?"

"I did. And there will be questions to answer with the Gestapo. I may have to be taken away, so I pray you will be all right, you and your brother and sister. I pray we will all be all right."

"How did you find me, Momma? How did you know I was in that barn?

"I had the lantern, and that man didn't. The things you two tripped over and moved, the tracks in the soft earth, well, you left quite a trail. You couldn't have done it better if you tried. Did you try to leave me a trail?"

"No, Momma. I was too afraid to do anything. He said he would kill you and Christoph and Konstanze if I resisted him. He told me how he would do it, and it was terrible."

"It's over now. Let's go get cleaned up. And I have to find something less bloody to put on."

"So, do I, Momma, I'm bleeding."

"Oh, dear Jesus!" Hedda cried.

Inga fished a tissue out of her bag when she finished telling Third the tale. She wiped her eyes.

Third was solemn, eyes on the road, heart aching for what this young teenager had gone through a half century before. This young, lovely girl had grown up, had a son, and then a grandson.

He shook his head as he considered the horror his grandmother had endured, and the strong, admirable woman he knew she had become.

It may have been ten minutes the two rode in silence. Inga reviewed the events in her memory as she had been doing for decades.

Joe reviewed them, too, with an admiration for his great-grandmother's strength that he would probably never admit. Peaceful people aren't supposed to admire those who murder others, even if the others are evil. But Joe didn't care. Great-grandmother Wentzel acted with courage and strength. He wished such strength was within him, but he doubted it was.

After a few minutes, Joe spoke. "I still don't know what this has to do with Chelsea?"

"Maybe nothing. I don't know the young lady well enough to say one way or the other. But I'll tell you what happened to me."

"Oh, my God! Something else happened to you?"

Inga smiled. "Yes, Third, it did. In those days there were no counselors, psychologists or psychiatrists you could go to when you had something like this happen. My mother was adamant that we keep it a secret. I had to deal with it myself and there was no magic pill to get over it." Inga looked out the window and wiped another tear.

"Grams, you don't have to talk about this if you don't want to."

Inga spoke as though she hadn't heard her grandson. "I started to laugh inappropriately. When someone would say something at home that was even slightly amusing, I would fall apart in hysterical laughter. I embarrassed myself at school, and at home everyone thought I had gone nuts.

Even my mother became disturbed, although she suspected the reason I changed. It was all about trying to force myself to be happy. I was living in a horrible time in history, in the middle of a war with little to eat and less to wear, freeloading in a borrowed home and scared to death to turn on a light in the house after dark." She paused. "And then this happened."

Joe didn't know what to say. He gripped the steering wheel with all his might and stared straight ahead at the road. When he heard his grandmother take a breath to continue, he braced himself for the rest of the tale.

"I tried to be strong, Third. I really did—for my mother—but it was too much. It wasn't a conscious thing, but I dealt with it by laughing at the least little thing. Sometimes, in honest moments, the laughter would turn to tears. I kept those moments private, though. I would go outside when the laughter began to change to grief. I don't think anyone ever knew. I never told a soul until years later when I met Joe."

"Gramps knows?"

"Of course. Certainly. He knows everything about me. That's how a relationship is supposed to be. He accepted me completely and never judged me for being dirty. He's a wonderful man. It was ironic that as Joe began to make me happy, I stopped the inappropriate laughing.

"Now it could very well be that your friend, Chelsea, simply has a hair trigger on her sense of humor. But it's just as probable that something is wrong in her life. I think she needs help

"What do you want me to do?"

"I don't know, Third. You can't very well outright ask her. You don't know her well enough. But if she knew you were sympathetic and a gentleman, maybe she would feel enough trust to confide in you. There are resources for young people who are in bad home situations."

"Grams, I don't know what to think. You and your mother were amazing women. You are still really amazing. But I just don't think I inherited the kind of courage you have. I don't think I could go through what you've been through, and I'm not sure I can help Chelsea."

The two fell quiet again, both deep in thought.

After twenty minutes, Chelsea Christmas was still on Joe's mind as the two crossed the small piece of real estate that comprised Monroe City. Joe told himself he would try to get the young woman to reveal herself in hopes that he could help.

Trying to get his mind off of Chelsea, Joe opened a new topic with Inga. She had been looking out the window, silently watching the scenery go by, her handbag in her lap, her sunglasses on.

"Grams, I've been thinking a lot about some of the things Gramps said. So, what about Stalin?" he asked.

"Hmm? What?" Inga returned, breaking from her reverie.

"Joseph Stalin. In school, we learned that he was a bad guy who brutalized and murdered a lot of Russians. He was an animal, and he was a communist. Dad says all the time that if we let communism come into this country, we would turn it into a Stalinist regime and then we'd all be prisoners, and we'd lose this country and all the freedoms that we have. What does Gramps think about that?" he asked with just a note of challenge in his voice.

"You'll have to ask Joe, Third. It's up to him to tell you what he thinks. But I can tell you what I think."

"Okay . . ."

"I think that any system, whether economic, governmental, or what have you, is only as good as the people who run it. Personally, I believe that socialism is a good system, if tempered with a certain amount of capitalism, but not too much. The key is that the powers that be in any system have to embrace the spirit of that system," Inga stated.

"I'm not sure I follow," Joe said.

"Well, look at it this way. I'm a Christian and I try to be the best Christian I can. So, I sure as blazes don't want my religion or my Savior blamed for the things people throughout the generations have done in Christ's name.

People who call themselves Christians, have killed and stolen, pillaged—done terrible things. It's gone on for centuries and isn't over yet. Should we blame Christianity for the actions of those people?"

"Maybe we should, Gram. I mean, if Christianity leads to acts like that, well, then maybe it's not so great."

"Are you kidding me, Third?"

"I'm not doing anything, Grams. I'm just trying to learn. It seems to me that if a system makes way for hurting people, it may not be a good system."

"What if it is a good system, but people use it for their own benefit to hurt others?"

"Then it's not so good," Joe insisted.

"Do you go to church at home, Joe?"

"Not if I can help it."

"How long have you not gone to church?"

"I don't remember ever going," Joe replied. "Dad never took me, and Liz doesn't care."

"That's disappointing. You've missed a lot."

"Like what? Not having my Sundays all to myself?" Joe asked, raising his voice a pitch higher.

After a few silent moments, Inga spoke again. "Socialism is not much different from religion, I think," she began.

"What? Socialism is completely different from religion," Joe contradicted.

"Not in all ways. In both systems, there is a great deal to be gained by accepting them, but people are frightened away by a society-wide perception based on misconceptions."

"What is to be gained by being a communist country?"

"Ideally, a more equal distribution of wealth so that the very, very wealthy don't exist side by side with people who have absolutely nothing. Capitalism strives to concentrate wealth."

"Okay, then what is to be gained by being a Christian?"

"Eternal life, for one thing."

Joe paused again, thinking. "I'm surprised that you seem to believe in both. I thought a lot of communists were atheists."

"Marx was a human. I understand his rejection of religion, but I suspect he didn't know Jesus the way I do. You take the best from anything, and leave the rest," Inga said.

"Besides," she continued, "the first Christians lived in communes and shared all they had in common. Their lifestyles were kind of a microcosm for a socialist utopia . And Jesus taught that, if you have two coats and your neighbor has none, give him one of yours."

"Third, Joe is the one who knows the most about this. You should ask him about it," Inga concluded. "Now, how about we stop in Hannibal, gas the car, and visit the restrooms?"

The two chatted lightly until the Welcome to Hannibal sign came into view. Joe took the exit and stopped at the first store with a filling station attached. Inga went inside while Joe filled the tank. She made use of the facilities and then filled a cup with iced tea and a slice of lemon just as her grandson joined her inside. She offered him the drink or snacks of his choice, and when he declined, she paid and they left.

When they returned to the car, Joe broached another new topic. "Jamal Armstead got invited over to some guy's house. He and Chief Armstead met the guy at their gym. The guy has a pool table, and is having a get-together next week. Jamal asked me if I want to go along with him."

"Do you?" Inga asked.

"I'd love to. I like Jamal, and I like to hang out with him," Joe replied. "It's not just that he's the only guy up here I know near my age, or that he's the only friend I've got. I mean, it is like that, but I like the way he thinks and talks. He's real easy to hang with."

"Joe and I have been concerned since you got here about you not knowing very many people your own age. It would be great for you to spend time with Jamal. He's a nice young man. I've always liked the Armsteads," Inga said. "Where is the get-together?" Inga was rummaging in her handbag.

"In Elsa."

Inga froze with her handbag still open. She looked at her grandson. "You're going to Elsa with Jamal?"

Joe became defensive. "Are you going to tell me not to go because Jamal is black? 'Cause Chief Armstead doesn't want him to go for the same reason, but I don't see a problem if we don't go looking for trouble. I mean, Gram, it's the nineties! Do people really go after each other in this day and age because of color?"

"I don't know. I want to believe that time in history has passed, but I'm not sure. Most places in this country, a cross hasn't been burned on anyone's lawn for fifty years, but one burned in Eleanor not ten years ago. The police caught up with the men who burned it. They were from Elsa. Eleanor is five miles from Elsa. A black family tried to move in there, and that was their housewarming gift."

"Wow," Joe said, his eyes wide. "Things in St. Louis aren't nearly that bad."

"Oh, I think they are, Third. I think they're worse. Worse, because it's more subtle and insidious."

"Mr. Armstead talked to Jamal and me about that."

"When your father first moved to the city, he told me about getting into an elevator with a black man.

After a few floors, the elevator stopped, and an elderly white lady stepped onto the elevator, and the door closed. She hadn't noticed the other two at first, but when she looked up and saw that black man, she very obviously grabbed at her purse and clutched it close to her chest.

" Your father said the black man looked like he'd been cold-cocked."

"I guess it would have been worse if she'd paid attention and refused to get on the elevator at all," Joe surmised.

"Probably. But I think that kind of thing happens to black people all the time and it wears on their sense of hope.

It must be exhausting," Inga concluded.

Joe, listening, noted the incongruity between the seriousness of her words and the passion with which she spoke versus the soprano timbre of her voice. It was like a civil rights speech put to music and played on a xylophone.

"I've never known my dad to have any sympathy or compassion for anyone other than the usual rich white people he hangs out with. That must have happened a long time ago. He's changed," Joe complained.

Inga said nothing.

"Gramps says that being black in this country is a lot like being an Okie was in the thirties—the same instant judgment of people just because of the way Okies looked," Joe said.

"And smelled," Inga agreed.

For another long while, the two rode quietly. South of Hannibal, there was abandoned road construction, and Joe slowed and maneuvered on the rough, uneven pavement. Inga watched the young man drive. She looked across the seat at his profile and marveled at his physical resemblance to her son. Don't all parents hope to infuse their own values into their children? she asked herself. Surely, they do, but this young man had a mind of his own. He questioned things, disagreed with certain ideas, but still gave them consideration. Third would grow to be a fine man if Inga had her way.

The thought startled her. This was not her child, and though he was a grandchild, she scarcely had any right to teach him her values or beliefs, especially as removed as they were from his father's.

Joe, meanwhile, thought of relationships and his growing fondness for Jamal and Chelsea, the only two friends he could claim in Sylvia. He thought briefly of Sarah, too, but he seldom saw her and feared becoming embroiled in her mess of a life.

Joe was beginning to recognize that friends enrich a person's life in a way that even family can't.

It occurred to him that his St. Louis friends may lack a certain quality because they were mostly potheads and drunks. Still, friends and the relationships a person has with them add definition, comfort, and value to life.

Joe's father believed that wealth and achievement and the kudos he won from his employer earmarked a successful life. He was wrong, Joe told himself. Those trappings were superficial.

Of course, Joe admitted to himself, anything his father valued or found important was an object of his own scorn, and he had no apology for that attitude. Yeah, he had a comfortable enough life on his father's paycheck. Still, he would rather have a father who was poor, but interested in his own son, than a father who chases his son off to learn life from his grandparents.

The familiar ember of rage lit in Joe's soul, but he tamped it down. He was starting to build a life in Sylvia, so he couldn't fairly damn the father who caused that life to become reality.

If he had to go home now to stay, he would miss Jamal. He would even be sorry to leave Chelsea. And he would especially miss Grams and Gramps.

It's people who matter.

CHAPTER 28

"God dammit! God dammit! Mother frig . . . How in hell did this happen?" Chief Ollman bellowed at Bill Fast. "I've got thousands invested in an investigation that this town can't afford, to shut down this meth lab, and this Sample skips town in the dead of night and is just gone?"

"The house is empty, Sheriff. There's furniture, but any personal effects are gone," Bill replied placidly. Bill was annoyed as well about the failure of the investigation and the flight of the perpetrator, but Ollman was such a loose cannon, Fast did not wish to add his own fire to stoke Ollman's.

"How do you know?"

"We searched it."

"How? There's no warrant that I'm aware of."

"No, no warrant. The landlord dropped over to clean up for the next tenant, and he let us in. The place was a mess. They left in a hurry, certainly, but they left."

"Did they give the landlord any forwarding address?"

"Of course not, and they didn't tell him jack about where they were moving. Obviously, they were onto us."

"Obviously. It's a solid bet Sample was onto us when he killed Mark Newstead."

"We don't know that he killed Newstead. It may well have been this Simpson maniac who shot Mark, or his minion, Soto."

"Who?"

"Ernesto Rodriguez Garcia Soto. I told you about him. Simpson's muscle," Fast reminded Ollman.

"Oh, yeah. From now on, Soto. Why do Mexicans have to use so many names, anyway?" Ollman complained.

"No doubt it's a plot to lengthen the time we spend on paperwork," Fast retorted. "Keep us off the street."

"Thoughtful of their parents to think of that ahead of time. Real foresight, if you ask me."

" Soto's a blood-thirsty goon. We know he's killed before, mostly over drugs, and he kills for Simpson on a whim.

"Sample isn't a killer. Not directly, anyway, despite what his chemical does. I think he lacks the stones to walk up to an unmarked car and off a cop," Bill advised.

"Mark wasn't offed ," Ollman said bitterly. "He was murdered."

"What's the difference?"

"Use terms of respect. He was a friend and colleague to you, and my daughter's husband. By the way, I'm going by Dottie's house tonight with some groceries. Do you want to send anything along?"

Bill Fast removed his wallet from his back pocket and handed Ollman five one-hundred-dollar bills.

Ollman was surprised. "You always carry so much cash?"

"I saw this coming."

"Well, thanks."

"Now, back to Jack Sample and his bimbo. We have no idea where they went. We don't even have a last name on the girl," Bill explained.

"Too bad. Dollars to donuts she rents the next house in her name. We've got to find them. I can't stinking believe this happened. Who fell asleep on the job?" Ollman bellowed again, passion renewed.

"Gary Abbott. He actually did fall asleep in his car while he was watching the house. Sample and the girl drove away under his nose."

"Why didn't he have a partner with him so one of them could stay awake?"

"You'd know better than I, Sheriff. You cut man hours to meet the budget."

"Mother of God!"

CHAPTER 29

The Seventh Inn was St. Louis' only restaurant consistently winning a five-star rating. It was intimate inside and out.

The dining room was designed for elegance and intimacy. Fresh-cut gladiolas that were changed daily, filled large vases in every corner. The dining room was mirrored and decorated with tiny white lights draped on artificial tree branches. The lush, thick oriental carpet sank slightly when stepped on, and the linen table-cloths were immaculately white—bleached to perfection.

The owner, a Danish immigrant, offered her tiny hand to each guest with a warm smile and a thickly accented welcome.

Her waiters wore black tuxedos, white gloves, and a sycophantic demeanor. No water glass could be sipped without an immediate refill. No cigarette could be lit by the smoker, but rather, the server.

No smudge on a snow-white glove was tolerated. The waiters bleached their own gloves by hand daily, and then submitted them for the owner's inspection.

The dining room was dark, lit mainly by the tiny white lights and the flickering candles on each table. A credit card and a pen-light were necessary for diners to see their food and pay for it.

The Seventh Inn was the place to go for the most special occasions: a milestone birthday, college graduation, a wedding anniversary, or a romantic marriage proposal.

At the very least, it was the place in St. Louis to take a visitor you want to impress, so it was a matter of some irritation to Joe MacDonald II that his mother never called to tell him that his father would not be coming. She would report back to the old man that his son was doing all right for himself, that being a stockbroker was more than just selling out to the ruling class. Still, it would have been more satisfying to rub it in the old man's face himself.

Joe II was itching to show his father that it was possible to be happy and successful while reveling in the capitalism his father despised. In his mind, this proved something.

Sitting at the table for four in the dark dining room, Inga was disinclined to tell her only son that the show of improvidence embarrassed her more than it impressed her, yet she lifted a small prayer of thanks that she had brought her sequined dark blue dress to wear to the symphony.

When the headwaiter had taken their orders, the four settled in for what would surely be an awkward conversation.

"How are things in Sylvia?" the elder Joe asked, turning to his son rather than his mother.

"Good," Third said noncommittally.

"Well, what are you doing on the farm?" his father probed further.

"Last week I learned to change the oil in the tractor," Third answered. "One Saturday Grams and I went to Monroe City and sold eggs at the farmers' market. And, of course, there is always chicken shit to shovel."

His father nodded. "I've shoveled my share of hen guano on that farm, too. Let me tell you, brokering stock portfolios is a lot more pleasant." The statement hung in the air with an unexpected sour note that the stockbroker didn't really understand until his son spoke.

"Sure, I guess it is very pleasant to use rich people's money to make them even richer while they don't do any work for it. I guess it's a big thrill to syphon off some of that wealth for yourself as you do something that has no real value for most of the world."

Third smiled contemptuously.

His father leaned back in his chair and looked at his son. After a moment, he said with thinly veiled regret, "I see you've been to Sylvia to see my father." Then, turning to Inga, he said between clenched teeth, "How is the old pinko?"

Inga took responsibility. After all, she thought, it was her own words that her grandson was parroting, not her husband's, and it would be up to her to steer this dialogue back to a pleasant tone.

"Joe's fine, though his eyesight isn't much better. I told you about that, didn't I?" Without waiting for an answer, she continued, "I'm sorry I didn't call you to say he wouldn't be coming down. He really wanted to come, but just couldn't get away from the farm."

"I very much doubt that," her son said, "but if I had at least known, I wouldn't have bought a fifth symphony ticket which will now be wasted."

Inga bit her lip. She could have called attention to the lavish waste of money this meal represented, all in an effort by her son to show off his wealth and standing, but she thought better of it. She told herself that the mission she had appointed herself was to be the blessed peacemaker. That said, it was time to step to the plate.

"Or, if we had thought of it, Third could have invited his girlfriend to take Joe's place!"

That was when Liz spoke up. "Joey has a girlfriend? Tell us about her!" Liz was also relieved for the change of topic.

"She's not my girlfriend yet," Joe explained, "but I'm working on it. I met her at the farmers' market when we were selling eggs, and I've already had her to the farm for dinner. Her name is Chelsea Christmas. She's beautiful. She looks a little like you, Liz, except her hair is black. She's smart and nice and has a great sense of humor."

"I'll say she does," Inga interrupted. "She laughs all the time about everything. She reminds me of my childhood in Germany." Inga's sharp, steady gaze rested on Third.

"From what I understand about your childhood, I am surprised there was so much to laugh about," Liz noted, sensing an underlying message between Inga and her grandson.

For Joe's father, Inga's gaze at his son represented a level of intimacy that had eluded him, and he felt left out. It was his own doing. His sense of failure clawed at his heart.

Mercifully, the food arrived. Inga tasted her braised scallops, and then quipped, "My, I hope this food looks as good as it tastes." Third laughed out loud, at his grandmother's indictment of the darkness. The others smiled behind their napkins.

"This Mayfair salad dressing is unusual," Inga continued. "The chef adds more anchovy paste than I put in mine, and I taste just a pinch of nutmeg.".

"My God, Momma," her son laughed. "You do sound exactly like Julia Child when you talk like that."

"You're not the first to notice that," she smiled back at him.

Joe then turned to his son. "Tell me more about this Chelsea," he coaxed. "Is this what you would call a first official girlfriend?"

"No, Dad," Third replied with a tone of fatigue. "I've gone out with lots of girls, but I don't expect you would be aware of them."

Inga was stunned by the query. Was her son so disconnected that he had no knowledge of Third's relationships? How was he so oblivious?

Her son retreated, embarrassed in front of his mother, but then he got a second wind and continued. "I hope you don't go getting one of these girls pregnant, because you know what will happen. You hook up with some poor white trash—or worse—some African-American, and she'll smell money. So will her family, and then we'll have real trouble."

"What!" Third raised his voice. "I can't believe you said that. God, Dad, take a chill pill."

"I can't believe you said that either!" Liz added.

Inga set down her fork and looked at her son. "That's not how you were taught to speak—or think of the less fortunate," she scolded in a quiet voice. It seemed her efforts to make peace had derailed.

"Oh, c'mon, Momma," Joe said. "It's not like we don't all know that the have-nots in the world want everything they can get from the rest of us. Don't be naïve. We have to protect what we have or it will be taken away by less deserving people."

No one at the table realized that their voices were raised until a bald, elderly man in an Armani suit at a neighboring table, called out to Joe II, "Here, here!" He raised his cocktail as if in a toast, and his gaudy diamond ring glinted in the candlelight.

Young Joe turned from his father. His eyes met Inga's astute, piercing stare. .Something passed between them.

Joe couldn't wait to go home and see his grandfather.

CHAPTER 30

The weather was getting warmer as late June approached. Inside Chelsea Christmas' trailer, the air conditioner ran during the day, and even then, only in severe heat. Fans buzzed in every room, yet Chelsea wore long pants and long sleeves. Despite the heat, she did not show her skin.

It was a genuine nuisance that her tiny, seven by eight-foot room was situated across the narrow hall from the bathroom, forcing her parents to traipse past her doorway on the way to and from. In lieu of privacy, she held a secret catalog of dreams about making good her escape from this home and this life.

The double-wide was old and worn, but new to her. She had once lived in a nice home in Hannibal, before her father's error at the Butler factory. Everything went downhill from there, including his drinking, his temperament, and his appetites.

Her mother, Virginia Christmas, was gone from morning until late at night, running the Monroe City boutique alone. Chelsea could only pitch in to help with customers when the store was open. Nights, after close, Virginia spent much of her time in the back office smoking cigarettes, crunching numbers, and trying to stretch the dollars.

The boutique was failing. The profit margin on Chinese crap, as Chelsea called it, was not substantial enough to keep the store solvent. In a small town like Monroe City, how many hair ribbons and ankle socks could you really expect to sell to the thirteen-year-old set? It was another example of the decline of the small-town merchant, exacerbated by the population shift to larger cities and the arrival of Walmart.

Chelsea was almost old enough to get a part-time job, but her birthday was months off. She had just turned sixteen, but it seemed employers preferred a first-time worker to be seventeen or older.

On occasion, she would babysit for neighbors, but everyone's money was tight, and parents of youngsters didn't go out much.

She hated her cramped living conditions, and counted the days until she had a job and a way out at least part of the time.

Her aspirations were real goals, she reminded herself–goals to be chased with fervor. Still, if she was honest, she had to admit that dreaming of them was a deliberate act designed to take her focus off of home and the trouble there, to distract her from her father and her loathing of him.

Immersed in her thoughts, Chelsea got up and went into the tiny kitchen. There was only one soda left—strawberry, not her favorite. She'd leave it for Mom. She wasn't exactly hungry; her craving was for an escape from this life.

Her father spoke to her from the living room. He sat in a ragged brown recliner with leaking upholstery stuffing, a beer can in his fist on the armrest. The television was on.

"Your mom'll be home late," he warned. "She called. Another two hours of work at the store."

"Yeah, okay," she said with an air of defeat.

"You getting ready for bed?"

"I hadn't thought about it. I thought I'd wait up for Mom."

The liquor was thickening his tongue. "Nah, she'll be real late," he slurred. "Why don't you get off your clothes and get in the bed? I'm just gonna finish my beer."

CHAPTER 31

"I need to teach you to cook," Jack Sample announced to Sarah Dednum, "if we're gonna meet demand from Dix. He's set up to ship meth to Mexico and make a load of money. We'll have to cook nearly twenty-four/seven."

"I don't want to learn to cook," Sarah resisted. "I don't want any part of that mess, and I wish you didn't, either. We have a son, Jack. What would happen to him if we both go to jail?"

"We won't go to jail. We slipped past the Shelby sheriffs, and we'll keep slipping by them. The folks who come here wanna protect their source. The whole community is behind our success."

"You're dreaming," Sarah accused. "You're nuts and we are going to get caught. The police won't stop just because they think we left the county. Some sky-high addict will give us up to cut a deal, and we'll be running again. I don't want to run anymore. This was my last move, Jack. I'm serious. I want a cleaner, safer life for little Dusty."

"Oh, for God's sake, Sarah, don't be ridiculous. This deal with Dix goes the way it's supposed to, and we can take Dusty to the French Riviera if we want to."

"Jack, I want you to quit the drugs and get a real job. It's not healthy for the baby breathing those fumes or for me—and the police probably think it was you who murdered that cop."

Jack looked at her and rubbed his chin. It was unlike Sarah to look to the future, care about consequences, or resist his say-so about much of anything. This sudden rebellion was not just surprising, it was ill-timed.

The two were sitting on the floor of their new home in Elsa. The boring beige rug, one overstuffed chair, and white walls were all there was to see. The two had little furniture, and left behind in Sylvia most of what they did have to make good their escape in the darkness.

He pulled a pipe out of his pocket, a short glass tube for liquefying meth and turning it to smoke. He lit it.

As he inhaled, Jack told Sarah not to worry. With the money they'd be making through Dix Simpson, she could buy any life for Dusty she wanted. "Look, I'm doing the best I can. I wrangled this tie to an actual cartel, and all I'm asking for is help with the cooking. This is an investment in time and effort. We can make a good life for all three of us if you do your part."

This time the usual stars in Sarah's eyes dimmed. The naiveté and short-sightedness that were her stock and trade had slammed directly into that dead cop.

"Sarah, if they thought I killed a cop, they would have arrested me already. Now, thanks to you, we have a new house in a quiet little town, and no one knows we're here. Word of mouth will bring back the usual crowd of customers over time. Dix knows where to find us, and he's all we need."

Sarah realized with that statement that the stars dimming in her eyes were shining brightly in Jack's.

"Stop clawing yourself, dammit!" she cried. "Your neck is bleeding and we're out of calamine again. Is there any gas in the car?"

CHAPTER 32

Powell Symphony Hall stood in the heart of St. Louis' arts district, surrounded by theaters and restaurants.

The first floor was a vision in gold, black, scarlet and white. The black and white tiles defined the perimeter of the lobby. The gilded woodwork on the windows, balconies, and ornately carved appointments were set off by the tall window treatments of perfectly draped scarlet velvet.

As patrons climb the plushly carpeted scarlet staircase to the second and third levels, and enter the theater, the vista is stunning.

The ceiling is inset with ovals some thirty feet across, recessed into the ceiling to carry the sound. Within the ovals are more ornate, gold-painted carvings that trace their way down every wall and column in the massive theater.

The seats are placed steeply, one level above the next, to maximize each patron's view of the stage.

As Joe, his wife, his mother, and his son entered the first balcony level and found their seats in the first row, they were delighted to learn that their seats were in the first balcony row. The balcony wrapped in a semi-circle halfway around the theater. Joe II sat between his mother and Liz. Once seated, he took Inga's hand and squeezed it. She squeezed it back and looked at her son. Her smile was mild, a little muted, he thought.

The theater's astounding acoustics carried the buzz of the audience as it settled into seats. Ushers stood at every entrance wearing pristine white shirts or blouses, black pants, and scarlet sashes.

On stage, several musicians played with their charts and warmed up.

Presently, the members of the orchestra entered from stage right and took their seats. They shuffled charts, tested sound, warmed their instruments, and then, as if on cue, fell silent. The concertmaster stood and played an open A on his violin and the musicians tuned their instruments one final time.

The conductor walked onto the stage and strode to the platform. He bowed to the applause and then turned to face his orchestra. He flipped through some papers before tapping his wand on the edge of the dais, raised his arms, and the music began.

Johan Sebastian Bach's music touched the soul of Inga MacDonald, but was unknown to her grandson. The music was as Inga remembered it from her record collection, and from a time many years ago when she had visited this very hall. She closed her eyes to listen, opening them only occasionally to drink in the elegance of the theater and the warmth of her son's company.

She took his hand again and laced his fingers in hers.

Brandenburg Concerto Number Five followed Number Four. Young Joe was begrudgingly appreciative of the craftsmanship that went into composing such a complex, stunning piece of music, but it was certainly nothing he would choose to listen to if he could listen to Mariah Carey or The Cranberries instead. At intermission, he admitted to himself that he was glad the concert was half over. He acknowledged his boredom, but reminded himself that this concert was not for his entertainment. It was for Grams. He brought her here as a small gift to her—not because he wanted a good time.

Following the intermission, the orchestra resumed with Richard Strauss' Four Last Songs. The boredom was renewed, but Third surmised, owing to his failure to get up and use the bathroom during intermission, that these would be the four last songs before he had to pee. He smiled at the connection, and Inga, next to him, noticed the smile. She interpreted it as pleasure from the music.

CHAPTER 33

Liz was up first on Sunday morning. God knows, she told herself, she was no Inga in the kitchen, but she'd be damned if she wouldn't try to make a nice breakfast for her visitor. Croissants, grapefruit halves, and southwestern omelets were on the menu, and having set the dining room table, she sipped coffee while she made the preparations.

Inga was the next to enter the kitchen. "Good morning," she said to Liz. Her lilting voice was beautiful, Liz thought.

"I guess the men aren't up yet," Liz said.

"Third is up. He's in the shower. Thank you for making me so comfortable. Your guest room is lovely. I love the lighthouse theme. Very colorful," Inga remarked.

"I hope you slept well."

"I slept okay, although the bed was empty. I haven't slept alone in many, many years."

In her own home on her own turf, Liz felt comfortable enough to speak frankly. "Inga, may I talk to you about something?"

"Of course, dear. What's the trouble?"

"I haven't slept alone for many years either, but I'm thinking about it," Liz confessed.

"Why?"

"I was very disturbed by a remark made last night at the dinner table. It is unlike Joe to say hateful things about certain groups of people. I don't really know where all that came from, but it isn't like him. If it is like him—if I simply do not know the man as well as I think I do—well, I can't be part of that." Liz cracked the eggs into a bowl and seasoned them before continuing. "I love him, Inga. I really do. But I can't accept hatred of others painted with such a broad stroke. I have never heard such a thing out of Joe's mouth."

"Why are you telling me this now?" Inga wanted to know. "You know my son better than I do. We haven't talked much in the last few years, and people change as they go along. I'm not sure what help I can offer."

Liz gazed at her mother-in-law for several seconds, considering her next words. Finally, she sighed. "I guess there are a couple of things. I need you to understand that I'm not like that, and he didn't get that attitude from me. Also, I want you to know that Joe has never influenced Joey to be that way at all–at least not that I've seen."

"Oh, I believe that," Inga interrupted. "What I get from Third is that he rejects everything his father says or does or believes. I don't know how that disconnect happened. Maybe it's just the age, but Third tells me his father doesn't really notice him or care what he does."

"Hmm," Liz nodded. "I can certainly see where you would get that from Joey. He'll never admit it, but he's very emotional about his father. He's been hurt in ways that may not be anyone's fault, but they still happened." Liz measured coffee and set out the bowls for sugar and cream.

"The problem I see is that Joe loves his son too much, and doesn't know how to express it. When Anne died, Joe kind of cocooned for several years. He was in such pain that he didn't reach out and grasp that Joey was hurt just as much. Joey looks so much like Anne that I believe it hurt Joe for years to even look at the boy. He admitted to me once that he wasn't there for Joey. They could have bonded and built a deep connection, but they didn't," Liz concluded.

"Liz, neither you nor I can fix what had been done in the past, but we can try to improve the present and future. I admit that I was also surprised at the dinner table last night. I was disgusted that my son's ugly words actually brought praise from that man at the table next to us. It's hard to imagine that a son of mine would turn out to be so opposite to the way he was raised, but maybe that's the point."

"What do you mean?" Liz laid raw bacon in a skillet and fired it. She was self-conscious, cooking for Inga, but she set that emotion aside to concentrate on this rare moment with her mother in law.

"Well, Third is not the only MacDonald son who has fallen out with his father, "Inga explained. "Joe wanted our son to be a farmer. He was terribly hurt when he chose to be in business instead, and while Joe understands now that the family farm is going the way of the dodo bird, he still takes your Joe's decision as a personal affront." Inga paused and smoothed her dress with her hands.

"There are a lot of fences to mend in this family," Inga added.

"That doesn't explain the racist remark," Liz objected.

"Yes, it does," Inga countered. "They're all the same—all three of them. Saying that hateful thing may have reflected how Joe feels, but it's more likely he said it as a way to hurt my husband. He believes the remark will get back to Sylvia. He knows I tell Joe everything that happens. On some level, I think Joe was striking out at his father through me," Inga explained. "He's been looking for payback for some perceived wrongdoing for a lot of years."

"I don't get it," Liz said. "Why would my husband's racist remark bother Joe? He didn't insult your husband, did he?"

"He actually insulted him in a pretty offensive way," Inga said. "Let me see if I can explain this correctly. It's kind of hard, but I'll try."

Liz stirred the scramble and dropped sliced mushrooms into it. Then she began to cut up the grapefruit.

Inga cleared her throat. "It isn't even enough that he speaks against it whenever it pops up in a conversation. Joe lives every day in his life in a positive, pro-active, deliberate, calculated fight against the practice of dividing people—whether it's race, religion, gender, whatever. He simply sees division among working-class people as a machination of the ruling class. It's his mission to knock down the dividers between people."

"Joe told me his father is a communist," Liz commented.

Inga nodded. "Joe believes that the power of the ruling class lies in its money. The power of the working class lies in our numbers. So, the divide and conquer strategy is a powerful tool of the ruling class, maybe the most powerful tool it has.

"So, for my son to say what he did goes to the core of his father's belief system. My husband would find our son's cavalier remark to be wrong, offensive, and awful in many ways, and against everything he lives for. I believe that's why he said it."

"Okay," Liz said, not completely understanding. "Is your Joe going to be offended when he hears what happened last night?"

"My son expects me to run to Joe with everything, but I see no reason to hurt him," Inga replied.

CHAPTER 34

"You need to come home now!"

"Lindsey? What's wrong?" Mitch Ollman asked his wife. "And why are you on the department radio?" It was ten p.m., Saturday night, and Lindsey should be nodding off in front of the television news.

"The house is gone. It collapsed on Emily. The fire department is here, but they can't find her in the wreckage. Your friend, Don, is here. A drug addict ran right through the house," Lindsey Ollman, now hysterical, cried and pleaded with her husband.

"Put Don Armstead on the radio." Ollman, with ratcheting fear, wanted the best of clear-headedness he could get. Don Armstead would have facts more than hysteria.

Ollman could hear his wife call to Don. There were shuffling noises and then Chief Armstead was on the radio.

"Mitch. There's been an accident here. Come on home. Now."

"What kind of accident?" Ollman was up from his chair and digging for his car keys in his pocket. He began pacing the floor in front of his desk.

"Mitch, a kid drove right into your house. He's high as a kite, apparently, and didn't even know he was off the road. According to his ID, he's Dale Denton out of Shelbina. I've got firemen and some of your guys searching for your little girl, but I can't let anyone very far inside. The roof could collapse any minute.

"This maniac drove in just to the right of your front door, and the car stopped in the back of the house in the garage. He's conscious but pinned in the car. I've got emergency equipment on the way," Don reported.

Mitch took a moment to let this sink in before he cried out, "Oh, God, Oh, God, Oh, God!" He dropped the radio handset and flew out the door.

In the car, his hands were shaking, but he managed to turn the ignition. As he slammed the car into reverse, Bill Fast knocked on his window.

"Scoot over," Bill said. "You're in no shape to drive."

Mitch took the car out of gear and complied, cursing the momentary delay. As they sped toward the Ollman house, he appreciated Bill's focus and haste. Fast turned on the siren and lights and beat a path. A normal thirteen-minute trip took only four.

Mitch and Lindsey Ollman lived outside of Sylvia on a piece of property with its own small lake, and several acres of rolling green hills. The house itself was large and beautiful. Three stories and a basement provided ample room, and the architectural features and decorative touches made the Ollman home a showcase worthy of *Better Homes and Gardens.* The house was far from commensurate with the salary of a sheriff in a depressed county like Shelby, but Lindsey's family money had allowed them to build their dream home.

Mitch spent the short trip home trying to control his emotions. He knew he was in trouble. A sheriff, an authority figure in a small town in a small county, would be looked upon unfavorably if he used his position to exact vengeance on a suspect who had done him wrong. He told himself on the way that the suspect was innocent until proven guilty.

Bullshit, his passion told him. The perp drove through his house, and now his baby girl was missing.

He told himself to be detached, to treat this like any other crime scene.

Bullshit, came the reply in his head again. His child is missing, maybe hurt, maybe worse.

When Bill pulled the car up in front of the house and shined the headlights on it, the two men gasped.

The right side of the house was badly mangled, and the first floor was partially collapsed.

Mitch was out of the car before it came to a stop, sprinting to the back of the house. Bill followed him in the squad car.

At the back, Bill pulled to a stop next to Mitch as he saw Don Armstead approach the car. Mitch was already trying to enter the garage, but a fireman warned him off. Bill saw Lindsey trying to get in, too, and as he noticed her, a fireman grabbed her by her waist to hold her back. Bill could hear her sobs.

"Hey, Don. Thanks for being here," Bill said. "What's the situation?"

"I've got guys searching, but the house isn't safe. I'm not going to call it structurally sound until I have daylight and quite a lot more time. Until we have more equipment, there will be no removing of debris, no real access inside the building.

"We're doing what we can to find the girl," Don explained.

"We have to find her!" Mitch implored. "Please, please, let me go in the house."

"Mitch, try to take it easy. Where's the driver of the car?" Bill asked Don, hoping to distract Mitch.

"Still in the car. We're keeping an eye on him. He's pretty well stuck, but that isn't fazing him. I'm not sure he knows where he is or what he did."

"You're kidding me."

"No, I'm serious as a heart attack. He's so stoned, he doesn't even recognize that he drove into a building."

"Don, the road he should have been on is a quarter mile away," Bill objected. "You're telling me he left the road and drove across a quarter mile of real estate without realizing it?"

"That's what it looks like. Look, a crew is on the way from Hannibal. Ordinarily, none would be available until daylight, but since there's a missing child—"

"My baby . . ." Ollman mumbled.

"Yeah," Don continued. "They're on the way tonight. Mitch, listen to me. There's not much you can do until we have heavy equipment and supplies. Why don't you and Lindsey let us take you to a hotel ?"

The suggestion, as ridiculous as it was, struck a chord in Mitch. It was the thing you say to a victim's father at times like these. His head new full well that there was nothing at all to do but wait, and the best he could do would be to gett in the way. But Mitch's heart was in command here. He turned and ran toward the gaping hole that had been the garage door. Lindsey had freed herself from the fireman and was running back and forth across the opening, sobbing and screaming, "Emily, Emily!"

A moment later, a fireman shouted from inside the garage, "Over here! I need light."

Ollman pushed his way into the garage, with Lindsey behind him. As he approached, he saw blood. Then he saw hair. Long blonde hair appeared as a fireman lifted a piece of crumbled sheetrock off of Emily's still form. Her head was caved in. The other fireman found her hand and felt for a pulse. There was nothing.

He looked up at Mitch. "Oh, God, I'm so sorry, Sheriff."

Mitch stepped back in disbelief. As his knees buckled, a hand came around his waist. It was Lindsey. She fell to the ground with her husband, and a mournful shriek began in her gut and filled the night air.

Mitch closed his eyes but continued to seeimage of his daughter's body, her hair and face shining with red liquid.

He turned his back to the horror and vomited. His heaves were punctuated with sobs and gasps.

Bill Fast and the firemen stood back and let the man and his wife have a few moments while shock and grief settled in.

When Lindsey choked, "I want to see her," and tried to stand, Mitch, still on his knees, reached up and grabbed her around her legs and pulled her down into the grass again.

"No, baby. No, no. Don't. It's better you don't. You don't want to see her that way." He held his wife and hugged her, rocking her and sobbing.

After a few moments, Mitch stood and pulled his wife to her feet. He led her clear of the collapsed garage, took her by the shoulders and set her at arm's length. He looked her over. "Are you all right? Are you hurt? Tell me! Is there anything wrong with you?"

Lindsey looked back at him in silence. When she began to speak, her eyes glazed over as if she had disconnected herself from this awful moment.

"I'm okay. I was in the kitchen making Jell-O. I spilled it all over the place, mopped it up with a towel. I sent Emily to the laundry room with the towel and told her to soak it in the machine in cold water. As soon as she was downstairs, I heard a crash. That's the last I saw of her. Oh, God! If I hadn't spilled that Jell-O . . ."

Mitch and Lindsey collapsed into sobs again. The sobbing continued until Mitch could control himself.

"Honey, I want you to sit in this car," he said, gesturing toward the department sedan he had arrived in. "I've got some things to do at this scene. I'll be back in a minute." He guided her to the car, opened the door and seated her.

What was left of a red Ford Tempo GL was sticking out of the garage. The garage door was collapsed around it. The car was crushed and the smell of air bag propellant hung in the air.

A fire truck was parked at the side of the garage, its flashing lights illuminating the scene.

Turning to Don Armstead standing next to him, Mitch asked, "Is the kid conscious?"

"That's a loaded question. He's awake, but he's pretty jacked up. You know, all full of himself and bulletproof like they get when they're on that shit. He's soaring, man, he's really out there."

"Can I talk to him?"

"Don't go back in the garage. It may not be safe. You can stand in front of the car and talk to him through the windshield—which is no longer there."

Bill Fast joined the two men. "Mitch," he said, "Don't approach the kid. Don is right to tell you to get out of here. The longer you're here, the better the chance of compromising whatever criminal case this turns out to be. I'll talk to the kid, and I'll tell you everything that's said. But, you need to stay out of this for a handful of reasons."

Mitch, ignoring Bill, approached the Tempo. The front quarter panel on the driver's side was lodged in the passenger door of Lindsey's copper-colored Dodge Caravan. The driver looked to be in his early twenties, with dark hair and terrible skin. He wore a dingy tee shirt and jeans. The "meth mouth" was evident as he sucked repeatedly on a Pepsi, baring stained, decaying teeth with a missing incisor, as he lifted the beverage to his lips.

He seemed alert and active, though pinned inside the car, and was repeatedly trying the door, banging on it with his fist.

"Hey," Mitch spoke loudly, "your name is Denton?"

The kid looked up from his efforts, and said, "Yeah, man, who are you?"

Bill intervened. "Mitch, I'm serious. The kid has not been mirandized, and the first two-bit lawyer will get quashed anything he says even if we do read him rights. He is in no condition to understand them, or even know what he's saying.

"I happen to be Mitchell Ollman, the sheriff of Shelby County," Mitch continued as though Bill had not spoken, "and this happens to be my house."

"Aw, shit, man," the young man said, and then resumed pounding on the door, dashboard, and window.

Don stepped up and spoke softly to Mitch. "Sheriff, do *not* interrogate this man. I will throw you over my shoulder and carry you off to protect this investigation. Your man, Fast, is right. Cease."

Ollman looked up at Armstead who stood a half a head taller and a good sixty pounds thicker. His eyes, glazed over in grief and pain, cleared for a moment as he understood the stakes. He walked away. As he did, Bill Fast stepped closer to the car and stated, for Denton, his rights. He knew that in the end it wouldn't matter, but the best he could do following the law, he would.

"Denton!" he said when he had finished. "I have one question. Where did you get the meth? Just tell me who you got it from."

"Huh? I don't know. I don't know about no meth. I never said I had meth. I was partying with some friends and they bought me a couple of . . .. It's okay, man, but I don't do meth. No, uh, I don't never do that. Uh, I was with some people and they wanted to party. I was already high, and I don't know where the house was. It was some good, strong glass, man. I feel good. Hey, what happened here? I can't get out of my car. I need to get home, man. Can you call my dad? Shit, he's gonna kill me when he sees the car. I need to get home."

"You don't know the name of the cook or where you went to get the glass?" Fast insisted.

"Uh, I heard one guy say we were going to see Jackie Blue. 'S all I know." The young man promptly vomited in his own lap.

"Hey, I need to call my dad, okay?" he complained, wiping his mouth with the hem of his tee shirt. "Where's a phone, man?"

"Who's your dad?"

"Uh, David Denton. I live in Shelbina. Could somebody call him to come get me? I'm sick."

"You're going to be staying right here, Mr. Denton. It may take most of the night to get you out of your car. Then, you'll be a guest of the county."

"No, man, I ain't going to no county. They really fuck you up in there, you know what I mean? Well, sorry, 'cause you're a cop or something, but I really don't want to go to no county. They really fuck you up. My dragon is white, man. I ride the white dragon, but no, I never touch no glass."

The nervous banging on the car door and attempts to roll down the driver's window absorbed Denton's attention. Fast doubted that he would get much else until the kid landed. Maybe not even then.

Bill strode back to the car where Mitch had seated Lindsey. Mitch was now sitting next to her, holding her, and joining her in sobs. As he approached, Deputy Nakamura joined him. "Look here, Nakamura, get a hold of David Denton in Shelbina and get him over here —"

"Already done. He's on the way," Nakamura said.

"Okay, good. Also, help me out by calling a board-up company. Try that one we used when that storefront was broken into a couple years ago and the owner was out of state. Get them out here to secure the building. Then, when you get that kid out of that car, take him to Moberly and have him checked out. I think his leg is probably broken. If I'm wrong, and the doctor signs off, lock him up. I'll be having words with him tomorrow."

Bill then leaned down into the car. "Go on, Sheriff. I'm going to get Jeckle to drive you to a hotel. I'll stay. I'll get this done. You need to take care of your wife and yourself."

Mitch thought for a moment and reluctantly agreed. "I'll call the office and let you know my whereabouts," Mitch said. "Keep me up to speed on anything that breaks. And thanks, Bill." Mitch choked on a sob, embarrassed in front of his second in command.

As Mitch nudged Lindsey out the door and helped her into the back seat, his thoughts were scattered and desperate. He knew Bill was right. He must stay clear of the investigation. But he would find

Jack Sample, even if he did it off the books, and the guy would pay for this and for every other life he had cost.

The meth crisis was new in Shelby County. Five years ago, it was unheard of. Now it had arrived, and taken off like a shot. With the isolated labs, the many ways it could be ingested, the comparatively low cost, and the nearly instantaneous addiction rate, Ollman saw the writing on the wall the first time he found a dead kid. Nineteen-year old girl, dead of a heart attack induced by methamphetamine.

Since then, there had been numerous explosions in labs, dozens of victims, and multiple associated crimes. There had been a half dozen deaths and even more maimings each of the last five years, some more violent than others.

There was one kid whose lab blew up in his face. He had been blinded and burned all over his head and torso. That kid had learned the hard way, but when would the rest of these stupid kids get wise? When would they learn to steer clear?

And now this. Meth had taken his own daughter. Mitch squeezed his eyes shut against the tears.

He looked at his wife as she cried, face red and flushed. He sifted through the recent events. Mark Newstead's funeral was scheduled for Monday. Mitch had planned a respectful and dignified send-off for his son-in-law, but he wouldn't even get through the one funeral before he started planning another.

A swell of sadness washed over him. He reached for Lindsey and enveloped her and held her in his arms as his tears fell with hers.

CHAPTER 35

Word spread swiftly through the county that the sheriff's daughter had been killed by a meth addict who tore into the Ollman home. Fire Chief Don Armstead broke the news to Joe MacDonald on Sunday morning. Joe was saddened, but even more angered.

"Why in blazes do kids start that shit?" Joe remarked in the narthex at Good Shepherd.

"You supposed to say 'shit' in church?" Don chided.

"If I really mean it."

"I don't know, Joe. Kids are stupid. Speaking of stupid things to do, did you know that my son invited your kid to a pool party Thursday?"

"Why is that stupid?"

"The party's in Elsa."

Joe's eyes widened. "I take it you don't think it's a good idea."

"Here's where I'm at with it, Joe. I don't really want him going, although the kid throwing the party is a nice enough kid. Obviously, my kid's color may mean trouble no one wants. On the other hand, I don't want to let him believe he has to run scared in his own community and in his own backyard. I want my son to grow up strong and confident, and not running with his tail between his knees. I don't want him to think there's a supremacist behind every bush."

"But there are a lot of supremacists behind a lot of bushes in this county," Joe countered.

"Don't I know it," Don said.

The two men looked at each other for a moment in silence.

"Understood," Joe said finally. "Let's do this. Let's let the youngsters go to their party, but let's you and me have their backs."

CHAPTER 36

"I was just making a point, Liz. For Pete's sake! You have no idea what growing up with that man was like. I was just trying to express how my views are different, and why." Joe's face was red and his voice was raised.

"I see. So, you're saying you meant every word of that hateful, ugly rant," Liz accused, pressing her lips together.

"No, I'm just sending him a message to let him know I think differently about some things," Joe insisted.

"If the things you said were to represent your so-called different viewpoint, then you meant them. What would be the point of sending a message that you don't mean?" Liz asked. She put her hands on her hips.

"Liz, I don't hate any one kind of person more than another. You know me better than anyone." Joe was yelling.

"Joe, I love you. I was telling your mother how much I love you. And I thought I knew you, but now I'm not sure I do. You were a stranger last night, and I can't live with a stranger ," Liz cried.

She looked at him with a pleading expression.

It took several seconds for her husband to grasp what she was saying, and he hoped with angst and desperation that he was reading her wrong.

"What are you saying?" he asked, fearing the worst.

"I'm trying to understand, and I'm trying to help you understand. Whether you think you meant it or not, last night I saw a side of you I didn't like. You crossed a line. I think that snide comments you have made about certain people for years I have mostly dismissed, overlooked, and ignored. But they came home to roost last night. I don't want to leave you, Joe, but I'm not sure I want to stay either. I think what I'm going to do is take a break. I'll call my sister and see if she'll put me up temporarily. I don't know. I just need space from you for a while. To think things through.."

CHAPTER 37

When Joe and Grams arrived at the farm late Sunday afternoon, Gramps met them at the car.

"We'd better go inside," he said to Inga without preamble as he opened the car door for her. "There's a storm coming in. Kirksville's got golf ball-sized hail."

"We know," she replied, kissing him. "We heard it on the radio."

"I've already got supplies in the storm cellar, but I thought you two might like to use the bathroom first," he told her.

"I do, Gramps. I drank too much soda on the way," Joe said, trotting into the house.

Gramps chuckled at his grandson, turned to Inga, and said, "I'm going to put the car in the barn with my truck and then we'll go down in the cellar. Hurry up and get anything you need. I'll meet you two there."

"Lady!" Inga hollered. "Lady, come!"

Lady tore around the side of the house and looked up to Inga, panting. Inga patted her thigh and the dog followed her into the house.

"Inside the barn, the older man noted the sudden change in temperature. He rolled up the windows on the car, but left the door open on the pickup truck just enough for the cat to get in there with her kittens if she chose to do so. If it got wet inside the truck, so be it, he decided.

Safe inside the cellar, Gram, Gramps and Joe heard plunk-plunks of hail hitting the large, heavy wooden door to the cellar not ten minutes after they entered. Lady whined and paced, panting, as Inga tried to comfort the frightened dog.

Joe had moved three kitchen chairs to the cellar, close to the far wall, but Inga and the boy chose to stand after the long car ride.

The small black and white TV was tuned to the news out of Quincy, but if the conditions got too bad, electricity would be lost. The nearing rumbles of violent thunder made that likelihood greater by the minute.

The Quincy station had interrupted reruns of "The Little House on the Prairie" as the storm headed south and east from Kirksville, The weather grew more severe. As the meteorologist reported minute by minute, the older man watched the expected change come over his wife as the storm descended.

With the first loud crack of thunder, Inga turned white. Her hands trembled and then she shook all over. Gramps stood and took her in his arms. He pulled her to the chair next to his and put her in it. He wrapped his arms around her and held her head under his chin.

The younger man, watching all of this, was at first flummoxed about why his strong, tireless grandmother was apparently going to pieces because of hail. Storms exhilarated him. Then he remembered her childhood, the bombings, the loss of her home, and all the terrors that war brought with it.

He picked up the third chair and positioned it on the other side of Inga. Sitting, he put one arm behind her chair on top of his grandfather's arm. He held his grandmother's hand with his free one.

Lady, having been through this many times, took her place on top of Inga's feet, lying on them as if to keep her mistress warm. Having been reassured by Inga in the beginning, it was now her turn to bring comfort.

As Inga whimpered and trembled, the four of them waited out the storm.

CHAPTER 38

Sarah was delighted that Sunday night her new roof didn't leak during the hailstorm like in the last place. She could put Dustin in his crib with little thought to any fears of a soaking wet ceiling tile landing on his little head.

In contrast, Sarah's fears, growing more acute by the day, A haunting, building dred began to assure her that this meth trade would come to no good end — and sooner than she would like to expect.

Jack was cooking almost constantly. He turned the burners off between batches only to eat, use the bathroom, and get high. He was averaging three hours of sleep, as the meth kept him awake. He scarcely noticed that the powerful stimulant was overwhelming his body's natural need for sleep.

It worried Sarah.

Dix Simpson had been by twice already and was pressuring Jack to get help so the cooking could continue around the clock without being interrupted by Jack's inevitable collapse from fatigue. Was he going to hire someone soon? Did he have a reliable supply of core ingredients? Was he going to honor his commitment and produce as prodigiously as he had promised?

Ernesto Soto had accompanied Dix on each visit. Ernesto said little, but his huge, menacing presence was sufficiently articulate.

Jack had entered into an agreement. Simpson and Soto would hold him to his obligation, or there would be serious consequences.

Ernesto's parting shot during the last visit had been ominous. His six-foot, five-inch body loomed over Jack's diminutive frame. He bared teeth and intoned with his Mexican accent, "I've got no fear of killing cops, and I've got no fear of you, capeesh?"

CHAPTER 39

The next week was somber in Sylvia. The town was stunned, not by another drug death, but by the death of a thirteen-year-old girl, the collateral damage of the meth epidemic.

The community's response manifested as a wellspring of casseroles, fruit salads, flowers, and candlelight vigils. The MacDonalds attended such a service, and the three signed a kindly-worded sympathy card. The card accompanied a dish of jambalaya, one of Inga's specialties.

Mark Newstead's funeral was Monday and Emily Ollman's funeral followed on Wednesday. The week was a blur to Mitch and Lindsey, and subject to get more surreal with each ensuing kindness from a stranger.

Lindsey cried until she vomited. Mitch was quiet, but his mind was not idle. He had devised plans for vengeance that unbecoming a member of law enforcement, but he didn't care. If it cost his career, his family, or his life, it made no difference. All that mattered was shutting down Jack Sample.

The next task would be to find the guy. He could be anywhere in the world, but Mitch would find him at any cost.

CHAPTER 40

Jamal called Joe Wednesday night. "You comin' tomorrow?" he asked.

"Sure, man, I'll pick you up. Gramps says I can use his truck. You know the way there?"

"Yeah, I got directions. But, hey, thanks for driving. My dad doesn't really want me to be driving in Elsa. Calls it 'borrowing trouble.' I may have to hunker down in the seat while we go through the town."

"You sure you wanna go somewhere you have to hunker down?" Joe asked.

"I'm not sure, but I told the guy we'd be there. My dad also doesn't want me to run scared every time Whitey rears his ugly head."

Joe paused for a moment considering the many possible responses he could make. He settled for "What time do you want me to swing by?"

When Joe pulled up to the Armstead home Thursday, Jamal was sitting on the stoop. He wore a baseball cap and sunglasses. Don Armstead was sitting on the stoop with him. The two rose and walked toward the MacDonald truck.

"Okay, you two," Don said with resignation. "You be careful. Any sign of trouble . . ."

"I know, Dad. I should call you. You better get back to work. I'll call you there."

"No, don't call me," Don corrected. "If it looks like there might be trouble, you call Okie Joe. Square?"

"Okay," Jamal agreed, but he looked confused.

The father and son fist-bumped, and Jamal got in the truck with Joe.

As they drove off, Joe asked Jamal, "You think the older generation is a little paranoid about Elsa? 'Cause I think this is 1992, not 1952, and people don't act so racist anymore."

"Spoken like a true white dude," Jamal retorted. "You'll never know 'cause you'll never live it."

"That's what Gramps tells me."

The two young men talked of girls, music, and basketball as they drove the ten miles into Elsa. As it turned out, the town was charming, sporting amazing architecture. Houses looked like they were plucked from the turn of the century and preserved throughout the decades. They were painted unusual colors: sienna gold, bright red, royal blue, and emerald green, as if each homeowner stood in competition with his or her neighbor to get the most attention. Cobblestone walkways added to the charm. In the midst of a wide swath of flat farmland, the town was a series of hills where a Native American village had stood in some past century.

Joe followed the directions Jamal read from a hand-scribbled piece of paper as they wound through the picturesque town.

Joe turned a corner of a small, narrow street and climbed the incline to the end of the block. A salmon-colored home, set back far off the street, got his attention. The white latticework was not unexpected, nor the unusual color of the building. The surprise was Sarah Dednum getting out of her car and carrying a grocery bag toward the house. He slowed for a better look and confirmed it was Sarah. He considered stopping and saying hello, but Jamal cautioned him not to.

"My dad said to get in town, to Tim's house, and out. No stops. Remember — borrowing trouble," he told his friend.

Joe wondered when and why Sarah had moved to Elsa, and if it had anything to do with the deputy who'd been killed.

Tim Flynn's house was set back from the road, surrounded on all sides by woods. The privacy set well with Joe, but Jamal was ambivalent. He didn't want to admit that his father's anxiety over his attendance at this gathering had been contagious.

Tim Flynn answered the door. "Hey, Armstead! Great you could come. Come on inside. I've got sandwiches, drinks, and some folks I'd like you to meet. Who's your bud?"

"Oh, this is Joe. He lives in Sylvia, too. He's cool," Jamal said.

Tim was a tall man in his early twenties. He sported a muscular frame and looked like he could take on any comers. His handlebar mustache was insufficient to compensate for his receding hair-line—or his baby face, ,but it did the best job it could to help him look mean. The mean look belied his friendliness, though, and Joe took a liking to him.

"Nice to meet you and thanks for the invite," Joe offered, shaking Tim's hand. "I notice you've got a hoop in the driveway. You play basketball?"

"I do, but not as well as I once did. I don't get a lot of company out here—no one to shoot with. I only bought the house a couple months ago. You play?"

"Yeah," Joe said with a grin.

"You got a ball?" Jamal asked Tim.

"Sure, I'll get it," Tim replied. "Come on in."

The two young men followed him into the main section of the house where eight or ten young men and a similar number of women surrounded a pool table, set up in what would otherwise have been the dining room.

The young brunette woman playing at the moment was good. She sank everything she hit, Joe observed, and her opponent, another muscular man, watched her with waning hope of a victory.

Joe said, "Hey," when one of the guests looked at him. "I'm Joe. My buddy, Jamal," he said, gesturing to his friend. "How're you all doing?"

Greetings were exchanged all around, but the names of people went in one of Joe's ears and out the other. He mentally scolded himself for his failure to remember names.

Presently, Tim returned with a basketball and handed it to Jamal. Jamal rested the ball on his hip and held it as he followed Joe around the room, greeting people.

Joe assessed that the guests, while friendly enough, had little common ground with him. Every conversation he started ended quickly with nothing left to say. Further, it became clear that Jamal was uncomfortable. Was he shy, or was it something else? He clung to Joe like they were duct-taped together.

After a half hour of forced civility, Joe had had enough.

"One-on-one?" he said to Jamal. Jamal smiled agreeably, and the two went back outside.

After twenty minutes of play, Jamal stopped, out of breath, and rested his hands on his knees. "That movie is dead stinking wrong, you know," he breathed to his friend.

"What movie?" Joe asked, also winded.

"Some white men can jump."

"Oh. Yeah, I guess. You see that movie yet? Woody Harrelson?"

"Nah, it just came out. It may not get up here to the boonies for a month," Jamal explained.

"When it does, you want to go with me?" Joe offered.

"Uh, sure, man."

Jamal clenched his fist and beat the air in victory. "Hey, you know the high school has a basketball team that's pretty good. Too bad you're going back to St. Louis in the fall. It could use a guy like you."

"Don't they have a point guard?" Joe asked as he resumed dribbling.

"Yeah, but he can't hit free throws. Not like you."

"You know the guy?"

"Nah, not too well. But I'm serious, man. The coach would love you."

After a few more minutes, the two let themselves back inside. Tim asked how the one-on-one had gone, and offered both a beer. Jamal waved him off, and pulled a Coke out of the cooler. Joe took the beer with thanks.

"White men can too jump," Jamal repeated, smiling. "Least, this one can."

The two friends played a little pool and made more small talk with the other guests. The fact was not lost on Joe that none of the guests, male or female, clicked with him as easily as Jamal had on their first meeting. It was a shame, indeed, Joe mused, that he would be going back home at the end of the summer.

"Hey, Tim, we're almost outta beer," one guy piped up.

"Already? Okay. There's a place just down the road a half-mile. I'll be right back."

Tim went to the door fingering his car keys. "Oh, man, I'm blocked in."

Joe, realizing that his truck was blocking Tim, spoke up. "No problem. I'll drive you down there."

The two went out the door, and Jamal followed.

The three piled into the cab of the truck. The half-mile was more like two or three miles, Joe noted, but eventually they came to a small intersection with a sundries store of some kind on the corner. Joe pulled in.

"Wow," Joe exclaimed as he climbed up the three or four wood stairs to the door. "This is real old-time."

Jamal nodded. "This is Mr. Drucker's General Store off of reruns of Green Acres. I wonder if guys are sitting around a pickle barrel on the floor playing poker."

Joe cracked up. "It sure looks like that. What a hoot."

When the three stepped into the store, the jingle bells hanging on the door announced their arrival. The rustic configuration of the building became more apparent as their eyes adjusted to the dim light. The hardwood floor creaked as they walked in.

Joe and Jamal were astonished and amused as they saw three men in plaid shirts and overalls at the store counter actually playing cards.

Their amusement was short-lived. One man behind the counter was most likely the proprietor, Joe assumed. The other two were sitting on stools in front. When they saw Jamal, their body language changed abruptly.

"What you doin' in here, nigger? Don't you got some goddamn window to wash in the city?"

The two men stood, and joined by the third, formed a line, shoulder to shoulder.

Fear paralyzed the three young men.

"You're not welcome here, boy," the tallest of the men drawled. "You need to get gone now before sump'n happens to you." He took a menacing step toward Jamal.

Joe stepped in front of his friend. "We don't want trouble, man," he said to the tall man. "We just came in for some beer. Nothing to it. Peaceful." He raised his palms in a gesture of conciliation, but his actions only seemed to enrage the three strangers.

"Hey, he's right," Tim Flynn agreed. "We just want beer and some snacks and we'll get out."

"Damn right you'll get out, but your little nigger is gonna get schooled on how folks are around here with his kind." The proprietor was confident. He obviously expected no outside intervention.

We've landed in the Twilight Zone, Joe told himself. This is unreal.

"And you, nigger-lover, you think you're gonna protect your nigger by standing in front of him? You're gonna get what he's gett'n.' You need a lesson, too. We don't like niggers, and we don't like nigger-lovers."

The three, shored up by the words of the largest and the three open beers on the counter, strode as one toward the three visitors. Joe could almost smell Jamal's fear, as well as his own. He also smelled the sweat of the guy nearest him who raised a fist and clocked him on the left cheek. He stumbled back, knocking Jamal down, and the other two descended on Jamal.

Tim ran out the door. The jingle bells marked his swift departure.

Jamal covered his head with his arms, assumed a fetal position and prayed to God for rescue.

God heard him.

As the first work-boot-kicks to his kidneys commenced, the jingle bells rang again. Jamal, tearful and terrified, wondered what new terrors had entered the room. He prepared for death.

But Joe, seeing stars, heard a familiar voice.

"That's about enough." The words were spoken with a calm, assured menace.

Joe rolled over to face the door. His grandfather stood there gripping the shotgun normally stored in the hall closet. He cocked it with a jerk of his arm.

The three assailants ceased motion and stared uncertainly at the shotgun. The tall one raised his hands in a gesture of peace and diplomacy exactly as Joe had done a moment before. "Uh, sorry, man. We just have our ways around here and don't wanna be bothered with ni—his kind. He just should'na come here, is all."

Joe's grandfather stared into the face of the speaker for a moment while Joe and Jamal gathered their senses and regained their feet.

"We'll be goin' right now," Gramps stated. "If anyone cares to follow, feel free. We'll be headin' to the sheriff's office. Come on along if you want." He grinned mockingly, but that sense of menace was still thick in the air.

The boys went out the door, with Okie Joe bringing up the rear, not too hurried, not looking back.

The MacDonald Taurus was parked behind the pickup truck. Don Armstead was at the wheel of the Taurus. Tim Flynn was nowhere in sight.

Jamal ran to his father who motioned him to get in. The two MacDonald men drove the truck back to Sylvia. The Taurus followed.

"How'd you find me, Dad? How'd you know to come? Oh, God, it was awful. I was scared shitless. Oh, God, oh, God."

Jamal was becoming hysterical. Don drove the car quietly, letting the child vent his emotions. Don raised a silent prayer of thanks. It was the sincerest, most ardent prayer of his life.

"Are you hurt, son?"

"I'm sore, but I think I'm okay. How's Joe? He got punched pretty good in his face. How'd you find us?" Jamal repeated.

"Joe and I followed the two of you to the house. We figured there'd be trouble at some point. We parked down the road and waited for you two to leave. What the hell did I tell you about staying out of sight?" Don wanted to know. "What did I say about going there directly and coming home directly? What in God's name told you it was okay to go into that town?" His voice was rising, and the teenager began to cry.

CHAPTER 41

Acting Sheriff Bill Fast sat in his office with Don Armstead, Joe MacDonald, and their two young men. It was Friday, and he had already been to the general store in Elsa to interview the proprietor, Ed Lammert. Lammert did not match the description that Joe and Jamal had provided of any of the men involved in the attack.

Mr. Lammert said that he had taken the day off Thursday, and left his cousin, Seth Flanagan, in charge of the store. Seth had since returned to Nebraska, and Ed didn't have an up-to-date phone number or address for his cousin.

Bill Fast, who didn't believe a syllable of this fiction, looked forward to meeting up with these three criminals.

"I'm sorry, that's all we know, gentlemen," Bill Fast said to the four. Hell of a time for Mitch Ollman to be out on bereavement leave.

The four men asked questions of Fast, but he explained that without the identities of the assailants, it would be difficult to make any arrests. The people of Elsa, a tightly knit community, would be less than eager to come forward with testimony.

Fast was sincere in his apology.

Don and Okie Joe looked at each other. Something passed between them, and Fast raised an eyebrow. .He knew Armstead well. Armstead was a good man.

"There is one thing. I'll report this to the Feds as a hate crime. If these jokers ever turn up again, the federal government can prosecute, and it'll go real hard on them," Fast promised.

"Okay, but no one was hurt very badly. Both boys have bruises, as you can see," Joe gestured at his grandson's black eye and swollen face, "but we got there before it got out of hand. No one was really hurt," he repeated.

"No one is really hurt when a cross is burned on their lawn, either," Fast said. "But, it's still a hate crime, and there are stiff penalties when the Feds get involved. The tough part will be finding out who to prosecute, and then handing them over." He reviewed his notes, tapping on his notebook. "By the way, I did talk to Flynn, and he corroborates everything you've told me. He feels real bad, too, Jamal, about the way he high-tailed it," Fast concluded.

"Yeah, fine," Jamal mumbled.

Putting up an apologetic hand, Fast excused himself to answer the phone.

"Hey, Mitch," Fast said. "How you doing? I was just thinking about you." He paused while Mitch replied.

"Well, yeah, since you bring it up, we have had an incident. Don Armstead's son was attacked in Elsa. He got away with minor injuries, but Joe MacDonald's grandson was with him and got clocked. Looks like a hate crime." Fast went on to explain briefly the incidents of the day before. "I'm wondering what they were doing in Elsa too, Sheriff." Fast looked at the two young men meaningfully as he said it.

"No, sir, we haven't had any Jack Sample sightings in town. I still think he's out of town and possibly out of the county. He's laying real low after Mark's death. All officers are being given daily reminders to watch for him, that he's a known meth chemist, a known associate of Dix Simpson and Ernesto Soto, but we have no leads on his whereabouts and we still don't know the identity of the girlfriend." Fast paused. "Yeah, exactly. We have close to nothing. Sorry, Sheriff. Look, I've got folks here. Let me call you back. Take care and don't worry about work. You have enough on your plate."

He disconnected. Turning his attention back to the Armstead and MacDonald men, Fast said, "Now then, where were we?"

"In Elsa," stated Joe III.

"I understand the attack was in Elsa, but are there any other details —"

"No," Joe interrupted. "Jack Sample is in Elsa. I saw his girlfriend yesterday on our way there."

Gramps turned and stared at his grandson. Don did, too. Even Jamal looked surprised.

Bill Fast caught his breath. He looked at the young man for a full ten seconds, with his mouth open. "How exactly do you know these people?"

"Well, I don't know *them*. I know her slightly. I met her at the post office and saw her at a dance in Macon."

"What's her name, Joe?"

"Sarah."

"Last name?"

"Um, I don't think I ever heard her last name."

"And you saw her doing what in Elsa?"

"She was walking into a house with a bag of groceries."

"Did you speak to her?"

"No. Jamal and I were told to go straight to the party without making any stops. I mean, I wanted to, but Jamal nixed the idea."

"Where is the house she was entering?"

"I don't remember what street it was on. Sorry. But it was orange. I mean, kind of a pinkish-orange. You know the houses in Elsa are mostly weird colors."

Bill Fast nodded, thinking. "I don't want to have to take you back there, after what's happened, but it would sure be great if you could specify where the house is."

Jamal leaned forward in his chair, reached behind him, and lifted a folded piece of paper from his back pocket. He handed it to Joe. Joe nodded at him, unfolded the paper and read it. "Here it is. We made a right on Taylor and then a left on Sycamore Street. She lives on the corner of Taylor and Sycamore. It's at the top of a hill. Elsa is very hilly."

"Yes, it is. And what do you know about meth chemistry? Are you a customer of Sample's?"

"Oh, God, no," Joe protested. "That's nasty. I made Jack as a chemist just from Sarah talking about him. He's got the itch real bad, and she ought to buy stock in calamine lotion, as much of it as she buys. I took her to Walmart one time to buy calamine lotion. She tried to shoplift cold pills, but I made her put them back."

Joe wondered why he could not make himself shut up. Just shut up, he told himself. If Liz were here, she'd call this over-sharing.

Bill Fast stared at Joe for several seconds. This unexpected windfall of information was made possible, in essence, by three white supremacists ten miles away with no better sense than to attack the son of the fire chief. What were the chances?

He rose from his chair, shook everyone's hand, and promised to call if anything came up. The four left the office.

"Do you see what I mean, Gramps?" Joe asked on the way to the car.

"About what?" Gramps replied.

"About the tiny little decisions, we make every day and how they can have great big results."

"You mean you went to a known supremacist community with a black kid and almost got yourself killed? That kind of decision and those results?"

"Joe," Don interrupted. "If this is anybody's fault, it's mine. I should have listened to my gut instead of trying to turn this into a life lesson for Jamal. I'm sorry, Jamal." He turned to his son, grabbed him and hugged him hard. He pressed Jamal's face to his shoulder and kissed his son on the top of his head.

The young man's arms came around Don's substantial waist and he hugged back.

"That's not even what I mean," Joe continued. "I mean about the decision to come here today, this afternoon, and be in the sheriff's office when we were. And the sheriff's decision to call in at that moment. If those two things had not happened just as they did, I might not have ever told the police where that guy and Sarah live. Seemed like they wanted to know pretty bad."

The two older men looked at the teenager. Don let go of Jamal and turned to the other teen. "I'll say they do, Joe. It is very likely that Sample made the meth that hopped up the kid who killed Mitch's daughter."

"No shit?" both Joes said at the same time.

"How do you know that?" Okie Joe asked.

"The hopped-up kid told Ollman, or as good as told him."

"No shit," he repeated.

Back inside the sheriff's office, Bill Fast sat in his chair, staring at the phone and thinking about Mitch.

He had to call him. Hell, he told the guy he'd call him back. As a crime victim, Mitch should not really be brought into this particular loop. But as Bill Fast's close associate and best friend . . .

Bill made the decision to tell Mitch of this unexpected gift, that the much-sought-after Jack Sample had been located.

Why, then, did every instinct tell him it was a bad idea for Oll-man, in his present state of mind, to know where to find his neme-sis?

CHAPTER 42

"Joe, I think we need to cut down some trees near the west cornfield. I noticed that storm last weekend cracked one or two of them," Inga told her husband at breakfast Saturday morning.

"I noticed that, too," he replied. "Third and I will take a ride out there. The wood ought to be good and dry by winter if we cut it up and stack it now."

"It takes me back to my high school days," she reminisced.

"I sense a story coming," the boy interjected.

"What do you mean, Third?" Inga asked.

"I don't see a connection. I thought you have storms all the time up here," he said. "Besides, Grams, you didn't go to high school here. I don't get it."

"It's more the cutting up of trees into firewood that reminds your grams of high school, I think," Gramps put in. Inga's gaze met her husband's.

"Oh, I see now," Third said with playful sarcasm. "That makes all the sense in the world." He rolled his eyes.

"Third, when I grew up in the war, heating fuel was in such short supply that each school child was asked to bring a piece of wood every day to heat the school. Sometimes there was enough wood, but most of the time we took our lessons in the cold. My feet still feel chilly when I think of it."

Inga Wentzel learned to knit when she was eight years old. The first winter she could remember, the half hour walk every day to classes was a miserable ordeal. If the rain came, or snow, or sleet, it was more miserable still. The only way to keep her feet warm was to wear the socks that she knitted for herself. The cold and the wetness were tolerable if she had a spare pair of socks in her pocket. Her feet may still be cold and wet, but not as much as many of the other children.

Inga learned early that she was gaining a valuable skill. She knitted socks for Konstanze and Christoph as well as herself, and then she made spares.

A neighbor in the town had given Hedda Wentzel a spinning wheel. After shearing sheep, herself, Inga learned to spin the yarn and knit the socks herself. Warm, dry feet were the dividend of a significant investment in time and effort.

Later, as Inga's skills grew, she added sweaters and scarves to her production, and she even learned to dye the yarn interesting colors with onion skins and other plant dyes.

Some of the older girls lacked the patience Inga was forced to employ. Some of the boys lacked it, too. Or else, they lacked the sheep. Some socks were bullied out of Inga, and some were given up deliberately to protect her younger siblings from bullying. She was made to understand by her mother that times were tough, and everyone needed socks whether they had access to them or not.

"When everyone is poor, any act of love takes a sacrifice," she would repeat. "No one has so much that a kind gesture goes unnoticed. It all costs." Repay cruelty with kindness was the lesson here.

Decades later, the truth about Hitler's Reich was publicized when it was discovered that the Nazi leadership had spent years lining its personal pockets with German wealth, as ordinary Germans lived on the cusp of economic crisis. But during Inga's childhood, it was a shared struggle, and everyone needed socks.

"But Grams, that was a long time ago in a different world. It's hard for me to believe that your cold feet stuck with you so long that you think about firewood still today," Third protested. "I haven't been here in wintertime, but I'm guessing you haven't been that cold in a long time."

Inga said nothing at first. She smiled and answered in a soft voice, "I was just telling about my childhood in Germany. You said you wanted to know."

"I do, I do, but . . ." Third paused, unsure where he was going or how this wool sock story applied until Gramps stepped in to help.

"Third, did you know that your grams double-pays the electric bill every month?" he said.

"No," Third replied, bewildered. "Why would she do that? My dad complains about the electric bill and the gas bill every month. He says they are highway robbers, the utility companies."

"Be that as it may, your grandmother pays twice the bill to help out poor people who can't keep their electric turned on.

"Really?" Third asked.

"We never see the people she helps, and she has kept this up during our own lean times, too. But that's the idea. We do it because, well, we've been cold in our lifetimes. Hungry and cold."

"That reminds me, Third, are you going to go to Monroe City and visit Chelsea like we talked about tomorrow while Joe and I are at church?" Inga asked.

"Oh, wow. I don't think so, Gram. I haven't talked to her and I don't really want her to see me with my face like this. Then I'd have to explain to her that I got punched by a . . . by that guy."

"Why don't you surprise her?" Inga suggested.

"Why?"

"Because your intent is to find out if anything is wrong in that trailer. You'll find out more if it is a surprise. We'll drop you off, and we'll take the truck so we can haul the ladder. I'd like to know what is troubling that girl," Inga decided.

"Grams, I don't think I want to go Sunday. Maybe the next Sunday after the swelling goes down a little."

"It's not like you to be so vain, Third," Inga said.

"Okay, what if I go over there and surprise the family and nothing at all is wrong? Everything is fine and I've shown up without an invitation with my left eye swollen shut, and I look like a damned fool. What would that help?" He paused, then added, "What if she just likes to laugh?"

Inga hesitated for a moment, then went into the kitchen.

Third followed her. His grandfather's words from weeks ago still stuck with him. "If a person is hurt, if a person is being mistreated . . . Speak up. Take action. Whatever it takes. I don't want to see you turn a blind eye to someone suffering."

"I'll call her, though, Grams," Third said. The onus was on him and he felt both burdened and challenged. "I'll talk to her and see if I can find anything out. Promise."

CHAPTER 43

Dix Simpson had an apartment in Columbia. He and Ernesto Soto relished the town where the University of Missouri campus drew young people from all over the state. Business was booming with a clientele of wealthy kids wanting a chemical escape from their studies. Simpson and Soto already provided crack cocaine and various opiates for entertainment purposes, and very shortly they would introduce methamphetamine to the college campus.

A mere hour and a half from Shelby County, Columbia was on a pipeline from the factory at Jack Sample's house. If Sample could keep his promises, there would be a fortune for the taking.

"So, you think he'll hold up his end?" Soto asked.

"He's got to," Simpson replied. "We've got this set up real righteous. He'd be the only variable. But I tell you this—he needs help. Either he puts on more shifts cooking, or we'll have to add a factory or two."

"He wouldn't be happy about that," Soto said, grinning. "And neither would I." He twisted his fist into the palm of his hand like a mortar and pestle.

"Honestly, Soto, I wish you didn't have to always beat somebody till they're stupid first and ask questions later."

"I wouldn't make a good enforcer if I asked questions first, would I?" Soto sneered.

"You wouldn't make a good business partner if you killed our only source of product in a hundred miles, would you?"

"Aw, I won't kill him unless he makes me. But, hey, if he won't produce the way he promised he could, I could kill his bitch. That might light a fire under him. And they got a baby, too, I think."

"Before we start killing babies, we ought to line up some other factories just in case."

The two men were having lunch in a pizza parlor at the edge of the Columbia campus across the street from the student center. Simpson looked out the window at students walking by. The semester was over; only a few summer classes were in session, and yet there was a lot of foot traffic. When the new semester got started, this campus would become an orchard of fruit ripe for plucking. Simpson noted that Soto's interest was only in his food. He didn't look out the window. He had no interest in potential new customers. Soto, Simpson acknowledged to himself, was an animal driven solely by his appetites. His appetite for violence was both a blessing and a curse.

"I got us invited to a party tomorrow night," Simpson revealed.

"Yeah? Where?"

"A half mile from campus. The apartment belongs to a co-ed. I expect to romance her into helping us out whether she intends to or not."

"I'll forget to mention it to your wife."sneered Soto.

"Appreciate. But as long as I put the bitch in big-ass cars, I doubt she'd care much."

"Which bitch you talking? The old one or the new one?"

"My lovely wife," Simpson said, noting that Soto wasn't following the conversation.

"I've always wondered what it would feel like to kill a baby," Soto sighed.

CHAPTER 44

As it happened, Monroe City was located at the intersection of three Missouri counties. Owing to budgetary constraints, each county was happy to put off expensive, troublesome complaints onto one or both of the other two, so it took some time for any anonymous report to be processed. The report in question said that a teenage girl in a trailer park in Monroe City might be a victim of incest.

"Why are we even looking into this?" questioned the Marion County sheriff, Wade MacAffee. "I heard the call. The report came in anonymously from a female with what sounded like a faked voice. I'll bet it was a teenager disguising her voice and pulling a prank."

"You can think that all you want to," replied Ralls County Sheriff Lisa Tucker, "but we still have to follow it up. More specifically, you have to follow it up. The residence in the report is in your jurisdiction."

"I don't think I'm going to, Lisa. It's my call, and I say it's a hoax."

"Based on the caller's voice?" Tucker said. It wasn't a question. She was appalled by the irresponsibility. She had only dealt with MacAffee occasionally in her eighteen-month tenure as Ralls County's sheriff. In that short time, she couldn't figure out if MacAfee feared overstepping any boundaries, if he disliked confrontation, if he simply eschewed work—or all of the above. It did seem clear to her, however, that in these domestic matters, he opted out of acting more often than not, and that could put families at risk.

She found him irritating. He boasted an exaggerated sense of his value to law enforcement, but the agreement among the three counties predicated that it was Sheriff MacAfee's call. There was little she could do about it other than to look out for more reports of this kind.

Of course, if this wasn't a hoax, and it came to light that a child was seriously injured, she could intervene, she thought, but it might be a case of locking the barn door after the horses escaped.

"All right, Sheriff MacAfee, I'll talk to you later." She put special emphasis on the title in hopes of sending him a subtle message that she did not wish to be called by her first name. Not by him. Not in this business relationship.

Sheriff Tucker hung up the phone without waiting for a reply.

CHAPTER 45

The Armstead lunch table was quiet Friday as it had been Thursday evening following the Elsa incident. Don normally ate at the fire station, but given what had happened, he had come home for lunch.

Jamal was thoughtful and quiet, and Don wished he could be a fly on the wall inside of his son's brain. Maybe, Don thought, he should soft-pedal this and wait until the boy was ready to talk.

Lynae was also reserved. Furious at her husband for allowing the two young men to go to a party in Elsa in the first place, she and Don had argued about the wisdom of preparing their son for the real world in such a way. She held her tongue now, but her silence was more a feature of her anger.

"Dad," Jamal finally began.

"Jamal," Don returned in the same timbre.

"Joe stood in front of me when those guys came after us. He tried to protect me."

Don raised his eyebrows and sat upright, surprised. Surely, he had expected, the kid would want to talk about the mentality of white supremacists. Or how to avoid them. Or how to understand them. Or something about them. Yet, the first words out of his son's mouth about the incident involved the MacDonald boy instead.

"Really? Why do you think he did that?" Don asked.

"Dunno. Maybe because when we were playing one-on-one, I showed him I'm not that much of an athlete and I needed protecting," Jamal surmised.

"Is Joe a good athlete?" Don asked.

"More than me. A lot more than me. He's no Larry Bird, but he can jump and shoot, all right."

"Jamal, I'm surprised at your reaction to what happened. I thought you'd want to talk about those people who attacked you—not Joe MacDonald. I wish you would talk to me about how you feel, I don't want to make assumptions about how the attack affected you, but if you don't tell me, assuming is all I'm left with."

"Oh, uh, I'm not saying it isn't a big deal, but it wasn't a new thing. Until a few years ago, I lived in Detroit, remember? I've seen racists before. They're like a song with only one note. There's nothing there to understand. They are what they are. But Joe is so, I don't know, white. He does surprise me. While we were on our way to Elsa, he told me he thought you and his gramps were out of line being all paranoid about the racism in Elsa."

"I guess he doesn't think that now, does he?" Don said with sorrow in his voice.

"No, I guess he doesn't. Why do you think he did that?"

"Did what? Try to protect you?"

"Yeah."

"I can't say. Maybe he's just his granddad's grandson. We talked about how Joe has a different take on things than most white folks."

"Why?" Jamal wanted to know. "I think most white folks are clueless."

"That's cause they are. But Joe, I don't know, I guess his life has brought him different experiences. He just seems to care enough to pay more attention.

"I mean he notices the subtle, insidious signs of oppression. He opposes requiring ID from voters at the polls."

"But what's wrong with that?" Jamal asked. "How is that a race thing if whites have to do it too?"

"That's what makes it subtle and insidious. Poor people—especially black folks—definitely see it as more of a threat if they have to show I.D. It scares people from the polls.

"Yeah, it does."

"Okie Joe grew up in a time and place where he got a big snootfull of being one of the people on the outside. He understands how tough it is to make your way when so many people treat you like a second-class citizen for things you can't help." Don reached for a second helping of green beans.

"Do you know that one of my firefighters recently told me that he, personally, has never enslaved anyone, and he hates being blamed for the slavery that there once was in this country?"

"Ha! Black folks are enslaved economically to this day," Lynae cut in.

"Sure, but the economic slavery is subtle and insidious, if it's not in your face. If you're white, you don't see it.

"Okie Joe always looks at society as one thing. He looks to find ways that everyone can be helped all at once. He's the opposite of most folks who worry about their job or their bills or their kids going off to college."

"So, you think he's taught Joe, my friend, to be like that, and sacrifice his own safety for someone else?"

"Probably not. Maybe God's left that job to you. We're all called to something."

"Me? Why me? I can't teach him nothin.'" Jamal objected. "You know what I wish?" he asked.

"You wish people wouldn't beat you and kick you anymore?"

Jamal chuckled. "Right, but I also wish Joe weren't going back to the city at the end of summer. He's the best friend I've made here."

"I don't know what I can do about that, son."

"You could talk to Big Mac," Jamal suggested.

"You think your friend is so good that Big Mac would want to meet him?"

"Yeah. Definitely."

CHAPTER 46

The conversation at the MacDonald house was different. Okie Joe came downstairs dressed to cut down trees on the far side of the property. Joe followed a minute later wearing shorts and a tee shirt.

"I need you to go back and put on long pants, Third," Gramps said without preamble. "You'll tear your legs up on the brambles in that. And a long sleeve shirt if you've got one."

Third returned in a few minutes with jeans, work boots, and a long-sleeved button down shirt.

Gramps sent him to the barn. "There's a gas-powered chainsaw on the left wall, son. It's yellow. The gas can is underneath it. Put 'em both in the truck."

When Joe returned from that chore, his grandfather studied him.

"We still need to work on your clothes, Third. That shirt won't survive this job. Let me get you one of mine." Gramps headed upstairs and returned with a long sleeved shirt with holes worn in the front. "Put this on instead," he said. Joe eagerly made the change. The shirt was way too big, but there was something about wearing his gramps' shirt that pleased him. A sense of closeness. The teenager liked it.

"You want a refill on coffee while I'm up?" Young Joe offered. Without waiting for an answer, Third picked up Gramps' near-empty coffee cup and took it from the dining room to the kitchen. Joe gazed at the cup for a moment and realized he had never once in his life, to his recollection, picked up a coffee cup of his father's—or Liz's for that matter—to refill it.

He set the mug on the counter and hugged his grandmother's shoulders.

"Morning."

"How are you feeling, Third?" Inga chirped.

"You mean about Thursday." It wasn't a question.

"Yes."

"Stunned, I guess. I never knew things like that happened in this day and age." He poured coffee for himself and Gramps.

"Do you have enough hands to carry the hash browns along with coffee?"

"Uh, sure."

Joe picked up the dish with one hand, and looping the fingers of the other through the handles of the coffee cups, strode back into the room where his gramps sat looking at the Quincy paper. Inga followed him.

"Joe, Third was just saying that he feels stunned about what happened in Elsa," Inga stated as she reached the table and set down a ham steak on a plate.

"Understandable," Gramps agreed. He had been reluctant to bring the incident up with Third. He thought he'd wait until the young man wanted to talk. Up until now, he had been silent on the topic, allowing it to remain the elephant in the room. But now, the kid would have to talk about it whether he wanted to or not. He'd reserve judgment whether to blame his wife or bless her.

"See, this is new for me," Third began. "It's hard to put into words, I guess." He squirmed.

"When you go into the cafeteria at Roosevelt High School in St. Louis, the black kids sit at some tables and the white kids sit at others. The Vietnamese kids sit together, too. It's how it's always been as long as I've been there, and I really don't see what's wrong with it. People sit where they're comfortable, and most folks are comfortable with their own kind. This whole thing with physical attacks is out of my . . ." he trailed off, looking for the word.

"Well," Gramps said, "That's how I remember St. Louis, only on a bigger scale. It's quite a polarized community racially. The last time I was there, there were only one or two major streets within the city limits that went all the way north and south, as if to encourage the polarization."

"What's wrong with that?" Third complained. "If society is as racist as, well, Elsa, then wouldn't blacks want to stay in their own groups?"

"It's kind of a vicious cycle, Third," Gramps explained. "Sure, people wanna feel safe, so they stay with what's familiar. But that sets a whole different thing in motion. When people stick with what's most familiar, then everybody is encouraged to build an us-versus-   them-mentality about it that then disintegrates into bigotry." Gramps took a drink of coffee and placed his cup on the table.

"What I want for the world is for all working people to cling together because the real us-versus-them is working people versus the ruling class."

"Here we go again." Joe expressed his exasperation by rolling his eyes.

"Yes, we do. We always do, because it's always just that way. As I told you, the isolation of minorities plays right into the rulers' hands. Divide and conquer."

"Okay, but what's being conquered, Gramps? What does this ruling class win if blacks and whites don't eat their lunch at the same table?"

"It distracts groups of people away from who the real enemy is."

Inga interrupted. "Joe," she said, "I'm not sure that the principles of Marxism are really what Third is interested in right now. I know that I would like to hear more about how he feels about the incident, not what it means to society."

"I'm not sure how I feel, Grams. I was so stinkin' scared, I couldn't think straight, and all I could do was stand in front of Jamal and try to shield him. It didn't work." Joe tried to smile sheepishly, but the tender side of his face convinced him otherwise.

"You shielded Jamal?" Inga asked, aghast.

"Not very well. I just hoped that these jackasses would rather not hit a fellow white guy, but I was wrong. They had no problem doing that. They called me a nigger-lover. "

Gramps nodded with understanding.

"Let me ask you this, son," Gramps said. "What would you do differently if you had it to do over?

"Not go to Elsa."

Gramps laughed. "Sure, sure. But if you did go to Elsa, not knowing what would happen, would you still stand in front of Jamal and shield him?"

"Damned right, I would!" Joe exclaimed. "Even though it didn't really do any good. Jamal was set to get beat up pretty good if you hadn't shown up when you did."

"It did do good, Third," Gramps said. "It taught you something about people, including yourself. And it may have taught Jamal something about you."

"Gramps, I'm never going to be the kind of man you are. Or the socialist. I don't have that in me."

"Be who you are, Third. That's all I ask."

CHAPTER 47

"Hey, it's Jamal."

Joe heard his friend on the phone, and noted the subdued tone in his voice.

"Hey, what's up?"

"Uh, you wanna go somewhere with me this afternoon about three? I'll pick you up."

"No, not at all," Joe replied, trying to keep the humor out of his voice.

"What? I mean, why?"

"Tell me what I'm signing up for first. Then I'll decide to go or not."

"Oh, yeah, sorry. My dad talked to Big Mac McIntyre about you, and he wants to meet you and see what you got."

"I see," Joe replied. "And who the hell is Big Mac McIntyre?"

"Oh, sorry. He's the basketball coach at the high school. Dad told him that you're great and he wants to check you out."

"Did he tell Big Mac that I'm leaving town when school starts?" Joe ventured.

"Yeah, he did, but he'd like to see you anyway."

"I dunno . . . I don't see much point in it."

"Ah, man, c'mon," Jamal objected, whining. "My dad went to some trouble. Don't be like that. I'm picking you up at two-thirty, okay?"

"All right, I guess."

"And one other thing . . ."

"What?"

"The way you stepped in front of me Thursday and tried to shield me from those mother fuckers . . . that was real dumb-ass of you," Jamal stated.

"Yep, sure was," Joe grinned.

"Yeah. You know, you're the first white dude I ever had for a friend."

"You're kiddin' me."

"No, I'm serious. When we were in Detroit, all my friends were black, and I haven't made any friends since we moved here," Jamal said.

"I'll try not to sour you on my entire race," Joe laughed.

"Too late. Thursday did that whole thing in."

"I'll see you at two-thirty."

CHAPTER 48

Chelsea Christmas' weekend started out on an unexpected note when the phone rang Friday just after noon. Dad was still asleep, and mom was at the boutique working her ass off, so Chelsea, nursing a summer cold, was in the trailer as good as alone.

She answered the phone on the first ring. "Hello?"

"Hi, Chelsea. This is Joe MacDonald. How're you doing?"

"Oh, hi," she said, checking the hallway to see that she still had privacy. "What's up?"

"Not a lot. Well, actually, a lot is going on, but it's nothing for you to worry about."

A queer thing to say, Chelsea thought. "I wouldn't think of worrying since I don't know what you're talking about."

"That makes two of us."

Chelsea began to laugh. The familiar despair she tamped down in her heart revealed itself as laughter as it typically did, and while the tears flowed with the guffaws, she hoped her dad was still passed out.

"Chelsea! Chelsea! Stop laughing for a minute. Earth to Chelsea! Come in, Chelsea!" Joe coaxed.

The girl forced herself sober. "Sorry. What? What'd you call me for?"

"A couple of things. I wondered if you would mind if I came by sometime to see you."

Awkward silence.

"I mean, I can't do it too soon 'cause, well, I've got some things going on personally, but I'd like to just stop by," Joe stammered.

"Why?"

Joe's mind raced trying to think of a way to skirt the truth, but he wasn't any good at it, and besides, he was nervous picturing this beautiful girl on the other end of the line.

"Well, um, I noticed before when I was over that you need some work done on your roof, and I thought I might bring by a ladder, get up there and clean out your gutters. . ."

"That's the craziest thing I've heard lately. Why are my gutters important?"

"When your gutters overflow, there can be water damage, and I, well, I assume your dad is too busy to take care of it. Plus, there are a lot of dead branches on your roof," Joe stammered. More silence followed, so he hastened to add, "It's not much, really, but I'd like to help."

Chelsea hesitated. "We don't have any money to pay you."

"No charge. I'd like to do it as a friend. Please? Say it's okay."

"When?"

"Well, that's just it. Depends on how fast the bruising goes away."

"What bruising?"

"Well, uh, I got into a little thing yesterday and got, um, bruised. So, when that clears up, I'd like to come by," Joe said, hoping he was sufficiently vague. Then he added, "Is there any reason I shouldn't come by, Chelsea? You can tell me if there is."

"The place is pretty messy right now," she said.

"So is my face."

"What?"

"I don't really care about the mess. Anyway, you are so pretty, you would outshine . . ." Joe didn't know how to finish the compliment. It hung in the air.

Chelsea, sensing the awkwardness of the attempt, relented. "Well, okay, I guess. I hope it will be all right."

"Chelsea, it really is okay to tell me if anything is wrong, if you don't want me to come over, or there is some reason I shouldn't come in your house. It's okay to tell me, I promise." Joe knew he was failing. He'd never get her to open up like this, and he was at a loss for a better strategy.

"Are you free next Saturday night?" he continued, trying a different approach. "There's always a dance in Macon on Saturday night. Do you like to dance?"

"I don't know how to dance at all."

"Neither do I. Not one step. We are perfect dance partners," he assured her.

The laughter resumed.

He tried distracting her. "What kind of music do you like? Country? R&B? I like Mariah Carey and Whitney Houston. I also like Boyz 2 Men. Chelsea?"

The change of topic sobered her, and she responded, "I like it when Kenny Rogers sings with Dolly Parton. Or with Dottie West. I used to have every Kenny Rogers record there is, but I don't anymore."

"What happened to them?" he wanted to know, feeling safe with a topic that probably wasn't funny.

"Oh, I did something a while ago that my dad didn't like, and he got rid of them all."

"Wow. What did you do?"

"I went out with a guy."

This time it was Joe's turn to respond with silence. After a moment, "I'm not sure how to answer that. Will you be in trouble for going out with me?"

"It's just that my dad gets a little bit . . ." she paused several seconds, "jealous at times."

Joe felt hair stand up on his neck. He thought immediately of Inga and her suspicions that the young woman was being molested. Nah, no way, he told himself. He was reading too much into it. He was ready to leap to that conclusion only because Inga had planted the suspicion.

"Jealous how, exactly? Why?"

"I think he wants me all to himself," she said vaguely. "He doesn't think I should see other males."

"This is your father we're talking about, right?" Joe demanded.

"Yes, but he drinks and doesn't always act right. Some of his attitudes are kind of off."

Joe wasn't sure what that meant, but he sensed that he had gone as far as he dared. "What about Saturday night next week? Are we on or off? And I'd still like to come by sometime and check on you and your roof. I'm worried."

Chelsea was quiet.

"Chelsea? Are you there?"

"Yeah, I'm just . . . I don't know. I've got to go now. See ya." Joe sensed that she was struggling to keep her composure. This girl was definitely in some kind of trouble. If she wasn't being molested, something else was happening to her. Without knowing more, though, what could he do? The phone had gone dead. He hung up and found Inga downstairs.

"Grams, I just talked to Chelsea, and you could be right. She might be in trouble." He explained the phone call briefly. When he finished, she went to the phone and picked up the phone directory next to it. She looked up the number for the Division of Family Services in Ralls County.

CHAPTER 49

Miles McIntyre had coached the Shelby High School basketball program for twelve years. He had won a state championship and sent several boys to college on basketball scholarships. His passion for the game and for the young men he coached was a force that drove his entire life, and he entertained notions of one day coaching at an NCAA school.

To that end, he used every opportunity to host college scouts, and make the best impression he could. Coach McIntyre prepared for any contingency that might advance the program at Shelby. But when a call came on a Friday morning from Don Armstead asking him to look at a kid, McIntyre was somewhat taken aback.

Big Mac, as he liked to be called, had actually worked with the Armstead kid who loved to play, and had enthusiasm. But at five foot, six inches, and without any upper body strength to speak of, he couldn't do much for Jamal.

While he was unable to help Jamal realize his dream of playing pro basketball, he had a lot of respect for Don, so, Big Mac agreed to look at a player from out of town in spite of learning the kid wasn't even going to stay for a semester.

He pulled into the back of the high school at ten minutes before three. James Freeman was with him. James, who had just graduated, had been Mac's best player the previous season, and now would be hard to replace. James was off to college in the fall and Mac wished him the best possible career. Nice of the kid to come with him on a wild goose chase this afternoon, Big Mac thought. He liked James, and didn't mind spending an afternoon with him.

A few minutes later, the Armstead parked behind Mac's truck. Jamal and a white kid got out of the car.

"Coach Mac! Thanks for meeting me," Jamal enthused. His voice was too ebullient, too anxious, Joe noted. He had never seen Jamal try so hard to impress someone.

"I'm Joe MacDonald," Joe extended his hand to Big Mac.

"Big Mac McIntyre." Mac stated, returning the handshake. "What's up with the shiner? You been in a bar fight?"

Joe, realizing his appearance would be off-putting, elected to go with the flow. "Yes, sir. Sure. Bar fight. You should see the other twenty guys."

Big Mac grinned at Joe, and continued the conversation without mentioning the shiner again. "This is my best player, James Freeman. I thought you might show me what you got with some one-on-one with him."

"Hey," Joe said to Josh.

The two bumped fists.

"Tell me about yourself, MacDonald," Mac said.

"Uh, well, I'm from St. Louis. I go to Roosevelt High School and I'll be a senior in September. I've played hoops there for three years, and I'm pretty good."

"Remains to be seen. Stats?" Mac asked.

"Okay, well, I play point guard with a 23 points-per-game average, an 82 percent free throw percentage, and last year I had about five assists per game."

As Joe spoke, the coach waved the three teenagers to follow him to the outdoor court. He walked with a basketball on his hip, his left arm holding it in place.

"My team won regionals the last two years and I was named MVP both years," Joe continued. "What else?"

"Rebounds?"

"Seven or eight per game, on average," Joe replied without hesitation.

"Sounds pretty good. Let's see your work."

"Let's do it," Joe replied, turning to James.

James had two inches of height on Joe, and quick hands. It took a few minutes for Joe to get a sense of the other young man's patterns and movements. It took James even longer to get a sense of Joe's.

The kid was good, Mac admitted to himself. Damned good. James Freeman was barely able to hold his own. Before long, MacDonald had Freeman's number and was anticipating each step. The MacDonald kid was pretty flawless.

Big Mac stepped in, halted the play, and grabbed the ball.

"Not bad, MacDonald. Let's see how you do with a little one-on-two." Big Mac began to dribble the ball. He passed it to Freeman, who took a shot, missed. Joe grabbed the loose ball, dribbled, leaped, and sank it.

The play continued for fifteen minutes. The double-teaming gave Joe a chance to show off his best stuff.

Jamal, watching, was off-put by the double-teaming, but realized that if he stepped in on his friend's behalf, he would do more harm than good. Jamal had learned a while back that as an athlete — even one in a nearly all-white school — he contradicted the stereotype of the strong athletic black dude. He forced himself to be content to watch.

When Mac called the play off, everyone was winded. He leaned forward, hands on knees, breathing hard. "Not too shabby, Mac-Donald. How sure are you that you're leaving the county before the season starts? 'Cause, if you don't, you'd be welcomed replacing Freeman as a point guard."

"What's Freeman leaving for?" Joe gasped.

"I graduated," Freeman answered. "I'm going to Vanderbilt. From there to the NBA, I hope."

Joe smiled and shrugged. He's got a ways to go to get to the NBA, Joe thought, but he didn't say anything. "Your folks must be real proud of that," he said instead.

"Nah," Freeman demurred. My mom doesn't know the difference between the NCAA and the NAACP. She's just happy I'm going to college."

"Hey, even I know what the NAACP is, and I'm white!" Joe smiled.

"No shit! I had no idea you were white," Freeman teased. "Did you, Coach?" He turned to Big Mac.

"Not by how he jumps," Jamal put in.

CHAPTER 50

After Chelsea concluded her phone call to Joe MacDonald, she went to her bedroom to try to calm down. Her face in her hands, she breathed deeply. A vague sense of dread gnawed at her insides. On some subliminal level, she knew Joe was onto her big secret. What she couldn't determine was whether that was a good thing or a bad thing.

Her father appeared in the door jamb to settle the matter.

"I heard you on the phone. Who was that?"

"Just a guy I know. You know him, too. We met him that one time at the farmers' market. He was selling eggs. He said that if we don't clean out the gutters, we could have water damage in the trailer, and that the tree branches on the roof aren't doing us any good either. Is that true?"

"Yeah, I guess. So, what did he want?"

"He wants to come over and clean the gutters."

"You told him you can't pay him, right?"

"Yeah. He doesn't care."

Dennis Christmas was careful, framing his next words to his daughter. "You know, Chels, ignorance in some ways is bliss," he began cryptically. "Your mother would be real, real hurt if we didn't go out the way to protect her from things."

Chelsea, still sitting on the side of the bed, looked up her dad, a fear mounting within her.

"It's real important that we take care of the things that go on around here and leave her out of it. There'd be no telling what she might do if we didn't. There'd be no telling what she'd do to you if everything that goes on came back on her. You understand?"

Chelsea nodded and put her head back in her hands. The hopelessness of her situation enveloped her. She waited until she heard her father go to the fridge for a beer before she let herself cry.

CHAPTER 51

While Simpson and Soto had a telephone in their motel room, the two relied on the developing technology of cellular phones to conduct business. They were expensive, and there were always problems with roaming, limited range, and the failure of one cell to connect to the adjacent one, but they offered more privacy. They offered bulk, too, as the instruments were large, heavy contraptions that rendered them not easily mobile. Simpson believed they'd improve over time, but right now, they weren't any more than they were.

Most of the time, they used the mobile phones to order pizzas. The pizzas were actually working girls, and the orders were placed in code with the brothel owner. The hope was that the girls were as easily addicted as they were easy, and that they would, in time, become addicted customers, as well as providers of their services.

"I've always wondered what it'd feel like to kill a whore," Soto remarked on Friday night.

"I wish you would stop saying that shit. It creeps me out. Killing people just for fun is nothing but trouble we don't need," Simpson replied.

"Hey, I never said it was fun, but, shit, sometimes it just needs done."

"Focus on Jack in Elsa. I've about had it with him. On the way there now. If he doesn't have all the product we want, then we'll talk about how much fun it could be to do him."

"Or the baby. Still think we can light a fire under him by offing the baby."

"You're freakin' nuts, man."

Simpson clicked the phone's off button as he drove toward Elsa.

Forty-five minutes later, he pulled up in front of the salmon-colored house where Sample and his little family had set up residence after leaving Sylvia.

Sarah let him in. She showed him the basement door and returned to the kitchen where macaroni and cheese and hot dogs were cooking.

When Dix Simpson reached the bottom stair, voices almost immediately rose to Sarah's unwilling ear.

"How can I hire help when there ain't no help to hire? I ditched most of my customers to move here, and I don't know anyone here yet who wants this kind of job," Jack complained.

"No one told you to move your kitchen, man," Dix scolded.

"Oh, really?" Jack countered. "Just what choice did I have after your business partner killed that cop?"

"Soto wouldn't have killed the cop if the cops weren't onto your operation. You brought it on yourself, man." Dix's voice got louder with each accusation until Sarah, upstairs in the kitchen, extinguished the burners, ran to the bedroom, picked up the sleepy Dustin, and carried him outside. She sat on the porch where the voices from down below were inaudible. She watched the trees flutter in the breeze.

She would just sit here, she decided, until that guy was gone.

While she sat there, she noticed a minivan parked halfway down the hill. It was an unusual copper color and its passenger door was pretty banged up.

She could see that the car was occupied, but she had to squint to see the driver's face. The face was familiar, but she couldn't place it. She thought he looked like someone she had seen in Sylvia at some time. Someone who wore a uniform. She wracked her brain. Where had she seen that face?

Dix Simpson, burst through the front door and ran down the front steps carrying a package under his arm, rolled up in a paper grocery sack. He rushed past Sarah so fast, the baby's blanket moved in the wind he created. Without speaking to Sarah, he got into his van and took off.

A moment later, Jack appeared on the porch. Sarah glanced up at him.

"He's upset that I didn't have all his product ready. I told him I need help and can't get any 'cause we had to move."

"I heard that much."

"I really need help, Sarah, and if you won't cook for me, I'm likely to lose this deal and then we'll have to go back to selling product to strangers. I'd much rather have one guy do all the buying so I don't have to worry that he's going to rat me out to the sheriff."

That's it! Sarah thought to herself. That guy in that copper-colored minivan was the sheriff! What's he doing up here?

Sarah lifted Dustin over her head and handed him to Jack. Without commenting further, she went in the house and resumed boiling the macaroni. The realization that her home was under surveillance—again—was not at all lost on Sarah. But she put it out of her mind as she did much of reality, and would think about it later.

CHAPTER 52

"I've got that meeting tonight, don't forget," Okie Joe said to Inga Friday afternoon.

"Okay. Thanks for the reminder," she stated.

"You want to come with me?"

"Not this time. I've got things to do. Maybe Third would want to go with you," she suggested.

"Really?" he asked. "I don't think I've exactly won him over to my viewpoint on politics."

"No, I don't think so, either, but his father did an excellent job of repelling Third from his viewpoint when he and I were in St. Louis."

"Really? What happened?"

"Let's just say that your son showed his true colors." Inga's voice trilled with amusement.

"Please explain."

"No. I won't. There's no good to come of it. I will allow, though, that if there was ever a time to explain our beliefs to Third, now might be it," Inga assured him.

"Don is going with me tonight," Joe said.

"Are visitors okay?" Inga asked.

"Oh, sure. It's open to the public. It's just a discussion meeting with a guest speaker. It's a poli-sci professor from St. Louis."

"Well, you three have fun."

Across town, a similar conversation transpired. "I'm going to Shelbina with Okie Joe tonight," Don Armstead told Lynae.

"What for?"

"Some sort of political meeting. I'm going to learn to be a rabble rouser, I suppose."

"All right then," Lynae said with sarcastic sweetness. "Call if you need to be bailed out."

"Ha!" Don laughed.

Jamal entered the kitchen where Don and Lynae were talking.

"I just talked to Joe," Jamal said. "He said he's going out with his grandfather and you tonight. Can I go?"

"Really?" Don said, somewhat surprised. "I didn't know his grandson was coming along."

"Can I go too, then?" Jamal repeated.

"Jamal, this is going to be a political meeting that won't interest you."

"I'm never bored around Joe—or you, Dad" he added with diplomacy. Don paused. He had never seen his son warm to any of the local Sylvia people. This was good.

"Kind of surprised you want to, but okay."

"I like Joe," Jamal confessed. "He's the only friend I've got who isn't in Detroit."

The Armsteads took note. They realized, of course, that their son had been isolated since moving from the city. This friendship with the MacDonald kid had done a lot for Jamal, and his parents worried that Jamal would fall into a funk when Joe returned to St. Louis. But for now, it was a good thing.

Don called Okie Joe and told him his kid would be joining the group. Okie Joe picked up the Armstead men at six-thirty, and headed into Shelbina to a storefront in the center of town. Joe noted that the business section of Shelbina resembled that of Sylvia except that it was square. The same collection of boarded up storefronts and deserted retail establishments with soaped up windows announced that Shelbina and Sylvia had suffered the same financial woes.

The place they entered was different. Several racks of books for sale were visible through the window. It was unlike any bookstore Joe had ever seen.

Titles jumped out at him with authors' names emblazoned across the fronts: Marx, Trotsky, Engel, and others. A collection of Fidel Castro's speeches was bound with a colorful cover, and there were a number of authors Joe did not recognize.

A book entitled *Silkwood* also caught his eye–the basis for that

Meryl Streep movie about the title character's battle with a nuclear plant.

Various titles had to do with conflicts throughout the world—the Israel-Palestine conflict, the one in Central America with the contras, the Irish trying to throw off British rule. A biography of Nelson Mandela, who had been released from prison in South Africa in 1990 sparked Joe's memory of the news coverage.

He smiled to himself. His father would have a cow if he were here, he told himself. Or if he knew Joe was.

And all these books, Joe realized with a quick glance at their summaries on the backs, took the opposite viewpoint of what most Americans had, and certainly the opposite of what he had been taught all his life.

At the back of the bookstore, a door led into a meeting room where fifty-odd folding chairs were set up.

When the four entered, Gramps was welcomed by many people. He shook hands all around and introduced his companions. Joe heard name after name and, again, he regretted his lack of memory for names.

The crowd was a cross-section of ethnicity, unlike the cultural homogeneity Joe was used to. He could detect no suggestion among the group of the strain that was evident at his school and elsewhere between ethnic groups. There seemed to be a warmth and camaraderie among the attendees.

He recognized that the racial tension in St. Louis he had lived with for years was invisible and "normal" feeling until he went somewhere that such tension was missing.

The warmth was similar to the friendly spirit at Good Shepherd Church, but this group was not religious.

As the evening progressed, his grandfather stated with pride some fifteen times that his grandson was with him, and the teen was obliged to shake hands over and over. Joe thought with sadness, throughout his grandfather's introductions, that he could never remember his own father introducing him to people with pride in his voice.

The formal meeting was late getting underway. People had taken seats in anticipation, but were soon disappointed by an announcement.

"Sorry to say," began the meeting leader, "there's been a bad accident on Highway 61 just outside of Troy. There are injuries, and traffic is snarled."

The group murmured sighs and sounds of concern. The meeting leader continued. "Professor Giles from the political science department of St. Louis University, who was scheduled to speak tonight, will be at least an hour late, so, we have a little time to kill. Please enjoy a beverage and explore the bookstore." With that, he left the podium.

Attendees resumed milling about, and Okie Joe, anxious that people not grow restless and begin leaving, spied an acoustic guitar leaning against a bookshelf in the far corner. He stepped away from his companions, snatched up the instrument, and went to the facilitator who had announced the delay.

"Hey, I've got an idea to kill a little time, Derek,"

Okie Joe said. "Let's do a sing-along. I found this guitar over in the corner."

"Yeah," Derek Phinney replied, "but I don't know many sing-along songs."

"Can I see what I can do? Borrow your box?"

"Uh, sure."

"Okay, thanks."

Joe returned to his companions, holding the guitar by the neck. "Don," he said to his friend, "let's entertain these folks with some music. You up for it?"

"You're kidding me," Don replied, aghast.

"No, man, I want you to sing that song you sang for me that one time. It would be perfect here."

"What song? That one my cousin Clinton wrote?"

"Yeah, that one. It would be perfect."

Don Armstead looked around the room. There were maybe fifty people, many his own age. He looked back at his friend.

"You really think I should?"

"I'll announce it. It's settled," Okie Joe stated.

Jamal turned to his friend. "C'mon, let's sit down. This is gonna be a hoot."

Okie Joe took the podium. As he did, Don strummed the guitar, measuring how well it was tuned, cocking his ear a little closer. He felt a good measure of trepidation, but, hell, he told himself, he'd been known to run into burning buildings! He could do this.

"Excuse me, everyone," Okie Joe MacDonald pronounced loudly. "To make the wait easier, we have some entertainment. Please take a seat for a special musical presentation." Joe's Oklahoma dialect rang with a note of pride. "Welcome my friend, Don Armstead."

There was mild applause as people sat down to listen.

Don Armstead swallowed hard as he stepped up to the podium. His hands shook as stage fright gripped him, but he ignored it.

Joe leaned to Jamal sitting next to him. "I didn't know your dad played."

"Yeah, he does. And he's good if you like his kind of music," Jamal said.

"I guess I'll know in a minute."

"Uh, hi, I'm Don Armstead," Don said at the podium. "I've got a song to share with you tonight. My cousin, Clint Gallagher, wrote it a few years ago, back in Detroit, and I think it might apply to the, uh, spirit of what we're doing right here. So, if you don't mind, I'd like to sing it for you."

More gentle applause.

Don began strumming chords, and after a minute, his baritone voice began:

"Some of us will get a little money/
Personality changes from good to funny/
You may be the most in fashion/
Head swollen, big as a watermelon/
What I have to say to you people/
Is true but cold/
Some might even say/
Yes, it's a little too bold/
But its full of wisdom and it could/
Save your soul/
Remember, you go to the bathroom just like me."

As the song continued, there was a mild titter in the crowd whenever Don sang, "You go to the bathroom just like me," but at the conclusion, the applause was more appreciative than polite.

Don started to set the guitar down against the bookshelf as Derek Phinney walked toward the podium, still clapping. On his way, Derek grabbed his guitar, strummed a little bit, and led the crowd in Bob Dylan's anti-war anthem, "Blowin' in the Wind."

Meanwhile, Jamal turned to Joe and deadpanned, "Well there's three minutes of my life I'll never get back."

Joe cracked up. "Hey, he's pretty good, your dad. And that was a great song. Great song. And true."

CHAPTER 53

Ernesto Soto's woman lived in Moberly. He had moved her to Missouri from Zapopan in west central Mexico after the second child was born. Moberly was convenient. A mere forty minutes due north of Columbia, the small town was far enough away to keep Rufina out of Ernesto's hair, but close enough for him to keep an eye on her.

She worked in a Dairy Queen and lived in a small apartment with Ernesto Jr. and young Rigoverto, ages seven and six.

Ernesto didn't believe he would ever make much of a father, owing to his fundamental dislike of children, but Rufina had carelessly gotten knocked up twice, and he was stuck with the outcome. He grudgingly supplemented her DQ income with court-ordered child support. Someone in Ernesto's chosen profession would be ill-advised to call attention to himself from the authorities. And while he didn't want this makeshift family hanging around his neck, it served his purpose to take the path of least resistance.

Rufina also got some food stamps and shopped for the boys in the local thrift store. While she made ends meet, she had no car and was therefore disinclined to visit Columbia, providing the perfect set-up for Ernesto.

The kids were a different story. Ernesto Jr. looked just like his father, and seemed to have his temperament, but the other one, Ernesto always had to think a few seconds to remember the kid's name … Rigoverto—he could be anybody's kid. That bitch was such a whore. And for now, he was stuck paying for it.

Ernesto's plan was to keep Rufina high whenever possible. He showed up weekly to drop off some drugs and a small amount of cash. He wanted her compliant and available to serve his baser needs in case the well of co-eds dried up.

Ernesto had gotten so damned mad the last time Rufina got knocked up, he had a vasectomy, so if she did it again, he'd kick all of them to the curb and let them be someone else's problem.

These musings killed the forty minutes Ernesto spent driving to Moberly on Friday night. They didn't serve his mood very well, but the people at fault— Rufina and the kids—deserved every morsel of his wrath.

When he pulled into the gravel driveway outside the apartment, he struggled to tamp down the rage that swelled whenever he came here. It was just damned unfair that these two kids kept him glued to a woman he didn't want. Them and Rufina's sweet kootch. But he could get kootch anywhere.

He let himself in the apartment. Naturally, it was a mess. Rufina was dancing to the radio in the kitchen with headphones on, and the kids were chasing each other in the living room as they jumped over a pile of laundry, and leaped feet first onto the unmade sofa bed.

Ernesto noticed a dish of meth pieces on the floor being scattered and stepped on by the running boys. Without greeting his children, Ernesto picked the older one up roughly and said, "Did you eat any of that?"

The child shook his head no.

"Good, because it's expensive. Where did you get it?"

"Mama," said the child.

"Of course, you did," he said, setting the kid down. "Get out of my way."

The child stepped aside as Ernesto strode into the kitchen where Rufina was oblivious to his presence. When he grasped her shoulder, she spun around, startled, and shrieked, "Ernesto, you scared the shit out of me! Don't sneak up on a person like that!" Her Spanish accent was becoming Americanized. This set an alarm off in his head about the future of controlling her, but his anger pushed it aside.

"These kids have meth!" Ernesto spat between clenched teeth. He gripped both of her shoulders as he bared teeth at her.

"What? What meth? I don't give those kids meth. What are you talking about?"

"I gave you five doses of glass before I left last time. I just found them on the floor in there. Those kids were playing with them. That is way too expensive to be wasting on them."

All of the things wrong with that statement hit Rufina at once. She didn't know where to start with her objections. She dared not tell this brutal, ugly man that she was trying to wean herself off the poison – and him. The drug didn't make for sound parenting or successful job-keeping, but the less he knew about her life, the better.

Before she could say anything, the shrieking of children at play broke in. The noise enraged Ernesto further. He pushed her away and marched into the living room to quiet the shriek.

He found one child chasing the other around the sofa. Clearly, the children were having some fun, but it was of no concern to Ernesto whose take on children was that they should be neither seen nor heard.

He grabbed Ernesto Jr. by the shoulders and pulled him close. He wrapped one meaty hand around the child's throat and squeezed, holding him immobile. He looked into the child's horrified face, scowling. "Shut the fuck up!"

His grip on the child tightened. The child was unable to speak, or breathe, but the boy's silent tears fell, dampening Ernesto's hand..

Rage welled inside Ernesto. Rage and hatred for the inconvenience these children and their mother posed by their very existence, rage for the time, money, and trouble, and rage for his loss of freedom.

Ernesto slapped the child across the face as hard as his considerable strength allowed. The boy's head snapped back and he lost consciousness.

Unsatisfied still, he wailed on the child, delivering punch after punch to the head and shoulders of the seven-year-old, as if he was the adversary in a bar fight.

Rufina clawed at Ernesto, screaming in Spanish and pulling at his waist and arms. When a backhand caught her squarely on the jaw, she reeled in pain.

Ernesto eventually dropped the child on the floor, limp. Blood oozed out of his eyes, ears and nose.

The younger child, Rigoverto, cried hysterically as he watched the beating, and tried to hide behind the sofa. He whimpered and begged for mercy.

Again, Rufina tried to intervene, but Ernesto was on a roll, and barely noticed the shrieking, hysterical woman. He grabbed Rigoverto by the waistband of his pants, pulled him out from behind the sofa, and punched him repeatedly in the head until Rufina pushed her way between the man and boy, prepared to take the punches herself. Somehow her screams, entreating him to stop, or else the abrupt change of target, distracted Soto momentarily.

"Why should I stop, bitch? It's not even my kid."

"Yes, he is. Yes, he is. And you know Ernesto Jr. is yours. Why would you do this? Oh, my God! Oh, my God!" Rufina dissolved in tears and curse words as she kneeled by Ernesto Jr., held him, tried to wipe away the blood, and begged him to wake up. He didn't.

"I need to take him to a hospital, Ernesto. We need to go now, with both boys. Ernesto won't wake up. You hurt him real bad. Oh, my God!"

An inarticulate growl was all Ernesto had to offer. He glared at the woman holding her child for a full fifteen seconds.

"Listen, bitch, I gave them both what they had coming. The next time I come here, you keep those cockroaches quiet or I'll shut them up for good."

He stepped toward the door.

"No, Ernesto!" Rufina shrieked. "I need you to take us to a hospital. You know I have no car. I cannot do it by myself. Ernesto Jr. is really hurt. Oh, my God! So is Rigoverto! Please, for God's sake, don't leave us. Oh, my God! Oh, my God!"

Ernesto, without another word, stepped outside the apartment and slammed the door behind him. He wasn't even going to leave her any meth this time, he told himself. That would serve her right.

CHAPTER 54

Joe knew his grandmother was right. It was vain and self-indulgent for him to fail to help Chelsea—whatever trouble she was in—just because he didn't want her to see him with his bruised face.

Fortunately, the issue was answered when he woke up Sunday morning and the bruising was significantly reduced. He stood in the bathroom for a long time looking in the mirror and gauging just how awful he looked.

He came downstairs as Inga was starting breakfast.

"Hi, Grams."

"Your face looks much better, Third," she proclaimed, hugging him. "You're almost back to normal. Why don't you reconsider—"

"I already have, Grams," he interrupted. "I'm going to load the ladder into the truck right now, if you still want to drop me at Chelsea's before you go to church."

"You know, I called the county office again about that situation. As of Friday, they haven't done anything yet. I don't think they believed me the first time I called. They said my report wasn't credible. I offered to come to their office and talk to someone in person, and when I said that, they said they would file another report.

"Like the Bible says," Inga continued, "For God so loved the world that he did not file another report."

Joe grinned broadly at the fractured Bible verse. While his knowledge of church-related things was nearly non-existent, he at least recognized that simple passage, as it was quoted at Good Shepherd nearly every Sunday.

"I'll show up and surprise her like you said," he vowed. "Maybe Chelsea will tell me what's going on or maybe she won't, but I'll try to help."

"My idea exactly," Inga agreed. "Now, what will it be: biscuits and gravy or waffles with peaches?"

When the MacDonald truck pulled up in front of the Christmas trailer, Gramps looked around at the property and nodded in understanding. "Yep," he agreed. "The place sure does need some work."

"I'm thinking it may need more work on the inside," Inga suggested, looking at her husband to reinforce her perspicacity.

"I just hope you aren't borrowing trouble, Inga," he said to his wife.

"You're spending too much time with Don. He's the one who always says that. And you, Mr. MacDonald, you borrow trouble every chance you get, so the pot is calling the kettle black, isn't it?" Inga smiled sweetly.

Okie Joe smiled back at her, but didn't reply. He winked at her instead, and she squeezed his hand.

"You ready, Third?" Inga said.

A few minutes later, Joe had set up the ladder outside the front door as Inga and Okie Joe drove off. They got as far as the gate to the trailer park when Joe stopped, turned the truck around, and came back.

Young Joe, curious, met the truck. "What's up?" he asked his grandfather.

"I've decided to stay and help you," Gramps answered.

"Why?"

"'Cause if I'm gonna borrow trouble, I reckon I'll borrow all I can." He stepped out of the truck as Inga scooted into the driver's seat. Without a word, she backed the truck up, turned around, and proceeded on her way.

"Go ahead, boy," he advised. "Let's see what we can do."

Young Joe's plan had been to work quietly and unnoticed. He half-hoped no one would notice he was doing the work. Or if they did notice, they would do so about the time he got finished.

Joe dreaded confrontation, as many people do. Whether the conflict occurs between himself and Chelsea, himself and Chelsea's father, or between himself and his own father, there was an off-putting aversion to it.

As such, he dreaded his mission here. But with Gramps' arrival, the mission took on new urgency. There would be no wimping out.

"All right," Joe said with some regret to his grandfather. "How do you plan to help me?"

"I'll hold the ladder steady while you climb up. Just like we did when we closed the shutters on our house."

"Right. I remember that day."

"And I'll keep an eyeball peeled and an ear cocked for anything unusual."

Gramps handed Joe a roll of large garbage bags he had brought in the truck. "When the truck comes back, we'll pile the yard waste in the truck bed."

"I'm glad you thought to bring those, Gramps," Joe said. "I never gave it a thought."

Joe placed the ladder at the corner of the house, climbed halfway up, and peeked over the edge of the gutter. It was packed with sticks and leaves. A huge mess. He would be surprised if any water ever reached a downspout. He pulled the debris out with a gloved hand.

Joe worked in six-foot sections, filling bags and dropping them on the ground next to Gramps.

Gramps braced the ladder, lending more moral support than physical. This was not the MacDonald home, and the farthest his grandson could fall would be about four feet.

The two worked, tracing most of the front of the building and heading around the corner.

Gramps heard a noise. He tugged on Third's jeans and signaled him to come down the ladder and follow him.

Gramps stepped eight feet in the direction the ladder had been heading, and paused under a window. He heard sounds coming from behind the window.

The two listened together at the sounds of people having sex. As they paused, embarrassed by their voyeurism, they heard the muffled cry of a man in the throes of his climax.

The two MacDonalds looked at each other. The younger man curled up his lip in a sign of disgust and walked away. His grandfather followed him.

When they had walked several paces and were assured of not being overheard, Gramps said in a low voice, "I hope you're not disgusted by what goes on in a man's bedroom, Third."

"No, Gramps, but I don't want to be a part of it. I feel real stupid being here, and I wish Grams hadn't pressured me."

"What are you going to do?"

"Well, I guess we're in for a penny, in for a pound. I guess I'll knock on the door."

"Really, Third? At a time like this?"

"Sure, Gramps. It sounded to me that the, um, activity is over with."

With that, Joe strode back to the trailer with his grandfather on his heels. He knocked on the door, even as his dread of the impending confrontation became a choking sensation in his throat.

It took three minutes before rustling came from behind the door. Joe heard a deadbolt being thrown back and Chelsea Christmas answered the door. She was scantily dressed in shorts and a tee shirt with no bra.

Her eyes widened. "What are you doing here?" she asked with a shaking voice. "I thought you weren't coming for a while." She greeted Okie Joe with her eyes lowered. "Hi."

"Um, yeah, well, I promised to do the gutters. I got an opportunity so I came, and my gramps was available to help me. I hope this is an okay time."

Chelsea's face was impossible to read in the mix of sunlight and shadows from the trailer.

"And, hey, while I'm here," Joe continued with a sudden idea, "I thought I'd meet your mom since I didn't get to meet her at the farmers' market. I thought I'd introduce myself and my gramps to her. Is she home?"

"Uh, no she's not. Nobody's here but my dad and me, and he's asleep right now, so some other time, okay?" Chelsea was easing the door closed in Joe's face.

Joe glanced at Gramps who met his gaze.

He turned back to the young woman. "Sure, no problem. Some other time. We'll just finish the gutters —"

"Finish them?" Chelsea asked, her eyes widening. She put her hand on her stomach "How long have you been here?"

Trapped, Joe went for broke. "Long enough, Chels. Is there anything you want to tell me? You can trust us. We're here to help."

A look came over Chelsea's obscured face that was unmistakable even in the dim light. She was terrified. "No, there's nothing to tell, and you should mind your own business. I mean, thanks for the gutters, but you should mind your own business."

With that, she shut the door on the two men. They stood frozen, looking at each other. Joe found himself as uncomfortable as he had been at any time in his young life. His grandfather's demeanor, however, was one of open rage.

"I'll be right back, Joe," Gramps promised. "You can finish by yourself. Be careful, but hurry, so we're ready when Inga comes back." With that, Gramps turned and walked away, his face reddening.

Joe understood his rage as he processed his own feelings. While the boy admired his grandparents' heroism, he had always been quick to deflect any notions of his own fortitude. Nevertheless, he craved that heroism for himself in a stylized fantasy.

Now, he learned, stepping in to do for others isn't always fanfare and headlines. Sometimes, like now, he told himself, it's pretty ugly.

Lost in thought, Joe climbed back up the ladder, continuing to work his way around the perimeter of the structure. Gramps seemed to have vanished, and Joe had no idea where he was.

When the gutters were finished, Joe hoisted himself onto the roof. Unable to conquer his fear of heights, he stayed on his knees, crawling around the roof, tossing branches off onto the ground.

She's going to have to pick up the debris herself, he told himself. He wanted to get the hell out of there.

Joe sighed with relief when he saw the MacDonald truck pull up near the trailer. Gramps was driving, and Inga was riding shotgun. Perfect timing, Joe thought. He climbed down the ladder, buckled its hinge and carried it to the truck. He slid it into the truck bed, tossed in the debris-filled bags, and closed the gate. A wave of nausea hit him, but he quelled it.

He climbed in the truck cab next to Inga. Neither grandparent greeted him. The three were quiet on the way back to Sylvia, and Joe realized his grandfather had met Inga as she returned to

the trailer park and told her what had happened before the two
retrieved their grandson.

CHAPTER 55

"Sheriff's office," Bill Fast barked into the phone.

"Uh, yeah, this is Sheriff Adam Kinsale in Randolph County. How are y'all today.

Kinsale's drawl was so charming, Fast was sure there was bad news coming. "Just fine, Sheriff. What can I do for you today?" Fast asked.

"Well, I got a report here, says you folks over in Shelby are looking for one Ernesto Soto. Says he's wanted for suspicion of killing a deputy. That right?"

"It may have been Soto or one of his associates. He's involved with a meth chemist and one of them may have killed one of our men in cold blood. We can't find any sign of this guy, and we only recently learned the location of the chemist's new lab. What's this about, Sheriff?"

"Well, it looks like I'm gonna have to have a talk with Soto, too, if you get hold of him. If I find him first, I'll sure give you a shout. It looks like he killed two children last weekend. His own children. Beat 'em to death. Left the mother there in the house with the two kids and wouldn't even take them to the hospital."

"Ah, shit, man. How old?"

"Brothers – seven and six."

"Jeez. How in hell do you kill a little kid?" Fast lamented. Sadness and rage rose in him.

"I guess you'd have to be a different kind of man," Kinsale replied with similar sorrow.

"Or else some other kind of animal altogether," Fast sighed.

CHAPTER 56

"Hey, man, I heard what happened," Jamal told Joe on the phone Monday morning.

"What? What do you mean?"

"Your grandfather told my dad that your girlfriend is having sex with her daddy."

Joe was quiet.

"You there, man?"

"Yeah, I don't really want to talk about this," Joe demurred.

"I get it. I'm not supposed to know, but I picked up the extension and just the wrong time," Jamal said, half agreeing. "It wouldn't have come up except that no one is doing anything about it, so your granddad called my dad, trying to find out how you rat out a bad sheriff, and now they're both upset."

"I'm not sure what anybody is supposed to do." Joe said.

"Your granddad told my dad that your grandma called the county at least twice to report it. So, my dad called a buddy at the county, and it's true: no one has done anything about this yet."

Again, Joe was silent, thinking. Gramps came in the house through the kitchen door, saw Joe, and signaled to him with a wave.

"Get off the phone, and let's go, Third," he said.

"I gotta go, Jamal. I'll call you." He hung up the phone without ceremony. There was an urgency in his grandfather's tone that alarmed Joe.

"Where are we going, Gramps?"

"Marion County sheriff's office," Gramps said tersely.

"What's there?"

"I guess the son of a bitch who won't arrest that child molester. Your grandmother is in the car already. Let's go."

"Gramps," Joe said walking to the car, "Jamal knows what happened at Chelsea's. He overheard you and Don on the phone. I don't appreciate that her private business is being told around."

"I agree with you, Third. It's not Jamal's business."

"And it's not Don's either," Joe insisted.

"And it's not yours and it's not mine, but we've been given a chance to help. Look Third, when a family in this county goes homeless because their house burned, it's the fire chief who contacts Division of Family Services to arrange housing. He's on a first name basis with those folks. If I want a fire lit under DFS, and if I want an inside track, he's the guy to ask."

"I see," Joe murmured.

When the three arrived at the office of the Marion County Sheriff's Department in Palmyra, Joe was unimpressed. The office was an old, run-down storefront on a street even more dilapidated than downtown Sylvia.

They parked in front. A lone sheriff department vehicle was parked on the side of the building, but they didn't see anyone.

"Why are we here, Gramps?" Joe whispered. His grandfather didn't hear him.

"Gramps, why did you want me to come?"

"Quit whisperin,' boy. My hearing is going as fast as my eyesight. "Why are you whispering?"

"I don't know. Why do you need me for this?"

"In case this sheriff doesn't believe me. I have you to back my appeal."

As the three approached the door, memories flooded Joe of unpleasant police encounters in his young life. The car he stole almost two years ago. The open beer can that was between his legs when a cop pulled him over in St. Louis. A stupid act of thirteen-year-old idiocy when he ripped off a pack of cigarettes from a convenience store and the clerk called the cops. He didn't even smoke. It was for a girl.

What if they knew about his criminal past, he worried, as they stepped through the door? What if they didn't believe him either because he was such a troublemaker?

Once inside, though, he was committed.

A uniformed man sat at a desk, typing on a computer that squeaked with every keystroke. He stopped typing as the MacDonalds approached.

He was a pudgy red-haired man with a wide, receding hairline and a ruddy complexion. His shirt puckered between the straining buttons, revealing a white tee shirt underneath, and his upper arms squeezed through the shirtsleeves.

"What can I do for you folks today?" the red-haired cop smiled.

"We're looking for Sheriff MacAfee. I'm Joe MacDonald, and we're from Sylvia," Okie Joe began.

"I'm Sheriff MacAfee. Sylvia is in Shelby County, Mr. MacDonald. Maybe you should talk to Sheriff Ollman over there."

"I'm here about something that's happening in Monroe City," Okie Joe answered. Inga stayed quiet and stood a step behind her husband. They had an idea about what had gone wrong with her report of child abuse, so the two of them had agreed to a plan.

Joe stayed quiet.

"Monroe City is shared by three counties. Perhaps you should talk to Monroe County's sheriff. I'm not sure I can help you," MacAfee said. "Already did, Sheriff," Okie Joe said. "Sheriff Tucker sent me to you."

"She did, did she?" MacAfee relented. "What's this about?"

"I have reason to think that a child in Monroe City is being sexually abused by her father, and I want to know why nothing has been done about it."

"Well, I did get a report from Division of Family Services earlier today," MacAfee admitted, "but the report wasn't credible, and I chose to set it aside until I had independent confirmation."

"What wasn't credible about the report?"

"The reports came in over the phone, Mr., um, MacDonald. I listened to the recordings. The source was an anonymous caller, and it certainly sounded like a little girl or at best a teenager disguising her voice. It's possible the caller intended to make trouble for one of our citizens, or wanted to pull a prank."

The MacDonalds stared at the sheriff and it made him uncomfortable. "The voice was so affected, so implausible, so highpitched and ridiculous that the report had no credibility. I had to dismiss it." His over-the-top attempt to convince sounded desperate and implausible.

"You're saying you'd rather let a child be hurt in that way—on a continuing basis—and not even look into it because the report came from someone with a high-pitched voice?" Okie Joe looked over his shoulder at his wife.

"Not just high-pitched, sir. The voice was so artificial, it couldn't be taken seriously," he repeated. "And I'll be damned if I'm going to accuse a citizen of something like what was suggested when all I've got to go on is an anonymous tip that's obviously a kid pulling a prank."

Joe watched the sheriff's face, but his concentration became a herculean effort to not dissolve into laughter. He realized that he was here to help his grandparents sting the sheriff.

The MacDonalds remained silent, observing the sheriff's mounting discomfort. Joe couldn't be sure, but it seemed that armpit stains were forming in the sheriff's pits. Joe concealed a smile.

Sheriff MacAfee scooted his chair back from his desk and stood up.

"Let me pull that tape for you, sir. I'm sure when you hear it, you'll agree it's probably a prankster. Give me a minute to find it."

"That won't be necessary, Sheriff," Inga MacDonald spoke for the first time. "I know what my voice sounds like. I've lived with it a long time. Much longer than any teenager."

Joe found it satisfying to watch the way MacAfee froze as his red face drained of color. Caught and humiliated, he began to back-pedal fast.

"I didn't realize, um, Mrs. MacDonald. I meant no disrespect at all, but the recording does sound to me like a teenager. I'm sorry I misunderstood." He gazed at the three and measured that his contrition was unconvincing. "I should not have said what I did. Obviously, the voice was not artificial."

That didn't work either, he gauged. These people were still upset. Then, in a ludicrous attempt to be charming, "Worse things could happen, you know, than to be a woman of maturity and still have such a youthful voice." He attempted a winning smile.

Inga heaved an exasperated breath, placed her hands on her hips, and looked at the floor. MacAfee, hoping for forgiveness awaited her next words.

But, the words came from Okie Joe.

"You will go lock that jackass up today."

His words bore that same quiet, menacing certainty that Joe first heard when he was on the floor of the Elsa general store and his grandfather had come to rescue him.

Sheriff MacAfee took his seat. "Mr. and Mrs. MacDonald, I'm sorry, but I can't lock people up without any more evidence than you appear to have. Can you give me something else to go on?"

Okie Joe explained the events of Sunday, from the sounds he and Joe overheard to the absence of Chelsea's mother.

Joe stepped forward and added that Chelsea had stated that her mother wasn't home, that only she and her father were in the trailer. He went on to detail the incriminating things Chelsea had told him in their conversations.

Inga spoke again, and alluded to the girl's obvious depression as evidenced at dinner in their home.

"This is all still pretty thin, I'm afraid," the sheriff stated, "but it's enough that I can authorize sending a counselor to the home to attempt to ascertain the truth. If the man admits to it, or if the child—how old is this child?"

"Sixteen," Joe stated.

"If the minor turns him in, then I will happily lock up the suspect. I'll do the best I can."

"So, you'll do better than you've done up until now," Inga stated. It wasn't a question or even a suggestion. "I'm afraid I'm disappointed, Sheriff MacAfee," she trilled. "I have sacrificed my anonymity to bring you this report in person, while your reluctance to act . . ."

"Mrs. MacDonald, again, I'm sorry for the misunderstanding. Teenagers in this county are bored and they like to pull pranks."

"Teenagers in this county and every county are bored and they like to get drunk and high," the younger Joe corrected.

With that, Gramps guided his family with his hands, shooing them toward the door. If he stayed much longer, he feared he'd be facing felony charges of his own.

CHAPTER 57

Gramps and Joe were hacking down brambles in the north section of their property, with the question of Chelsea Christmas' welfare still on their minds.

"I hope that sheriff does something soon. Like, today," Gramps stated.

"Me, too, Gramps, but even if he does, it won't mean shit if Chelsea doesn't speak up and help herself.

And speaking of things not meaning shit, I want to ask you something , okay?"

Without waiting for a reply, he continued. "My dad would be all over me if he heard me say "shit." He never says bad words, and thinks it some sort of sin against God and man if anyone says a four-letter word. Why does it bother him, but it doesn't bother you? I mean, it's like the two of you don't even know each other, you're so different."

Gramps grinned and chuckled. "I never say bad words, boy. You'll never hear me say an offensive word unless I am quotin' someone who's offensive. Your dad and me are just the same in that."

"Gramps, you say four-letter words all the time. You don't even excuse yourself afterward."

"What four-letter words have you heard me say, Third?"

"Well, when we came out of the sheriff's office — I mean the Shelby County sheriff's office, and Mr. Armstead was telling us about the meth cook and the sheriff's daughter, you said, 'Oh, shit,' You said it right along with me."

"Oh, I see what you mean. Third. My list of words that are bad is different from a lot of folks.' See, I don't think words that describe a bodily function are bad words. You know why?"

"No. Tell me why," Third said, smelling a sermon coming.

"Cause everybody has them. Everybody shits. It's a thing that, if it does anything, brings us together. In that way, they're good words. They don't divide us.

"A lot of words bother me, but I don't say words that divide us."

"Like what? What words divide us? I'm not following."

"Oh, there's a million of them. 'Nigger,' 'spic,' 'faggot,' and 'bitch,' to name a few. Those words divide. You understand? They hurt people —"

"Yeah, I think one of them hurt Jamal the other day."

"So, you see what I mean. I don't say words like that. It's part of the process of cleansing my heart and soul. The tendency to hate rears up in all of us from time to time. Honestly, Joe, earlier today, I felt some hate for that sheriff in Marion County."

"You mean that fat, lazy jackass who didn't want to ruffle Dennis Christmas' feathers?" Third ventured.

"Well . . . yep. So, it's always a struggle to fight the hatred within me. I don't use those words because they open the door for hating. I wrestle with that within myself. I hope you do, too."

"Hey, Gramps. I'm best friends with a black guy!"

"Yeah, well, it's easy to love the people we love. Anyone can do that. The trick is to love the people we find unlovable. That takes a little more work. Hand me that wire cutter."

Joe complied, and held a stretch of barbed wire in his fists as Gramps snipped through it.

CHAPTER 58

Joe lay in bed Monday night, staring at the ceiling. He'd been in Sylvia two full months, and hadn't a lot changed?

He'd gone from dealing with a father whose love was scarce, who barely knew him and wanted no part of him, to Gramps and Grams. Joe's grandparents were the best. Okay, Joe thought, the Marxism was weird, but it sure didn't keep him from being a good person. Gramps had been there to probably save Joe's life—and Jamal's.

He had hit it off with Jamal on the first meeting as if they'd known each other from birth. Theirs was a friendship based on values and beliefs, not just a common drive to get high or get laid. Joe realized this was the kind of friendship he wanted. He could see new sights through Jamal's eyes.

Joe thought of Chelsea and what a puzzle she was. His feelings about her were ambiguous. Sure, when he first met her he was very attracted, and he recognized that he had dozed off more than one night thinking of fun things he could be doing with her right here in his father's bed, but now his approach to her was tentative. Of course, he didn't think less of her because she had been trapped in her home with that father. Still, his sexual attraction was muted now,, and he wasn't sure why.

Then there was this church-going thing that he didn't understand. But he was looking at it objectively. If his grandparents were the people they were, people willing to sacrifice and do for strangers, maybe the Lutherans had something to say after all. He was far less willing to dismiss religion as a manipulation and a farce than he had been when he arrived in Sylvia.

Grams, still beautiful, even in her sixties, was, Joe thought, an astonishing person. Strong and resilient, the product of an insane childhood Joe could scarcely imagine, had come into her own with a huge heart for strangers, and a love within her that enveloped him like a warm fleece blanket. She treated him with love and respect, didn't judge him, and fed him the best meals he'd ever had. And she did it all while facing her crippling fears head-on.

He remembered his trip up here. Liz had told him he would get a kick out of his grandparents, that they had lived extraordinary lives.

She wasn't kidding. Joe came to realize that his grandparents were the model of the person he wanted to be.

He didn't respect his father's values—in fact, his anger dismissed those values—but the heroism he had seen from Gramps and Grams, a heroism that had manifested in their lives early, was a quality he wanted to emulate.

Joe's fear was that he didn't have their strength. He was weak and insipid, like his dad.

Then it dawned on him. He hadn't spoken to Dad or Liz since he'd come home from St. Louis.

Wow. Another surprise. He was calling Sylvia home.

A lot had changed in two months.

He'd call St. Louis in the morning. Early. Before his dad and Liz left for work.

CHAPTER 59

"Hey, Dad. It's Joey."

"Hey, hi, Joey," his father said cheerfully. "How are things north? Are you settling in?"

Something was wrong. His father was uncharacteristically congenial.

"Settling in? No, Dad. I've been here two months. The settling in is over. Now, it's just life."

"You eating good food, getting some sunshine and fresh air? Bet it beats the smog here in the city, and Liz's cooking."

"Yeah, where is Liz? She around? I just want to say hi to her."

"No, Joe, she's not here."

"Really? Did she go to work early?"

"Hard to say. Joe, I didn't know how to tell you. She doesn't, well, she's not staying here anymore."

Joe was silent, disbelieving. The only thing he ever liked about his father was his wife—and she had left? The teenager reeled physically, spinning in circles in Inga's kitchen. It was the wildest of disclosures. He stepped down into the dining room and collapsed into a chair around the table. Elbows propped on the table, he tried to absorb.

"What happened?" he said after a long delay.

"We just came to a parting of the ways. She's gone to stay with her sister. She left just after you were here with Mom. I didn't know how to break the news to you. I know you love her."

"Don't you, Dad? Love her?"

"Of course, I love her. I begged her to stay—for both our sakes."

"Then why'd she go?"

"It's a long story."

"Yeah, okay. Do you have a phone number for her?" He left the suggestion hanging in the air that he would rather hear it from Liz. He didn't care if that stung his father.

His father paused before offering the information. When he did, it was a placid resignation to defeat.

"She's living in west county? That's a west county prefix," Joe said.

"She's living in St. Charles."

"So, do you see her?"

"Not very often, son."

Another silence.

"Dad, get her back. Whatever it takes. You've got to get her back. I don't want to lose another mom."

Those words sliced Joe II open at the heart. His eyes closed in grief and pain as he fought back his tears. How many other ways would he find, he wondered, to hurt and alienate his only son?

CHAPTER 60

Dix Simpson stewed on his latest report for hours. He sat in the hotel room he sometimes shared with Ernesto Soto, livid and fuming, waiting on his hot-tempered partner. He hadn't seen the joker in two days, and wasn't sure what he would do if the guy ever showed up.

Damn him, Simpson thought. How fucking stupid can you get?

When the key turned in the lock, Simpson braced for a fight, all the while reminding himself that Soto was a raging madman who won fights. Calm, clear-headed reason was Soto's Kryptonite. Dix needed calm. A composed approach. He couldn't show anger. Certainly, don't yell. That would just set Soto off.

"Hey, man, how you doing?" Ernesto said when he stepped into the room.

Simpson saw that the guy was high as a kite, and probably drunk as well. It was ten o'clock Monday morning, and Soto was already wasted.

"Not that great, man. We've got some things to work out, you and me."

"We do?" Soto laughed and laughed. "Like what? Which bitch to nail next? Which student to get hooked? Which hooker to order up? Whatchoo wanna talk 'bout?"

When Soto was drunk, his Mexican accent was pronounced. At this point, between the accent and the drunken slur, his speech was almost unintelligible to Simpson, but it didn't matter. Nothing he had to say was of any interest.

"Soto, you've racked up new murder charges. They're looking for you now, not just for wasting that cop, but for killing two kids. Did you honestly kill your own boys?"

Simpson became more appalled as the words left his mouth.

"What?" Soto slurred. "I didn't kill no damned kids. Ha! I might have wanted to real bad, but I just tanned their hides. Wait—how do you know about that?"

"Hiro Nakamura called me. You're wanted in Randolph County and Shelby County on murder charges. You just became a red flashing light to the cops. What are we going to do about that?" Dix started out calm and reasonable as he had intended, but as the narrative went on, his voice rose to a scarcely contained scream. He stared at Ernesto as his partner staggered around the room, sat on the bed, and blinked repeatedly in an unsuccessful attempt to appear sober.

After a moment, he slurred, "Who the hell is Hiro Naka—what?"

"Oh, jeez," Simpson said, throwing up his hands in exasperation. "Nakamura. Our guy in the Shelby sheriff's department. The one I pay a grand to every month for information. He told me you killed those kids."

"Oh, that Hiro Nakamura!" Soto slurred. He started to laugh. He would be passing out any minute, Simpson knew, and then there would be no answers.

"Hiro Nakamura! Hiro Nakamura!" Soto repeated, laughing between words. "What a fucked up name!" He then dissolved in laughter and collapsed on the bed.

"Oh, I'm not done. There's more," Simpson continued, as if his audience was lucid. Forced into an inevitable departure, Simpson began shoving his clothes into a gym bag, dirty and clean together. He knocked over a chair and then nearly tripped over it. A grocery sack became the recipient of everything in the bathroom.

"Hiro also tells me that they found Jack Sample's new lab," he continued. "They'll be busting him soon. So, we have all this potential business and no product." He raised a leg and kicked Soto in the knee. The brute was fading out of consciousness fast. "We have to find a new supplier+. There's a hell of a lot to do and you're off getting high and killing babies!

Pack your bags, man, We're leaving now—before the police get here. We'll take my car since Rufina gave the cops your license plate. Get a move on! Throw what you need in the car and let's go."

CHAPTER 61

Mitch Ollman's focus was the salmon-colored house. It was a small, one-story frame house with a basement. The driveway provided easy access. Shouldn't be too hard to take down.

Ollman was conflicted. He was tempted to simply drive his damaged minivan at top speed into the Elsa home, destroying it. It would be real payback, doing unto Sample what Sample's customer had done to him. It was sweet. Very symmetrical. Very fitting.

But too uncertain, he thought. He might get himself killed in the process and Sample could get away alive.

He struggled with his more reasoned nature that still valued law and order, due process, and the criminal justice system. That part of him said it might be best to just let the inevitable happen—the arrest, the charges, the prosecution.

Still, Ollman's level of rage and sense of injustice would not permit a laissez-faire approach. He wanted to see Sample die, and the ramifications be damned.

A full assault and a hail of bullets, an explosion made to look like your basic meth lab accident, a sound beating rendered as "resisting arrest" or the work of a disgruntled customer–lots of scenarios.

Ollman weighed his choices. The only thing that mattered was Sample's death. He no longer cared about his own welfare, and he scarcely gave a thought to Lindsey's. He might spend his life in prison, and it would be a horrible life, but Mitch's tunnel vision was set in place. He wanted a hand in Samples death. He craved the chance to look into Sample's eyes as he ended the cook. Emily's smiling, innocent face loomed in his thoughts and haunted his dreams, and his rage grew as he grieved for her. Nothing mattered to him except avenging her senseless death, and expunging this evil from the world.

Ollman had been watching the house in Elsa for days. He had learned an important fact: the business centered solely on one buyer. Good. Less collateral damage. No foot traffic on Saturday nights, and no stray victims to consider. It's almost as if Sample wanted to be busted, Ollman convinced himself.

In the madness of anger and grief, he had forgotten all about Sarah and her baby.

CHAPTER 62

Inga made chicken salad sandwiches for lunch for her husband and grandson, as she whistled a favorite gospel hymn, Blessed Assurance. A Jell-O salad with fruit made the night before, and lunch was ready. For some reason, though, they didn't seem hungry when they came into the house. Inga was alarmed at her husband's appearance. Third also didn't seem himself.

"What's happened?" she asked.

"Well, sit down, baby," her husband said, taking her hand and leading her to a chair. "Third has some upsetting news."

Inga knit her brows and allowed her husband to help her sit.

"I called my dad this morning," Joe stated. "My step-mom, Liz, left him. She's moved in with her sister, Aunt Jean." Joe took the seat across from his grandmother.

"So, I called Aunt Jean, and talked to Liz. She told me that she felt very bad after our trip to St. Louis. Since we got back, she has been stewing—that's her word, stewing—about the remarks my father made about minorities and poor people at dinner. She decided she couldn't live with someone with so much hate. She told me hate is infectious, and she didn't want to catch it. And there's other stuff. She got the idea that my dad was deliberately trying to be vindictive and mean, and it changed how Liz feels about Dad." Joe fidgeted, and picked at his fingernails.

"I already told him he has to get her back," Joe stared at the floor, and blinked back tears.

Inga looked away and shook her head, squeezing her lips together.

"What happened, Inga?" Gramps asked with that unnerving calmness Joe now recognized.

She looked at her husband, but her mind was far away.

"I don't remember exactly. Joe took us to a fancy, expensive restaurant. During the conversation, one thing led to another and he said something about how people who don't have anything want to get everything that's ours. I think that ticked Liz off. The next morning, Liz talked to me about it, and I got a scent off of her that this might be coming," she explained.

"Why is this the first I've heard of it?" Gramps asked.

Inga took a deep breath. "I kept it from you because I knew what he was doing. He went off against disadvantaged people at the same time he was trying to show me all his money. That meal probably set him back three hundred dollars, and he wanted me to know how wealthy he's become and how much he reviles those he feels are less than he is. It was awful, but what he was doing was . . ." she paused, and sighed, gathering herself.

Gramps finished her sentence. "Sending a message to me. And you didn't convey the message just to defeat him..."

Inga nodded and hung her head.

"How did we raise a child so hateful, Joe?" Inga asked, looking up at her husband.

As his grandfather considered his answer, Joe was contemplating his own take on his parents' split. He recalled Gramps' words—that the task was to fight the hatred within yourself. Fight it because hatred divides.

On the other hand, his father, alone in St. Louis, abandoned by everyone, still took pride in his hatred, exploited it and used it as a weapon to strike out at his own family.

Inga interrupted Third's reverie. She rose from her chair suddenly, and went to the kitchen. "I'm calling Joe right now," she said over her shoulder.

CHAPTER 63

On Monday morning, a combined task force gathered in the cramped office of Bill Fast. "Jeckle, Nakamura, Dansbury, and Fishman will take the front door," Bill Fast directed. "I'll lead Reisman and our friends from Randolph County, Brucker and Spann.

You should all be up to speed. Remember, Soto and Sample are both suspected of killing Mark Newstead, so they should be regarded as armed and dangerous. Take appropriate precautions and communicate with team members constantly." He looked at each of the men. "Questions?"

"Sheriff Fast?" Deputy Nakamura raised his hand. "Why isn't Sheriff Ollman leading this team?"

Nakamura, a two-year veteran of Shelby County's sheriff's department was swift and adept. Fast and Ollman believed him to be on the fast track to a promotion. They liked his initiative and his humility. They were impressed that he seemed to handle his money well, scoring a nice place to live on a deputy's salary, living modestly, and there appeared to be none of the drinking and carrying on during off-hours evident among many in the department. Fast and Ollman approved of Nakamura as a model cop–sober, dedicated, serious professional.

"Sure," Fast replied. "We believe Sample's lab produced the drugs that led to the death of Sheriff Ollman's daughter. That's for the court to determine, not us, and our job is not to exact vengeance. Let me be extremely clear on that. If there's a causal relationship, we'll protect the prosecutor's case against Sample by avoiding any conflict of interest."

Bill Fast poured a cup of coffee and looked around the room. "Anything else?" No one responded. "Good. The raid is scheduled for seven a.m. in Elsa. This is the last tour where I'll have you all together, so I'm briefing you now. We'll assemble here at six a.m., and head over there."

Bill stood. "Remember, there may be a very young child in the house. Avoid the use of force if at all possible. Dismissed."

The team left the sheriff's office. Ollman, who had been sitting to the side and listening during the meeting, appreciated Nakamura's question. Fast had handled it well, he thought.

His job, however, would be to show up at the Sample house before the deputies got there. Long before. Fast and his men would be too late to save Sample.

As for Fast's remark about the child in the house, Ollman either tuned that out, or had ceased to care.

On the way to the squad car, Nakamura stepped aside from his partner, Dean Jeckle. "I need to call home," Nakamura said, turning back into the building. "I will meet you at the car."

CHAPTER 64

Late Monday afternoon, a stern-faced woman knocked on the front door of the Christmas trailer in Monroe City. Bonnie Wallace stood at the door, determined to learn the truth of what went on behind the door. Bonnie's identification badge announced she was employed by the Social Services Division. She found Marion County, upon first impressions, to be filled with well-meaning, competent people who did their jobs with a few exceptions, notably the sluggish response the sheriff's department had offered to the initial report of possible child abuse. That didn't rest well with Bonnie, but at least now things were on track.

Bonnie hailed from Birmingham, Alabama where the energies of a social worker were taxed beyond reason. Calloway County with its university kids in Columbia and their associated affluence was a cakewalk in comparison to what she had seen in the South. Now in Randolph County, the poor, disadvantaged, and dysfunctioning were widespread, and it was beginning to feel like Birmingham again. The prospect of a sexually abused teenager rankled her to a degree that nearly derailed her objectivity.

After a minute, the deadbolt was released on the trailer's front door. A middle-aged woman appeared. The woman's eyes were puffy and dull with dark circles under them. Her skin was sallow and showed the merciless effects of gravity. While she may have once been pretty, time had been unkind to her and her face bore substantial evidence of stress and worry.

The woman's blonde hair was pulled back in a ponytail, and its dark roots were long overdue for a touch up. Her eyes were clear blue, but framed with wrinkles.

"Good morning. My name is Bonnie Wallace. I'm with the Division of Family Services. Are you Mrs. Christmas?"

"I'm Virginia Christmas. What's this about?" Virginia asked in a hoarse voice. She had just pulled an all-nighter at the boutique in town, juggling the bills and going over the books. She was completely exhausted.

"Mrs. Christmas, I am investigating a report that our office received. Do you have a sixteen-year-old daughter living in this residence?"

"Yes. Chelsea. Why?"

"There's been a report that Chelsea has been the victim of an assault. I'm here to find out what, if anything, has happened to her," Bonnie said. She was soft-pedaling the presentation as was her habit. Being too abrupt often jarred the family into silence.

Virginia looked completely bewildered. "What kind of an assault? What do you mean? Chelsea never said anything . . ."

"Is Chelsea here, Mrs. Christmas? I'd like to ask her some questions."

Virginia opened the screen door to let her come in. Bonnie entered the small trailer and looked around. It was shabby. The brown shag rug was threadbare in places, and the furnishings were sparse.

The tiny kitchen's avocado appliances dated them as vintage 1970s, and the refrigerator was making an rattling noise as if the engine was struggling.

"Wait here a minute," Virginia said. She went down a narrow hallway to the back of the trailer. "Chelsea?" she called, her voice raised in alarm. "There's a woman here from the government and she wants to talk to you."

Bonnie heard a muffled conversation she couldn't make out, but the tone was one of bewilderment and alarm.

The teenager followed her mother into the main living area where Bonnie watched as the girl approached. Bonnie noted the girl's body language and demeanor. The teen kept her head down until she reached Bonnie, then her eyes registered unmistakable fear and dread. This is not uncommon among family members who don't know the reason for the visit yet, Bonnie reminded herself. But it is also not uncommon among family members who absolutely do. Bonnie determined something was wrong.

The girl was pretty. Her dark hair framed a long face with high cheekbones and perfect skin, along with her mother's clear blue eyes.

"Hello, Chelsea," Bonnie said. She hoped her stance was warm, friendly, and disarming. "How are you today? My name is Mrs. Wallace, and I need to ask you some questions."

Chelsea's eyes widened with confusion and fear.

"I'm with the Division of Family Services." Bonnie paused, waiting for the young woman to react.

"Okay . . . ?" Chelsea said. "What do you want with me?" she asked.

"Mrs. Christmas," Bonnie ventured, hoping to get lucky, "I need to speak to Chelsea alone.."

"Up to you, Chels," Virginia said to her daughter. "You want me to stay or go?"

"I don't even know what this is about. Probably just a misunderstanding." She paused, remembering having been aroused at four a.m. when her mother got home from work. "Look, why don't I go for a walk with this lady, but I'll stay close and I'll call you if I need you, k?"

"Okay, if you're sure. I'm going to lie down." With that, Virginia went back down the hallway toward her bedroom.

"Where's your father, Chelsea?" Bonnie probed.

"Job interview."

"Oh, good. I mean, is he changing jobs, or is he between jobs now?"

"Between. Let's go outside."

"Sure." Bonnie followed the young woman out the door. The day was growing sultry, and dark clouds were forming. Bonnie didn't want to be caught outside in a storm.

Bonnie's thoughts rested for a moment on the work that is usually involved following severe storms. Displaced, newly homeless families needing accommodations had already absorbed hundreds of man-hours in Bonnie's office.

Chelsea took a right outside the door, the opposite direction of the hallway leading to her mother.

"What are you here for?" Chelsea asked. "What have you heard about me?"

"My office got a call from the sheriff's office. Actually, someone visited the sheriff. The visitor had reason to think that you may be a victim of incest. Is that possible? Remember that I'm here to help you. As a minor, you are not responsible for anything that may have happened, but I need to know the truth."

Chelsea stopped and turned to the caseworker. She studied her face, weighing her options. The older woman was overweight, and bloated-looking. Her dark face was littered with numerous moles, and her yellow flowered dress and discordant brown blazer did nothing for her blotchy, uneven skin tone. Her small eyes were encased in puffy flesh. Her black hair, graying at the temples, was pulled back severely into a little knot at the back of her head as if to show off the moles to their best advantage. This woman needed help herself, at least with her appearance, Chelsea noted. And here, the woman was trying to help Chelsea.

Chelsea hesitated. Bonnie waited, knowing she had struck some sort of a nerve. She smelled pay dirt, but she still needed Chelsea to trust her. She stood silently near the girl, smiling gentle, and patient.

Chelsea's thoughts were mixed. This was a chance to get out of the house and away from her dad—a worthy goal she had dreamed of achieving. But where would she go? The state would place her somewhere that may or may not be worse than her living situation now.

No, wait, she told herself. There could be very few living situations worse. Flashes of memory that included her father flitted through her reluctant mind. She pushed them away.

But what of her mom? Dad had warned her that if she found out what Chelsea was doing with him, it would break her mom in half. Flashes of his threats crossed her mind, and as they did, they seemed feigned and disingenuous for the first time. Her father gloried in suggesting that if her mother found out, she would surely blame Chelsea. But Mrs. Wallace's words suggested something else. Chelsea added manipulation to the indictments against her father.

Know the truth and the truth will set you free, she had heard. That was from the Bible or something.

But telling this truth would add a monstrous weight to her mother's already staggering burden. Could she do that to her?

"Chelsea?" Bonnie prompted.

"Well, um," she began tentatively, "Is everything I tell you in complete confidence?"

"I will protect you, Chelsea. If a crime has been committed, then I'm required to report it to law enforcement."

"What would happen then?"

"The perpetrator would be arrested and criminal charges would be filed, and you, if you're a victim, would be sent to a safe environment."

"Such as?"

"Possibly foster care."

"It would kill my mother if I went to a foster home," Chelsea stated.

"Believe me, I have dealt with hundreds of mothers. It kills all of them much more to know their kids are in danger and nothing is being done to help them. Are you in danger, Chelsea?"

"I guess not. I don't really know. What kind of danger could I be in?"

The young woman seemed confused to Bonnie, so Bonnie tried a different approach.

"Let me ask you this. It's a very personal question, and you can refuse to answer if you want. But I've been at this a long while, and if you choose not to answer me, that will be an answer in itself. Ready?"

The young woman nodded and frowned.

"Are you sexually active? This is not judgment. A lot of people your age are and I'm not sitting in judgment, but I'd like to know," Bonnie said.

The young woman looked down at her feet, again battling her emotions. Again, Bonnie waited.

It took a full half a minute before a feeble "Yes" emerged from Chelsea's mouth.

"And who is your boyfriend?"

Chelsea looked up at Bonnie. More uncertainty registered on her face. She shook her head, or it could have been a tremble. Bonnie wasn't sure, but she sensed the time was now.

"Chelsea, has your father been having sex with you?"

The young woman's eyes lit up with craven fear.

Pay dirt it is, then, Bonnie thought. "You look scared. What are you afraid of?" Bonnie continued.

"It will kill my mother to find this out," Chelsea whimpered.

"It will hurt her more if she doesn't know the truth. How long has this been going on?" Bonnie probed.

"My dad lost his job about a year ago. He worked at the Butler factory in Hannibal and it was his fault that there was an accident. A woman was hurt. Her arm got cut off. After that, he began drinking even more, and that's when it started," Chelsea stammered.

"Chelsea, when did you turn sixteen?"

"A few weeks ago.

"Not a very sweet sixteen." Bonnie said. Her voice was kind and sympathetic. "I'm going to have to talk to your mother, and you'll need to come with me. Pack some clothes. You won't be coming home tonight."

Chelsea's mouth fell open with shock and disbelief. "No, I can't go anywhere. No! I won't go! You can't do this!" The tears started.

The rising panic muted Chelsea's inner voice—the one that told her that escaping this home was her objective. Getting out of this situation was what she had wanted for the last year. This was her escape, and part of her didn't know why she was afraid to take it.

Maybe Dad told her the truth, that her mom would be mad at her, devastated and destroyed.

On the other hand, if it was destined to come out, and if Mom survived the news, she would certainly want to be with her mother to assure her that it would all be okay someday.

The tears, at first tentative, found their rhythm, and Chelsea heaved and sobbed.

As she cried, her palm over her face, Bonnie Wallace wrapped a pudgy hand around Chelsea's wrist, and cooed that everything was going to be okay, all the while giving the girl time to gather herself.

As she did, a plan began to form in Chelsea's mind.

"Okay," Chelsea told the woman between sniffles. "I'll pack a bag."

"I'll need to talk to your mother. We'll have to wake her up."

"I know."

The two entered the trailer and turned right down the narrow hallway.

Chelsea entered her sleeping area, grabbed two tote bags, and filled them with three pairs of undies, three tops, a spare bra, three pairs of socks, and one pair of jeans.

She darted into the bathroom where she retrieved her toothbrush, the lone tube of toothpaste, mascara, deodorant, and lip gloss. She set her bags by the front door.

Chelsea knocked on her mother's door and told her she needed to speak to Bonnie, and asked if Bonnie could come and talk to her. She waved the social worker in, and stepped back into the hallways, where she could hear Bonnie speaking in a gentle voice to her mother. Chelsea, knowing that her mother was dead tired, and that she sleeps like a rock, gauged that she would have a few minutes before Bonnie would realize Chelsea was gone.

Bags in hand, Chelsea grabbed her purse and darted out the front door. She took off at a sprint under the blackening sky, never looking back.

CHAPTER 65

Soto was passed out in the front seat as Simpson drove to Elsa. He would stop for the rest of his order from Sample and then head due south. Unsure of his destination or his eventual plan, the most pressing need was to get Soto out of the area until the heat let up. Surely, a bulletin had gone out for them in all Missouri counties—probably Kansas, Nebraska, Illinois, and Iowa as well—but with Soto now a cop- and baby-killer, the territory the two men frequented would be acting with a vengeance .

Soto snored so loudly, Simpson almost didn't hear his cellular phone ring.

"Yeah," he answered.

"Mr. Simpson? This is Nakamura."

"Yeah, what you got for me?"

"Yes, the drug lab will be raided Wednesday morning at seven. The sheriff is looking for Sample and Soto, both wanted for murder," Hiro told him.

"Are you sure it's set for seven Wednesday?" Simpson asked. This was news he could use.

"Yes," Hiro stated. "I'm on the team to raid the home."

"Thanks for the heads-up."

"Maybe you ought to thank me with a bonus this month?"

"Sure, man. Expect double your normal retainer," Simpson promised. Simpson knew he'd be out of the state by the first of the month, and would never see Nakamura again.

He turned off his cell phone and focused on his next step.

The sky overhead was turning an eerie blackish green. The weather had been weird this spring, he mused.

As he thought through his next move, speeding toward Elsa, his anger toward Soto gained steam. He reached a decision as he passed a dead raccoon on the side of the road. The raccoon represented a milestone for the next phase of his business dealings. And it gave him an idea.

He came around a corner on the two-lane highway and saw a picnic area sign. Further up, there was indeed a picnic table, a stone barbecue pit, and a lush, green wooded area.

Simpson slowed to a stop. As he pulled over into the picnic area, he considered the pros and cons of Soto's attributes. What Soto provided was muscle and rage. He was a decent enforcer, and an adequate Man Friday, but he had the common sense and self-control of a rabid dog. That turned a plus into a minus, and added to the long list of negatives that began with three murder charges and ended with perennial body odor, which Soto attempted to control by wearing enough cheap aftershave to drown a hamster. His unpredictability and appetite for purposeless violence made him less of an asset, and more of an unwanted liability.

As Simpson parked and got out, Soto's snores continued. He wouldn't be waking up any time soon. Simpson opened the passenger door of the car as raindrops began to fall lightly. He grabbed Soto under his sweaty armpits, and dragged him out. Once on the ground, Simpson searched his pockets, divesting him of a significant bankroll. He found Soto's gun and considered taking it. He watched Soto snore for a full minute and a half before changing his mind. He wiped his prints off the handle and left the gun where it was, tucked in Soto's waistband. The reasoning was clear: the gun was likely a murder weapon, and while it might be handy to have, Simpson wanted no part of it, given the likelihood of future prosecution.

Simpson removed Soto's wallet. Then he dragged the unconscious drunk into the woods. The snoring continued without interruption. He left Soto hidden by foliage, and got back in the car. Given the weather, he doubted anyone would find Soto before he woke up on his own.

Five miles down the road, the rain started in earnest and came down in blinding torrents in a matter of seconds. Simpson pulled into a gas station to wait out the weather. He searched Soto's wallet and found another hundred dollars and a Mobil Oil credit card that had belonged to one Laquitia Anderson at some point in history. There was also a lottery ticket, a membership card to Blockbuster, a driver's license, which Simpson removed, a membership card to a gym in Zapopan, and a condom .

When Soto woke up, Simpson chuckled, he'd be plenty steamed about being stranded in a storm. Fortunately for Simpson, his conscience, such as it was, had been seared years ago. There was no room for one in his business.

Another thirty miles to Elsa. After a few more miles, he opened the window and tossed out the wallet. Another mile, and he tossed out Soto's driver's license.

Chapter 66

Inga was pleased to receive a dinner invitation from Lynae Armstead. As her husband and Lynae's husband had intensified their friendship, Inga felt a gnawing urgency to grow close to the wife and mother of her own men's best friends. She accepted the invitation, even as she put the pork roast she was thawing back in the refrigerator.

She looked out the back door to check on the men. They were out of sight, but the darkening sky made Inga's breath catch. She tamped down her nerves as she closed the windows in anticipation of rain.

When the men came in from the field, she hurried them to shower and dress. They would be off to the Armsteads in an hour.

She didn't have to tell Third twice. He'd seemed pleased at the prospect of spending an evening with Jamal. He took with him some of the CDs Liz had sent him weeks ago.

As it turned out, Lynae was not the cook Inga was, but Joe had to admit that his first experience with soul food was not too bad. He was unsure what chitins were, and it was disturbing when he asked Inga. She explained the difference in spelling and pronunciation, but evaded a definition. All the flavors and textures were something new, and quite pleasing. The collard greens, while bitter and almost sour, were an interesting experience, though admittedly, the hot sauce didn't hurt.

Lynae smiled during the discussion, her teeth white and perfect. When Lynae smiled, her full, plump cheeks receded to each side of her mouth and dimples formed. She was a cute older woman, Third acknowledged, and her cuteness was not lost on Don who smiled back at her with an air of conspiracy.

Joe could do without the okra. He ate only a polite portion, and if he never ate it again, he'd be okay with that. It was slimy and kind of gross.

Worse things could happen to a guy than cornbread. He buttered a big hunk of it and added a dollop of honey.

After dinner, Lynae excused herself to tend to the baby, then the adults settled into the living room for drinks and conversation. A storm was raging outside, and in the living room, Gramps sat with Grams, his comforting arm around her shoulders. The Armsteads needn't know, Joe thought, that his grandmother would rather be in the cellar.

Inga was engaged in the lively discussion, and Joe was proud that the storm didn't distract her.

Joe went upstairs with Jamal while Lynae breastfed the baby in front of God and everyone. Joe confided to Jamal that he was uncomfortable with Jamal knowing what was happening to Chelsea. "I don't think it's your business, but it's not your fault you picked up the phone. It's not my business, either, but I'm in it and I found out she's being, well, used. So, I'm torn between wanting to help her and wanting to keep things private for her.

"Okay, that's sad," Jamal replied. "But did you get you anywhere with her?"

"What do you mean?"

"You know damn well what I mean. Did she give you any of that?"

"Ah, man, no." Joe paused for a minute. "She's real hot and all, but I just don't know if I could. It doesn't feel right after all she's been through."

"Bullshit," retorted Jamal. "You're just like me. You can do anything anytime any way. If she's that easy, why don't you take a shot?"

"What? Wait. I don't think I said she's easy. Probably she has no choice in the matter. I really think she's a victim, and she needs help.

He described the events of Sunday, and how the three MacDonalds had later driven to the sheriff's office to make their stand. Jamal thought it was crazy, and Joe admitted that it might have been, but if the girl was in trouble, he reasoned, the thing to do was to step up. "That's what we do in my family," he had stated with pride.

Jamal looked at Joe and frowned. "How's that?"

Joe seized the moment. He told the tale of his grandfather jumping trains, living in a drought with dust pneumonia and starvation while fighting for survival on the Great Plains. He painted a sepia-colored image of Okie Joe, his struggles, and his drive toward socialism. Jamal listened with his usual perfunctory air, saying little.

Joe described his grandfather's experience on the road to California, as he offered his rudimentary understanding of class struggle and its connection to racial prejudice. The rest of his grandfather's philosophy would be harder to explain, so Joe hoped Jamal wouldn't ask questions.

Instead, at the conclusion of the narrative, Jamal said, "That explains a lot of what my dad says about your grandpa."

"Really? What does he say?"

"Aw, you heard my dad talk about him, saying he gets minorities more than most whites."

"That's cause the Okies were treated with the same kind of prejudice," Joe replied.

"Yeah, I know.

"So, do you believe in this socialist shit?" Jamal asked.

Joe looked at his friend. "Nah," he said. "I've been told all my life that it doesn't work and it leads to our rights being taken away. All I'm saying is my gramps believes it, and he's the best person I ever knew, so if that's what made him the person he is, then . . ."

The two were silent for a moment. Then Joe said, "Hey, how am I doing on understanding the race thing?"

Jamal grinned. "I guess the fact that you know there is a race thing to understand puts you ahead of some folks."

"You should go into politics, Jamal," Joe smiled. "You talk out both sides of your mouth with the best of them."

Despite the lingering rain and the occasional rumble from the sky, Inga congratulated herself on the ride home for getting through the evening without revealing to her friends the extent of her fear.

Everyone's belly was full. Gramps reveled in the tales Don told of life in Detroit and the attempts to bring knowledge to young people who had forgotten—or never learned—about the Civil Rights Movement.

Lynae and Inga exchanged recipes. Lynae's knowledge of soul food was more than technical. While she cooked it well, she also employed a historical perspective. Inga repeated to her husband and grandson Lynae's tales of slave ships and turnip heads, of voodoo practices and ox tails, of slave revolts hushed by historians and ham hocks with beans. Inga remarked that she should have known, but didn't, that much of the history of soul food had to do with garbage.

"What? In what way?" her husband asked.

"I mean that ox tails, mustard greens, and similar foods were what was left after the slave owners took the good meats and vegetables. What was left, whites regarded as garbage, but the enslaved people of the South turned it into delicacies.

"I learned a lot tonight from my new friend, Lynae," Inga concluded.

When the MacDonalds got home that night, the headlights revealed Chelsea Christmas sitting on the front stoop, with two tote bags and her purse. She was drenched with rainwater, and appeared to be shivering. She looked relieved to see the car.

Gramps glanced at his watch. It was nearly ten o'clock. "How long has she been sitting there, I wonder?" he asked.

Inga got out of the car and rushed to the stoop. "We weren't expecting company," she enthused in her most welcoming chirp.

"I wasn't expecting to be company, Mrs. MacDonald," Chelsea replied, her teeth chattering. "I need a place to stay, and I wondered if I could stay with you just for tonight."

"Of course, of course, you're most welcome," Inga said, helping Chelsea to her feet. "Let's get you inside and get you some warm, dry clothes."

By that time, Third had come up behind his grams. "You can sleep in my room, after I put on clean sheets, and I'll take the couch."

Inga glanced at her grandson approvingly.

"I don't want to be trouble. I can take the couch," Chelsea offered.

"No, you take the bed," Inga said. "First, Third will get you towels and whatever you need in the bathroom. I'm sure you could use a hot shower, and I'll warm up a bite to eat for you."

Joe led Chelsea to the bathroom by way of his bedroom, where he stopped and grabbed a pair of sweatpants and a tee shirt for her.

Following her hot shower, Chelsea found all three MacDonalds sitting at the dining table waiting for her, along with a steaming bowl of leftover beef stew.

Chelsea ate as though she was starving, but between bites, she filled her hosts in with the latest news. "I came here because, apparently, you already know about my situation. Anywhere else I went, I'd have to tell it to someone fresh, and I'd like to keep this quiet as long as I can. My poor mother. This is going to kill her." Chelsea paused. "Gosh, I haven't eaten since this morning," she segued. "Thanks so much for the stew."

"You're welcome," Inga replied. "I went ahead and washed the things you brought. They were soaking wet. They'll be dry by morning."

"Thanks," Chelsea said. As she ate, Joe admired the girl's feminine gestures, her pretty smile, her beauty. Though his curiosity was mounting, he was determined to leave the interviewing to his grams.

As Chelsea set aside her bowl, Joe used the opportunity to take Chelsea's empty dish to the kitchen and give his grandmother the chance to probe further.

"Now tell us, please," Inga began, "What is it that we apparently already know?"

Chelsea looked in her lap for a moment. "When Mr. MacDonald and Joe were at my place, I believe that they overheard, um, something. The next thing I knew, there was a caseworker at my door from the government trying to take me away from my mom. She told me that someone had made a report to the sheriff. I'm pretty sure that was you."

"Yes, it was us," Gramps stated. "You may be upset at us, but we had to do what's right. We were right . . . right?"

She nodded, not meeting anyone's gaze.

"What's going to happen now?" Inga asked.

"I don't really know. I think my dad might be arrested. I guess he committed a crime . . ."

Grams and Gramps glanced at each other. "Don't *you* think it's a crime?" he asked.

"Oh, I think it's horrible what he's done to me. Horrible. I was always worried what it would do to my mom, but I just . . . I don't know . . . I never thought it would be something the government would get into."

"If he's arrested, will you go home then?" Joe asked.

"I...I don't know," Chelsea stammered. "I don't know much of anything. That woman from the government wanted to take me away right then and there. I just ran before I had any questions answered."

"How did you get here?" Okie Joe asked.

"I walked when I couldn't hitch a ride."

"Did you tell your mother where you were going?" Inga asked.

"No, I had to run. I didn't have a chance to say anything to her."

"You must call her on the phone right now. Tell her you're all right. Do it now," Inga commanded.

"C'mon," Joe said. "I'll show you where the phone is."

When the two teens had left the room, Inga turned to her husband. "Joe, if she ends up in foster care . . ."

"You want us to be the foster parents." It wasn't a question.

"I don't know that it will come to that. It may just be that she should stay here tonight and go home tomorrow if that man is arrested as he should be," she reasoned.

"She won't go home tomorrow or anytime soon, ," Gramps said with certainty. "The county will investigate to be sure that the mother didn't have a part in this."

"Oh, yes. I suppose that's right. I'll call the foster care office first thing in the morning."

Meanwhile, in the kitchen, Chelsea dialed her home number. She couldn't get through. She hung up and tried again. No luck. "Huh, I wonder what's going on with the phone," she told Joe.

CHAPTER 67

Jack Sample sat in the basement with the burners off. There was some sort of an obstruction in one of the propane lines to one of the burners, and the stove was off until he could clear the blockage. Sure, he could have kept cooking with three burners, but he made a judgment call that taking the time to fix the bad burner would take less time than cooking the same amount of meth with only three burners.

Simpson and Soto were bound to show up soon, so Jack was under pressure to produce. That, combined with angst, exhaustion, and irritation at Sarah for refusing to help, put him in an ill temper. He was working around the clock, thanks to the effects of the meth, but the fatigue was wearing on him and a loss of concentration could be fatal. His irritation with Sarah was acute. He needed help, and he knew that he couldn't go without sleep forever. He would stop functioning. He felt lousy. Plus, there was the matter of Jack's own jones. He'd feel better, and probably lose this nagging headache, if he could stay high, but doing so meant dipping into some of the glass he needed to give to Simpson.

The slow pace was maddening. He had to get back to full speed.

His mood worsened when he heard pounding on the front door.

"Sarah! Get that!" he bellowed, not taking his eyes off his work.

Dix Simpson tromped down the plywood basement stairs a few moments later and landed in front of Jack. Sample noticed that Ernesto Soto was not with Dix for the second time, and this was unusual. Dix was much more intimidating with his muscle alongside, and both he and Jack knew it. Jack wondered why Dix left his enforcer behind.

"Hi, Dix. Got a little problem right here I'm working on," Jack explained as casually as he dared.

"Yeah? Whaddup?" Dix replied. He was testy. "You got my glass or not?"

"Not. I'd o' been done by now, but this burner went out yesterday. Put me a little behind, but I'm workin' on it."

Dix had no response. "How much you got?"

"I'm about thirty short. It'll take me another few hours to knock them out if I get this burner going. Longer if it doesn't.

"I am so fucking sick of you and your excuses," Simpson boiled. "Give me what you got and I'm outta here," he growled.

Jack stood up and turned his back on Dix while he gathered the completed product. Handing it to him, he repeated that he could have the rest in a few hours if Dix wanted to stop by again.

"No, I'm not stopping by again, asshole. I'm . . . " he paused, thinking. "I'm going to be gone for a couple of days. Maybe you ought to think about taking off a few days, too. I got a tip today from one of my, uh, sources, who tells me . . ." he paused again.

"Tells you what?" Jack asked, curiosity aroused.

"Uh, nothin.' Never mind. The semester in Columbia will start in a few weeks and demand will be high. I'd just like you rested, and by then I think you need to have some help lined up. It'll take time to do that." The feigned interest he expressed in Jack's welfare fooled no one.

Dix picked up the bag of drugs, tucked it under his arm and trotted back up the stairs. He left without speaking to Sarah.

So, that was it, Simpson mused as he flew out the front door. He was a lone businessman again. He had dropped Soto and had dropped Sample. Sample would be in county lock-up or dead this time Wednesday. Sure, he could have warned him to get out right now. But the guy was totally unreliable, Dix rationalized. He didn't deserve the courtesy. He'd get what he had coming.

CHAPTER 68

It was mid-afternoon when Ernesto Soto stirred awake. His hangover was ripe. He sat up in the grass. Where in hell was he? How long had he been here? It was drizzling, but had been heavy during his nap, as evidenced by his sopping wet clothes. Where was Simpson? He struggled to his feet and looked around.

Suddenly, a wave of nausea hit him and he vomited in the grass.

Looking up, Soto made out that he was about fifty yards from the highway. But what highway?

"Dix!" he called out several times. Only the distant rumbling thunder answered him. That must have been some bender, he told himself as he made his way to the highway.

He checked his pockets. He'd been robbed. Seventeen hundred dollars in cash was missing along with his wallet. The killer searched his memory, trying to piece together the events of the last day. He had made it back to the hotel in Columbia, as he recalled. Simpson was there and told him something important. What was it? Oh, yeah. He'd killed those damned kids. That was all that was clear. The rest was bits and pieces.

On a hunch, Soto sat down on the highway shoulder and yanked off his left shoe. His emergency $100-dollar bill was still in the wax paper envelope he kept there. Good. He wasn't completely helpless.

He turned right, and as he walked on the side of the road, small snippets of memory returned. He came to the realization that Simpson had been in the car with him, and he figured Simpson had dumped him and robbed him.

Soto's soggy shoes squished as he walked. His wet clothes stuck to him, and the cool air made him cold and uncomfortable. As misery settled in with each step, his anger at Dix Simpson gained momentum. Vengeance was certainly called for, but he knew he'd never set eyes on Simpson again.

CHAPTER 69

By a quarter after midnight, Joe's room was ready for Chelsea.

As Joe worked upstairs, Chelsea sat in the living room with his grandparents trying to solve the mystery with the phone at the trailer. Was it out of order? Why else would her mother not answer?

"Maybe the power is out due to the storm," Gramps suggested.

"No, I don't think so," Chelsea replied. "I'm pretty sure our old-fashioned model still works when the power is out. Could be the lines are down, but that's never happened before. I wonder what's wrong."

"Tell you what, Chelsea," Okie Joe said. "I'll drive to Monroe City tomorrow and tell your mom where you are so she won't worry. You don't have to come with me. I'm thinking' you don't want to see your father, just in case he hasn't been arrested yet. Okay? I'll make sure she doesn't worry.

"Let's turn in, all of us."

CHAPTER 70

Ernesto Soto walked five miles to the gas station where his former partner had stopped. He asked directions to Elsa, and the location of the nearest pay phone.

He broke the C-note and got change. At his size, fitting into the cramped phone booth was a challenge. He called Simpson's cell phone. There was no answer. He tried several more times and then gave up. He realized that Simpson wouldn't answer an unexpected call on his business phone. He found the frayed, ancient phone book under the pay phone and looked up another number. Dropping more coins in the slot, he dialed and waited for an answer.

"Shelby County Sheriff's Department, Abbott," answered a man.

"Hello," Ernesto said with his best possible American accent. "May I speak to Deputy Hiro Nakamura?"

"Deputy Nakamura is about to start his tour. Let me see if he's left yet. I'm going to put you on hold for a minute."

The minute turned into three minutes, four minutes, five minutes, and Soto deposited more money with each delay. He was about to hang up in disgust when Nakamura answered the phone. "Yes, this is Nakamura."

"Yeah, man, it's Soto."

"Who is this?"

"This is So - to," Soto articulated. "Dix Simpson's partner."

"I can't talk to you on this phone. I gotta go now," Nakamura whispered.

"No, don't hang up. I'm on a pay phone," Soto objected. "What's your home number? I'll call you whenever you say it's okay."

Nakamura said the number quickly and Soto did his best to memorize it, repeating it to himself several times after Nakamura hung up.

CHAPTER 71

Dix Simpson was conflicted. Where should he go? He could use an alliance somewhere in the business, but he had no real connections, let alone friends. Nobody has friends in those cartels, he reminded himself. It would be more a question of which cartel would be least likely to eliminate him. Some enemies were less hostile than others.

If he were a cartel, he'd have himself offed. Blowing a sweet deal like the one he'd set up with those college kids was a stinking shame. No one to blame but Soto. And himself. He'd known Soto was a loose cannon from the beginning. He should've chosen a better goon.

A thought occurred to him. He could go home. Dix's wife lived in a condo in Mesa, Arizona, and that condo would be as good a place as any to crash and regroup. Hell, he was already paying for the place, he might as well use it. He'd have to endure rants about his long absences and demands for money, but he'd handle it. It would mean several days on the road, but if he kept his nose clean and paid cash for everything, maybe he could stay off the radar. He had the cash he'd taken off Soto's snoring carcass, so there'd be plenty for gas, food, and lodging. He could do this.

Plus, there was Renee. His nine-year-old daughter was a matter to which Simpson seldom gave a glancing thought. It would be good to see her. At the very least, it would be a pleasant diversion while he got his business going again. The girl was cute, as he recalled. Looked just like him, and smart, too. Quite a mouth on her, though. She got that from her mother.

Dix mused with satisfaction that Soto's penchant for carrying around cash was a good thing. His full pockets had been a godsend, and without any reserves, Soto would not be catching up to him any time soon.

Dix turned west.

CHAPTER 72

The elder Joe got up early in the morning, grabbed a bagel out of the kitchen, and got in his truck. He looked out over the vista before him—endless plains of farmland barely illuminated by the sun grazing the horizon.

No, he decided. He couldn't do it.

Old Joe's vision had been slowly declining for years. It would come and go, but this morning it was not good, and he opted out of driving into the rising sun. The glare would be blinding. He'd be foolish to try.

He'd have to take the boy with him.

He went back in the house and stepped into the living room where his grandson lay on the sofa. He touched the boy's elbow. "Third?" There was no movement. "Third?" he said a little louder. The youngster leaped off the sofa reminding him of a startled armadillo sleeping on a warm Oklahoma highway.

"What?!? Holy crap!" The kid blurted when he came to. He blinked and rubbed his eyes through the darkness at his grandfather.

"What's up, Gramps?" he asked at last.

"Sorry, Third. I need you to get up and drive the truck to Chelsea's house. I can't drive east right now, and I want to get there before Chelsea's mom leaves for her job."

"Do I have time for a shower?"

"Nope. You can grab a bagel on your way out, though."

"Okay." Joe stepped into the downstairs bathroom with last night's clothes and dressed. He snatched the bagel and ran to meet his grandfather in the truck.

Third glanced at his watch. It would be around seven when they arrived at the trailer park. Young Joe, in the driver's seat, turned on the radio. The AM radio stations near Sylvia offered two choices: news or country music. Joe turned up his nose, always, at the latter and set the dial for a news station out of Quincy, unprepared to be startled so early in the morning. While the MacDonalds had been socializing at the Armsteads' the night before, the storm that blew through the Highway 36 corridor had been intense. The high winds hadn't quite reached tornado strength, but there had been property damage straight into Quincy.

Joe felt sick to his stomach. He recalled Chelsea's failed attempt to reach home by phone. The trouble signal on the line could indicate the phone was left off the hook, or it could mean something worse.

"Gramps? Gramps, did you hear that?" .

The old man didn't respond. He was sound asleep. The late night last night must have robbed him of his usual rest. Gramps was normally up before the sun, but he and Grams typically turned in by nine p.m. Country folks, Joe mused. He smiled to himself.

Gramps, meanwhile, was dreaming.

Inga was as she always was whenever Joe dreamed of her: strong, capable, sensible and good. She stood at his side in most of his dreams as a helper and friend, completely trusted and trusting, defining companionship the waking Joe had reveled in for decades. She seldom spoke in his dreams, but she needn't. Her thoughts were his.

In this dream, he found himself in a humble brown shack in northern Oklahoma. It was the dirty thirties again, but now Okie Joe was a grown man, and his wife, who had still been in Germany during these years, was, in his dream, battling the infestation of caterpillars, spiders, and assorted insects that all the Okies battled. Insects invaded most homes looking for moisture and food in the barren Plains. They fed on the structures in such numbers that the "shh, shh" sound of a few insects grew thunderous when they feasted by the thousands.

In the dream, Inga had a large towel in her hands and was crushing and smearing the bodies of the creatures against the wall. The bugs weren't within the walls as they had been in his childhood reality, but on the insides of the house, systematically destroying it with a continuous, unwavering roar.

It may have been that the sleeping Okie Joe was hearing the roar of his own truck engine. The mind uses the tools it has to tell us stories.

He went to help Inga, but as he approached her, he found himself in another place in the house. Of course, the house he occupied as a child had only one small room, but this dream house resembled his home in Sylvia.

Then he saw his grandson on a mat on the floor with his hands pressed over the sides of his head to both block out the noise and keep the bugs from crawling into his ears. Bugs were attacking the boy, and Okie Joe, panicked and desperate, beat at them with a pillow that abruptly appeared in his hands. Okie Joe knew without watching, of the torn, eaten flesh on the youngster's arms and legs. The blood oozed around the creatures, flowing and dripping. He felt the bleeding boy's pain and fear. Meanwhile, Third, in the way that dream figures often do, took the form of both Don Armstead and Derek Phinney from his socialist group. The ambiguous identity of this dream character made no sense, but Okie Joe's job was clearly to save him —or them — from being devoured.

As desperation rose within him, and he observed the advance of the creatures, Joe's heart raced, and his feet began to itch. He looked down to see the bugs starting their inevitable advance up his legs. Still, the unswerving focus was to save his grandson, his colleague, and his best friend. Though the identities of this helpless person shifted in his mind, the intent to help did not.

He screamed at Inga to come and help him, but she didn't come to him. He began smashing the bugs with the pillow, but there were too many. The Armstead-Phinney-Third person was thrashing at the attackers, and Okie Joe kept up his efforts until a giant caterpillar appeared. It was about the size of a large dog and it sank its pincers into his hand.

The image awakened him with a start.

"Are you okay, Gramps? Did you have a dream?"

"Uh, yeah, son, I did. You were in it. It was more like a nightmare."

"Sounded like it. You yelled, 'Inga!' at one point. You sounded real afraid. What happened in the dream?"

"Uh, I don't remember. Where are we?"

"About eight miles to go," his grandson told him. "I had the news on while you were sleeping. Sounds like the storm did a lot of damage. I'm wondering if that's why Chelsea couldn't reach her mother on the phone. I wonder if phone lines were down or some-thing."

"Or something," Gramps echoed. "We'll find out shortly."

CHAPTER 73

Inga awoke not long after her men left. She could have used a few more winks, she mused, after the late night, but she had a house guest to tend to. She donned her jeans and a t-shirt, her sneakers, and her warmest demeanor, and went to the kitchen to make coffee and wait for Chelsea to get up.

Tiptoeing past the sofa, she found her grandson gone, and realized that he must have gone with her husband.

She folded up his bed sheets and put them aside. He could use them again tonight if necessary. That reminded her to call DFS as soon as their offices opened and to make her case for taking in Chelsea . It might be that Okie Joe and Inga wouldn't qualify, and a fear nagged at her, but she'd start the process when offices opened.

Also on her to-do list was the task of cleaning out her knitting room and converting it back into a bedroom, just in case Chelsea was allowed to stay.

She hoped the person at the agency would not regard her as a teenager pulling a prank and dismiss her.

As the coffee pot filled, Inga considered breakfast options. Waffles would be a good welcoming breakfast, she decided, and odds were that fresh peaches and whipped cream would appeal to her young guest.

She started to take a bowl out of the cabinet but then reasoned that the girl might want to sleep for a while. No telling when she'd be up.

Inga poured herself a cup of coffee and sat at the dining room table. As she made plans, she noticed the photo of her childhood home propped up against the centerpiece. It had been there for weeks after she had shown it to Third. He had been so fascinated with it that she had never returned it to its drawer. She picked it up and studied it, stirring memories.

Inga's mother was an undisputed beauty. Blue-eyed and Aryan, she embodied the ideals Hitler sought to present to the world of the super race. She was tiny and trim, standing merely 1.6 meters, and weighing only 51 kg. She nevertheless sported the upper body strength of a much larger person. She had to. Her life called for it.

When Inga was sixteen, and the war had been over for a few months, Hedda Wentzel had a visitor. Dr. Irving Sartorius, once a distant neighbor and more-distant cousin, was back in Germany after emigrating to the United States. He had followed the teachings of Dietrich Bonhoeffer, the renowned Christian author and philosopher, and had embraced Bonhoeffer's mandate to wear one's faith in Jesus Christ on one's sleeve in every word and deed. The call was for sacrifice, courage, and righteousness — to stand for good, even in the face of extraordinary evil. Bonhoeffer's stand against Hitler, vociferous and public, had cost the man his life.

Much of the church in Germany had embraced Hitler, and had postulated that his leadership would actually help the church to facilitate the cause of Christ, but Bonhoeffer knew better. Hitler was a madman and a tyrant, Rev. Bonhoeffer proclaimed in many sermons, and he must be stopped.

Sartorious lived by Bonhoeffer's beliefs and by the Christian doctrines he gleaned from his worn and well-thumbed Bible. He had heard from as far away as Hannibal, Missouri, the tale of his distant cousin, Hedda, widowed with young children, and he sought to reach out.

As it turned out, when they met, little courage was required to make the righteous sacrifice. The fall into love with Hedda was a short and steep one.

Letters were exchanged over the months. Gifts of cash to help with expenses crossed the ocean, and before Inga's seventeenth birthday, Irving returned to Germany to marry Hedda, gather his new family, and take them all to America.

Dr. Sartorius had a general medical practice in Hannibal. He sold his cottage shortly after the family arrived. He bought a much larger home on a nice street to accommodate his bride and her children.

"Papa Irv" as the children called him, was a kind and loving stepfather. He saw to it that by reading and speaking only English, the children and their mother had a polished grasp of the language in

short order. Good schools and nice clothes became a part of life. Hedda had a pretty new dress whenever the fancy took her, and while she was not vain, an occasional nicety served as a gentle reminder of the struggles of her past. She sought to not lose what she had learned from struggle. She wanted to teach her children — and remind herself — that in times of need as well as in times of plenty, showing kindness to others was how civilized people live.

The bounty from the backyard vegetable garden was shared with less fortunate neighbors, while Inga, having also learned from her life in Germany, knitted socks for children of less-affluent neighbors.

Seems, though, that Fate is a fickle friend. The family had been in the United States a mere two years when the worst happened.

Dr. Sartorius was walking home from the barbershop late one Friday evening. After getting his shave and a haircut, he had stayed past closing and had gotten in a card game with some of his American friends. He had won twenty bucks and was feeling pretty good. His footfalls were light as he strolled home where he intended to greet his beautiful wife at the door and look in on his sleeping children. He would enjoy a short snifter of brandy and retire for the night.

But it wasn't to be. Along the way, someone who would never be identified wanted that twenty dollar bill. It might have been a desperate father needing to feed his flock. It might have been a young drug addict, desperate to feed his jones. All that would be known was that, when the sun came up Saturday morning, Dr. Sartorius lay lifeless in a pool of his own blood. He didn't have a dime on him, his watch and glasses were missing, and Hedda Wentzel Sartorius was widowed once again.

The tiny titan of Korbach who had raised and comforted her children, neighbors, and friends through Europe's darkest period, crumbled with this tremendous blow. Her amazing strength disintegrated into exhaustion. Tears flowed for months as the savings evaporated, and despair settled on her like a shroud.

This time, the children were old enough to help out, and they did, each sensing that this tragedy was different from the others. The family was on unfamiliar turf with cultural barriers and a matriarch in denial. Young Christoph mowed lawns for fifty cents each. Konstanz began her career as a nanny for a wealthy family. Inga, having inherited her mother's beauty, earned good tips waiting tables at a diner in town, but she faced a cruel reality. Hedda had been the source of indefatigable strength for all of Inga's short life. It was bizarre and unnatural for this able woman to fall into such a depression. Her strength and optimism had always flowed through Hedda and into Inga and the younger children as naturally as breathing. There was nothing over which they could not claim at least a small victory. Now, the once-indefatigable Hedda had lost this last battle. Her white flag took the form of her husband's brandy bottle, and as she drank herself into forgetting, the onus fell to her eldest daughter.

Inga picked up hours at the diner and went to secretarial school at night. She assumed the role of head of the household while her mother descended into a liquored abyss. For Inga, the battle was on. She was determined to become like the Hedda she had once known, to gather the siblings close and to use their pooled strengths to hold the family strong.

The biggest break for the family came one Saturday afternoon when a tall, strapping man with an Oklahoma dialect named Joe MacDonald strode into the diner looking for a decent cup of coffee.

Inga's musings continued until she heard footfalls on the back staircase. She rose with her empty coffee cup and went into the kitchen to greet her guest. She could almost smell the waffles.

CHAPTER 74

Honestly, Soto had to admit to himself that it was unrealistic to expect to be picked up as a hitchhiker. Naturally mean-looking, and huge, the criminal would terrify any sane driver. Hell, he wouldn't pick himself up if he saw himself on the side of the road.

Nevertheless, he needed a ride. He had walked at least eight miles and tried Nakamura at his house. No answer. He had tried Simpson again from a different pay phone. Same result.

He tried his cousin in El Paso, calling collect. To his surprise, Rodolfo answered and agreed to accept the charges. He even agreed to wire some money, but Soto didn't have much faith in the promise.

The rest of his C-note could allow him to sleep indoors tonight. A bus ticket south might also be a good idea, but there were some things to take care of first.

He went into a bar in whatever tiny burg he occupied, ordered a beer, and sat down. He'd wait until some like-minded soul wandered in. It took another an hour.

They were good ole' boys, sure enough. But they had a reasonable amount of ink on their arms, one of a largely fanged rattlesnake, a skull, and the other guy had a dagger plunged into the heart of a busty, topless woman.

My kind of guys, Ernesto thought. He struck up a conversation.

Toby and Jiz were the brothers' names, and they hailed from Paris, Missouri where their farm produced corn, soybeans, methamphetamine, and potatoes. Ernesto actually surmised the methamphetamine based on verbal clues and the fact that soybeans wouldn't buy the gauge of gold chain that Toby had around his thick neck.

Sure would be good if Dix were here to meet these boys, Soto thought. Old habits die hard, he mused. His days of considering Dix were long gone, he realized.

He caught the boys' attention as he told the tale of how he and his partner had a fine deal set up for Columbia, but their meth supplier couldn't keep up. They were looking for a better meth cook, and they would buy in quantity.

Toby and Jiz listened with rapturous attention.

Soto spun this fiction less for a drug relationship, and more for a ride east. Birds of a feather, he thought.

"Your name ain't really Jiz, is it?" Soto asked.

"Nah, it's John. They call me Jiz 'cause I knocked up my first whore when I was eleven."

"Nice work," Soto laughed. "Did the court stick you with supporting the bitch and her kid?"

"Nah, man, I was eleven."

"Hey, where you going when you leave outta here?" Soto asked.

"Why?" Toby interjected. "You wanna ride?"

"Yeah, man, depending. I can buy a gallon or two of gas," Soto offered.

"Where're you trying to git to?" Toby asked.

"Elsa, if I can, or close to it."

"Hell, why you wanna go there? You're just brown enough to cause a commotion," Jiz remarked.

"I ain't had no trouble, but I bring trouble with me if I can," Soto sneered.

"Yeah," Toby chuckled, acknowledging a kindred spirit. "We can drop you off."

CHAPTER 75

"Yes, Joe, I know who you are. I understand that you want to protect what you've achieved. Most people do. But that speech at the restaurant that night was just ugly, and I was embarrassed to be seen with you." Liz MacDonald was on the phone with her husband. It was not going well.

"Liz, c'mon. In my line of work, I can't help a client spend his whole career amassing a fortune and then turn around and tell him that some welfare leech has the same right to it as he does. I can't live that kind of lie. My entire career has involved helping people invest in companies that pay dividends, people and companies who produce, not people who think the world owes them because they're black, or gay, or poor, or whatever."

"I know, Joe. I hear you. But you can't go spewing hatred in front of Joey. You have to set a better example," Liz argued.

"Better example than what?"

"Maybe a little compassion for those who aren't as well off," Liz suggested. Hell, she thought, she was sounding shrill and irrational, even to herself.

"You've been talking to my father," he accused.

"I really haven't, but if I did, am I now forbidden to do that?"

"Liz, baby, I have compassion for poor people. But you and I would be poor people too if I didn't work my ass off to get us ahead. Am I supposed to give all our money away to some poor schmuck just because he thinks he's entitled because of his skin color or his accent? I don't think so."

"An argument can be made that people in this country with a certain skin color have had everything taken from them for many, many years. Maybe those people deserve a stinking break once in a while." Liz's voice was rising. "No, no," she continued. "I take that back. Maybe people should get help when they need it just because they are humans."

"Fine. But not on my dime, okay? Not from what I've worked for. Listen, Liz, I have never enslaved anyone."

"Haven't you, Joe, really? Don't you advise your clients to invest in companies where the stocks are climbing in value?"

"Of course. That's my job."

"And don't stocks climb in value when profits go up? And don't profits go up the most when labor costs are held down?" Liz didn't wait for a reply. "So in essence, you're advising clients to invest in companies that economically enslave their own employees. And you are rewarded accordingly. It seems to me that you enslave people as a matter of course."

"Liz, it's not that simple. We can debate economics all day long. There's such a thing as profit-sharing for employees. Profits don't just go to shareholders. Workers have a vested interest in seeing a well-run company make a profit so they can take a share of the success for themselves. People can make their own success. Not everyone is exploited by the big, bad boss.

"It's my job to turn my clients toward profitable companies. That's what I do, and you can't tell me that's wrong or immoral. And what I mean is, I don't enslave black people. Black people haven't been enslaved for a hundred and thirty years."

"You're kidding me, right?" Liz said. The shock registered in her voice. "Where were you a year ago?"

"What? I was in our home with my wife and son . . . "

"When that man in Los Angeles was beaten to within an inch of his life by the police. That Rodney King."

"I remember," Joe said. "He started race riots and lots of people were hurt and had their businesses ripped apart. What's your point?"

"He started race riots?" she shrieked. "How's about the police started race riots by brutalizing a man for possibly, just possibly driving while he was black."

"He was also drunk," Joe stated.

"Fine. He was drunk. If a white guy was dragged from his car and beaten with clubs because he was drunk, what form of civil unrest would that cause? How many people would be up in arms about that, huh?" Liz was near to screaming.

"What does that have to do with this? You're not making any sense, Liz. Let's talk again after you calm down." Joe hung up the phone.

Liz, on the other end, looked at the phone's handset for several seconds before she returned it to its cradle. She had to admit to herself that she did sound unreasonable. Why was she so hysterical about an issue she had lived peacefully with for as long as she had known her husband? She wasn't sure. She kept going back to the discussion in the restaurant. It was ugly, and she knew the ugliness was something Joe directed to his father by using his mother to carry the sentiment to Sylvia. And that was plenty ugly in itself, she mused. Something else was bothering her, though. She searched her heart until the answer dawned. It's just that poor people, black people, disenfranchised people of all stripes including Rodney King, live a different paradigm. The knowledge settled on her like a weight. She knew she didn't understand that paradigm, and she wouldn't see the world clearly until she did.

CHAPTER 76

"Hi, Momma," Joe II said to Inga minutes later. His conflicted, jarred emotions after his fight with Liz had moved him to seek comfort from his mother. "How're you all doing up there?"

"Well, we've had a few adventures lately," she told her son. "Third's girlfriend is here. There's a situation at home, and she can't stay there for the foreseeable future. As soon as I'm off the phone with you, I'm going to apply to become her foster parent."

"That's what I love about you, Momma," her son exclaimed. "You can say a lot with just a few words. I can't wait to hear all about this."

"Another time, Joseph," Inga stated dismissively. "What's going on with you and Liz?"

"We're talking," he lied. "We're even kind of dating. I took her out to eat last night, and we have plans to go to the zoo over the weekend. I'm trying very hard to be the man she loves, but she kind of pulled a fast one after that night we went to the symphony."

"How's that?"

"You know, Momma, I never tried to hide from Liz who I am or what I believe, but she came out of nowhere with this emotional objection to my views of society. I think it's obvious—human nature—that there are many poor, desperate people. If they could, they would take everything I've worked for, and I can't stand for that. It's no wonder I'm cautious about people looking for an inroad through my son or any kind of way they could find."

"I certainly agree," Inga said, "that there are a lot of poor people who need help." She went no further on the topic. Instead, she switched gears, "You know that Third was interviewed by Big Mac McIntyre. Did he tell you about that?"

"I've barely talked to him. Who is Big Mac McIntyre?" her son asked.

"He's the high school basketball coach. Third played one-to-one, I think you call it, with a star player who just graduated, and Big Mac was really impressed. Told Third he could join his team in the fall if he wanted to. You know, Joe and Third put up a basketball, what do you call it — hoop on the side of the barn. Third plays with that thing every day. Joe bought him a ball."

"One-on-one, I think you mean. Third, as you call him, will be back home in a few weeks, and the sooner the better," Joe said.

"What do you mean, son? Third is having a wonderful time, and so are we. We're in no hurry to send him home. He can stay as long as he wants to," she said.

"I know that, Momma, and it was wonderful of you to take him in for the summer and keep him away from his trouble-making friends. But I miss him. This big house is lonely, especially without Liz. . ." His voice broke and the sadness was evident to his mother's ear.

"So, you want Third back because you miss Liz, is that right? It sounds to me like you need to get Liz back, not Third," Inga noted.

"That's what Joey says, too."

Inga changed the subject. "Third has a new friend here. A really nice kid. His father and your father are close friends. The family goes to our church."

"Wouldn't that make this friend of Joey's a lot older than he is?"

"No, they're about the same age. They like the same music, and they both like basketball, and they go places together. I guess his father had him late in life. His wife just had another baby. He seems to be a very involved father, which is good, because Jamal doesn't have many friends here other than Third. Don, the father, spends a lot of time with both young men. He's a born mentor." Inga wondered if her son was getting her subtle point. "And I am starting to get close to his wife, Lynae. Did Third tell you about the party they attended?"

"No. What party?"

"Well, I guess one of us should have let you know. There was an incident."

Joe remained quiet, so Inga plunged in and described the near-catastrophe in the convenience store in Elsa.

"I thought Third would have told you all about this," Inga concluded.

"No, not a word, Momma," Joe answered in a low voice. He sighed again. "I guess he couldn't be bothered."

Inga stayed quiet. Finally, her son continued, "So, Joey is best friends with a black kid."

"Yes," she answered.

"Who'd a thunk it?"

CHAPTER 77

Gramps and Joe pulled into the trailer park at seven forty in the morning. Joe made a mental note of the time and the date because it was something he would not want to forget for a long time.

The thunderstorm with "tornadic motion" had ripped apart the trailer park with a malevolence that seemed almost sentient to the teenage boy. The cyclone fence that enclosed the park was completely uprooted, flattened, and covered with debris from shredded trailers.

Joe wanted to gun the engine and speed toward Chelsea's home as fast as the truck would carry him, but he was impeded by fractured furniture, bicycle parts, a mangled refrigerator and somebody's 33 rpm record collection strewn all over the road. Two fat, healthy raccoons picked through the debris with no apparent fear of the people nearby—somebody's escaped pets, Joe surmised. He was forced to be patient as he circumnavigated wreckage, his thoughts in turmoil.

"Holy God." Gramps exclaimed, awestruck.

Joe's mouth gaped open.

As the Christmas trailer came into view, both men took a sharp breath. The troublesome sycamore tree that had dropped leaves and branches into the gutters of the trailer could be counted upon to cease doing so. It had been struck by lightning, split in half, and the largest half had collapsed on top of the trailer, cutting it in half.

Dozens of people stood around, observing the wreckage. Joe stopped the truck, killed the engine and jumped out. Gramps looked around from his seat for a moment before stepping out.

Joe dashed to the first person he saw, a thirty-year-old red-headed woman with a child on her hip. "Excuse me, do you know what happened to the people who live here? Are they okay?"

"I just got here a few minutes ago. My trailer is banged up pretty good, too. I saw an ambulance drive off from here, so that's why I came on over."

"Oh, uh, I'm sorry about your trailer. There were two people living here. Do you know how many were carried out?" Joe asked.

"Nah, I just got here myself," she repeated.

"All right, thanks." Joe sought another spectator, and another, but no one knew much. He traveled around the perimeter of the trailer, asking folks at random. As he turned a corner, he nearly collided with the portly form of Sheriff MacAfee.

Joe's heart sank. "Excuse me, Sheriff," Joe began, hoping the sheriff wouldn't recognize him. He hoped to get the most possible from the sheriff without the bad blood between him and the Mac-Donalds clogging the flow of information. "Can you tell me where the people are who were living in this trailer?"

The sheriff's face darkened when he looked at Joe. No doubt about it. He recognized the teen.

MacAfee was direct. "Is this the home you and your parents came to see me about?"

"My grandparents, yes," Joe replied. He didn't care for the sheriff's tone.

"A neighbor tells us that there was a young girl living here, but she's missing. Rescue workers were here at nine last night, but they only pulled out two people, an adult male and an adult female."

"How are those people?"

"We don't know yet. Both were alive when they left here, but were pretty messed up. One more than the other. I don't know which is worse. The radio message was garbled, I guess because of the storm, so that's all the detail I have. If you have any information on the girl . . ."

"I do, I do," Joe interrupted. "She stayed at my house last night. She's fine, okay. My gramps and I came here this morning to tell her mom that she's okay, and we found all this."

Okie Joe came around the corner at that moment and saw Joe talking to the sheriff. "Sheriff," he said placidly.

"Mr. MacDonald," the sheriff replied in the same tone.

"What hospital are they in?" Okie Joe asked.

CHAPTER 78

Soto had used his stolen credit card to buy most of the party in the bar. No matter. He'd tossed the card in the bathroom trash as he and the Rowe brothers headed out. He'd be on the way somewhere soon, back to his usual routine. It might turn out that his new liaison with these Rowe brothers would offer new business opportunities. Ernesto never thought of himself as an entrepreneur, but if Dix Simpson was going to ditch him the way he did, well, it wasn't as if Soto hadn't learned a few things about starting his own cartel. The Rowes might be a great find indeed.

The Rowes had dropped him in downtown Elsa, and Soto stopped at a pay phone.

H dialed Nakamura's house. Nakamura answered. "Yeah, Nakamura. This is Soto. Can you talk now?"

"Yes. Soto, hello. Mr. Simpson said you're not partners now. What happened?"

"Oh, nothin. Just a difference of opinion," Soto lied. "Everything's fine. What did you have to tell him? You can tell me, too, in case I don't connect with him."

"I told him nothing, except about the drug house raid tomorrow. That's all."

"What drug house raid?" Soto demanded, his pulse quickening.

"The one at Sample's house."

"No shit," Soto said, half to himself. "What time tomorrow?"

"It's for seven tomorrow morning. I told Simpson. I'm on the assault team," Nakamura bragged.

"Sample moved his lab. How does the sheriff know where the new lab is?"

Nakamura hesitated. Soto tried again, and raised his voice. "I said, how does the sheriff know the location?"

"Some kid saw Sample's wife at the new house and he told the sheriff."

"Really. Who's is this guy?" Soto asked.

"A Sylvia resident. Joseph MacDonald ," Nakamura reported.

CHAPTER 79

"Sarah Dednum," Fast said. "It took forever and a day for the County to respond, but we finally got the word."

Fast was on the phone with Sheriff Mitch Ollman, and the topic was Jack Sample. Fast had kept Ollman abreast of the developments in Shelby County even though Ollman was still on leave.

Fast had contacted the Recorder of Deeds for Shelby County to ascertain who owned the house in Elsa where Jack Sample was staying. Even between agencies there was the inevitable senseless paperwork. After the delay, the person who owned the home was identified as Jack Carson, who stated that the name on the lease was Sarah Dednum. The cooperative landlord was happy to report that he had met the other occupant, a young man with the same first name as his own. He remembered joking with the couple about the irony.

After hearing the report from Fast, Sheriff Ollman sought confirmation. He wanted to be sure on timing and intent. "Okay. So, your team is on for the morning?"

"Yes, sir. I've got a team of six with full gear. We're proceeding with the armed and dangerous protocol as a precaution," Fast promised, "although we actually expect a minimum of resistance. Mitch, we're going to get this done. For Mark and for Emily," Fast vowed. "We have high hopes that we can conclude this action with no harm to Dednum or her baby. There is only one uncertain aspect. . . ."

"What is that?"

"The weather report looks less than friendly for tonight through the morning. There's a report of a storm system blowing in from the northwest," Fast reported.

"Oh, God, no, not again," Ollman said, but his distress was feigned, and Fast picked up on it.

"Are you okay, Mitch?" Fast asked. "I thought I'd hear more out of you on the eve of the capture of Jack Sample. You don't seem quite with this process , if you know what I mean."

CHAPTER 80

Bonnie Wallace took the call from Inga. Having heard the tape of the original call, she understood that Inga was the woman who had acted to report the abuse of Chelsea Christmas. The elderly woman's voice was like no other.

"I'm familiar with the situation, Mrs. MacDonald. We're glad to hear that Chelsea has a safe place to stay. It was most disturbing that Chelsea took off before I could help her. Now, because of the storm last night, my hands are full with displaced families.

"Normally, there is a procedure for certifying a household as a foster care facility, but I'm going to fast-track this in Chelsea's case," Bonnie explained.

"Oh, that would be wonderful," Inga trilled. "I really appreciate it."

"Honestly, Mrs. MacDonald, this is no favor to you or to Chelsea," Bonnie went on. "The storm last night left at least 80 families homeless, and I'm doing my best to find temporary housing for them. Plus, the forecast says we're in for more tonight. Your offer to help is very much appreciated. I'll get back to you as soon as I can."

Bonnie sounded dismissive, and Inga realized she wanted to get off the phone, but Inga wasn't satisfied. "What about the father?" Inga asked. "Is he going to be arrested?"

Bonnie did not answer right away. After a few moments of silence, which annoyed Inga, she answered. "Mrs. MacDonald, the Christmas home was among those damaged in last night's storm. Mr. Christmas is, well, contained. That's all the detail I can give you. Thanks for calling. Good-bye."

Inga heard a click, and the line went dead. She hung up the phone and paced the floor for several minutes. She tried without success to shake off a sense of impending doom, but she needed word from Joe and Third before she could make any decisions.

"Chelsea," Inga said as she stepped down into the dining room. "I have a little news, but I don't know what to make of it."

Chelsea was finishing her breakfast, and looked up at Inga with her eyebrows furrowed. "What?"

"According to Ms. Wallace at DFS, your house was damaged by the storm. I couldn't find out if your parents are okay, just that your father is 'contained,' whatever that means. We have to wait for the men to get back. They may know more."

Chelsea set her elbows at each side of her plate and rested her head in her hands.

CHAPTER 81

The two MacDonald men headed to Moberly Regional Medical Center, the hospital serving the area. The highway was flat, tedious, and surrounded by green, lush, repetitive farmland. An occasional windmill, barn, or herd of livestock broke up the tedium.

"What do you think about Chelsea?" Joe asked Gramps.

"What do you mean?" his grandfather replied.

"She's been abused by her father. That's pretty awful. What if she got pregnant?"

"I reckon she's been through a rough time, and has more ahead of her.

"Grams wants to be her foster parent. What do you think about that?"

Joe didn't answer right away. He was trying to figure out what he did think, exactly, about the beautiful young woman with the terrible secret.

Gramps didn't pressure him. It wasn't an easy thing to sort out.

Joe set his jaw for several seconds before responding. "Gramps, our family helps people. Isn't that what you've been telling me? I really didn't consider that before I came here. In my house, people look out for themselves, and don't get involved in other people's personal business. Especially when it's this personal. " Joe took a deep breath and glanced over at his grandfather.

"There was a neighbor girl when I was little," he continued. "She was younger than me. Most of the kids didn't like her because she sometimes acted weird. Like an animal. Once she used our bathroom and I found shit on the floor right next to the stool." Joe recoiled at the memory.

"Her mother was a head case. She was angry and sweet all at the same time, and you never knew when her kind words would suddenly stop and she would burst into some kind of rage. I saw her hit the daughter across the face for doing nearly nothing that could be thought of as wrong." Joe shook his head.

"I told my dad and Liz what I had seen, and I said that I thought the girl was real mixed up and kind of, I don't know, wild because she was being abused.

Dad said that the girl's father was a respected doctor in the community and that I should shut up and mind my own business. It wasn't my place to interfere in other people's affairs.

"That was a few years ago, and the girl is now about 14, I think. I never see her with friends, and she's a hundred pounds over-weight."

"What are you getting at, Third?"

"I think we should have helped her before it was too late. I don't think the father knows what's going on. He's at the hospital all the time. I think I should have spoken to him about things I'd seen, but I was told to stay out of it." Joe looked away and sighed.

"I failed the family mission."

"How did you fail the family mission?" Gramps asked with a knit brow.

"Well, our family looks out for people who are treated unfairly, doesn't it? Doesn't our family worry about strangers?"

"But you didn't know that when you met this young girl."

"I know I didn't, Gramps, but I do now, and I know how to be a MacDonald. I just wasn't taught it at the time.

"You know, I was really attracted to Chelsea. I wanted to date her. A lot. I wanted to be with her. Really. But now, the whole thing is so, well, uncomfortable knowing what she's been doing. My whole attraction to her is gone, and I feel guilty about that. I mean, it isn't her fault that this happened, and I shouldn't look down on her, but I kind of do. And I think that's against our family mission, too," Joe explained.

"Third, I'm real proud that you're are trying to be a better person but, son, I think there's more to this than a family mission," Gramps said.

"Like what?"

Gramps pursed his lips for several seconds. "Well, truth is, I know you've had some trouble at home, and I think your dad sent you to us because you were hangin' out with kids who are trouble, and he wanted to keep you from getting any deeper in it."

"He wanted to get rid of me for a few months," Joe corrected.

Gramps ignored the remark and went on. "I know about the stolen car and the assault charge. I know there's been shoplifting and some other troubles."

Joe was silent, dreading the next words. "And you know what I think is the trouble with you, Third?" Gramps asked.

Joe didn't answer, so Gramps continued. "I think you just haven't been taught exactly right about who you're supposed to be. Sure, you're young, and you got you some growin' up to do, but it seems to me that you have needed a family mission and haven't had one. I think that's all that's wrong with you." Gramps reached over and squeezed his grandson on his shoulder.

"Since you've been here, I haven't seen much trouble in you. You've worked hard, made some friends, and been a pretty good kid. Inga thinks so, too. Maybe all you need to stay out of trouble is something to believe in."

"Like what?"

"Well, yourself, for one, but also what we call a worldview, a belief in doing right as an end in itself." Gramps explained.

"You mean a religion."

"No, not quite. See, religion tells us to do good things, good works, to please God, and try to earn Heaven. You can't do that. No one can. I mean, Heaven is a gift we receive when we believe in Jesus Christ. His blood bought our entrance to Heaven, not our deeds."

"Gramps, you're a communist. What're you talking to me about Jesus Christ for?" Joe asked.

"Yeah, I've heard that before," he said. "Marx was an atheist, and all that. But do you know the first-century Christians lived in communes and shared all they had? In fact, St. Paul slammed the commune in Corinth because some of the Christians there were not sharing everything equally . There's no automatic conflict between my worldview and my faith. You know John the Baptist taught that if a man has two coats, he should give one of them to someone who hasn't got any. I think the two philosophies are far more compatible than it might seem. Sure as hell more than, say, religious faith and capitalism which pretty much wants to help the fewest, richest people.

"Look, I don't want to preach at you, boy," Gramps said. "You can ask Inga if you want to know more. She's real good at explaining."

The two rode in silence for the last two miles. As they pulled into the hospital parking lot, Gramps spoke again.

"As soon as we can, Joe, I want you to find a phone and call home, tell your grandmother what we know so far."

"Shouldn't we wait, Gramps? We may know more once we talk to someone inside. Then we'll have something to tell Grams and Chelsea."

"Okay. Good thinkin.' Drop me off at the front door, then go park."

Gramps stepped down from the truck and strode inside to the information desk.

"Good morning," he greeted the front desk clerk. "I'm here to check on a couple of storm victims. Can you help me?"

The clerk was a pretty young woman with long auburn hair who wore an emerald green button down shirt and a nametag that read "Roxy." She replied. "Just a minute sir. What's the patient's name?"

"Christmas. There may be two people. A tree fell on their trailer."

"Oh, that sounds awful. Just a moment. I have a Dennis Christmas and I have a Virginia Christmas. Both are in critical condition, and in ICU."

"That's them," Gramps replied, his Oklahoma accent at its homiest.

Roxy continued, "And, sir, the woman in ICU is in very grave condition. I have a note here from the staff to notify family. She might not make it. I'm sorry."

"Can we see her?"

"Visitors must be a relative of the patient," Roxy recited.

The phone rang, and Roxy answered it. As she did, Joe strode up to his grandfather. "What'd you find out?"

"Third, get back in the truck right now and go home. Get Chelsea and bring her back here quick as you can. Her parents are in ICU, and it looks bad, especially for the mother. Try to get Chelsea back here before something happens. Go! I'll wait here. I'll call Inga and tell her you're coming."

Joe ran back to the truck, and Gramps found a payphone. Inga answered on the first ring.

"Yes, Joe," she chirped when she heard his voice. "We heard that the trailer was damaged by the storm. How bad is it?"

"It's bad, Baby. The story gets worse. Chelsea's parents are in critical condition in ICU, Moberly. I gather from the desk clerk that Chelsea's mother is in bad shape."

Inga was quiet and Joe spoke again. "I sent Third back to get Chelsea and bring her here before it's too late. But, it may be hard to get her into ICU because she's underage and has no blood relative handy."

"Why am I waiting for Third?" Inga asked. "I have a car. Why don't I just bring Chelsea right now?"

"I don't know, Baby. That's a good idea. I guess I was thinking that 'cause I couldn't drive it this morning, you shouldn't. Come on, then. Hurry. But leave a note for Third. He's on the way to you."

CHAPTER 82

Ernesto Soto had vowed to keep in touch with the Rowes. If he wanted to succeed in the drug industry, he would need partners to do the manufacturing. He hadn't decided that he wanted to be his own cartel, but, he reasoned, best to maximize his options.

It was not lost on Soto that he wasn't much of a businessman, and he would have to stretch his reach to do what Dix had done these last couple of years. He'd have to drink less, think more, and be his own muscle.

Soto knew he was better suited to taking orders and swinging his fists. It would be a change for him, but if he didn't step up, who would do it? He'd have to stay out of the reach of the law, which might be tricky. After all, there was the matter of these murder charges. *Damn those stinking kids,* he mused to himself.

Energized by his internal rage, Soto strode to the front door of the little house and pounded on it. Again. Again. Finally, Jack Sample answered and let him in. Sample was high, of course, and looked like hell. There was an undercurrent of exhaustion. Soto's could see that the guy hadn't slept in a week.

From Jack's perspective, there was more agitation to Soto than usual. The observation sparked less curiosity than increased un-ease with the goon.

"Where's Dix?" he demanded of Jack. "Has he been here yet?"

"Uh, yeah, man. C'mon in. He was here yesterday, I think. Not sure. Time flies when you're having fun, you know." He flashed Soto a brown-toothed grin that repelled even the likes of Soto. "He said something about you and him not being in business or some-thing. That right?" Jack asked.

Soto's anger flared. "Well, since the asshole dumped me in bushes on the side of the road and drove off without me, yeah, I'd say our partnership is over."

"Why did he . . . never mind. What can I get you? Beer?" Jack asked.

"Yeah, I'll take a beer. It's stinkin' hot out."

Jack disappeared and returned with a can of cheap grocery store beer. Soto made a disgruntled sound as he popped it open.

A vague sense of dread penetrated Jack's exhaustion. "So, um, what are you and Dix gonna do about the stuff I'm cooking? You gonna divide it up, or what?"

"Nah, there's no use in that. If I see him again, I won't be dividing anything but his head from his shoulders."

Jack was stunned by the realization that he was out of business. Through no fault of his own, all the careful courting of Simpson he had done, the promises made, the exhausting amount of work he had completed – it all meant nothing. He would never see Simpson again, and he'd have to return to cooking for the users who came to buy from him directly. He'd have to begin again building a clientele, and the word of mouth might not be enough to keep his family's head above water. Damn! Whatever had happened between Soto and Simpson would impact Jack and Sarah more than anyone.

But he didn't say anything to the muscleman.

"Well, hey," he said, shifting gears, "Dix left behind some product, so I guess he doesn't want it. You want it?"

"Why'd he leave it? Something wrong with it?"

"No, man," Sample answered. "It's good stuff. I just didn't have it all the way done when he was here, but I finished it a while ago. It's paid for, so you can have it if you want."

Soto looked at him with narrowed eyes. "You lyin' to me, man?" Soto accused. "I never seen Simpson leave behind product he'd paid for. What'd he do that for?"

"I think he was in a hurry to go. That's all, I think. I got the impression he was heading out of town."

To Jack Sample's deep regret, Sarah Dednum chose that moment to return home. She opened the front door encumbered with several grocery bags while she held Dustin poised on one hip.

She saw Soto and her whole body tensed. She looked at Jack and raised her eyebrows before heading to the kitchen to unpack groceries. On her way, she handed the baby to his father, freeing her hands.

"So, your little girlfriend's still here?" Soto ventured as he watched the young woman move about the house.

"Sure. Why wouldn't she be?"

"I dunno. If Dix has been here, I thought you might be gone," Soto answered.

Jack ignored the cryptic words, feeling sure that Soto was nuts, and never knew what he was talking about.

Soto noted the grocery bags and said, "Hey man, Dix took my car and money and I got nowhere to stay and nothin' to eat. You got any food around here?"

"Uh, I'll see. Hold on a minute. Sit down if you want."

Jack went into the kitchen and spoke to Sarah. "Sarah, Ernesto wants something to eat." His tone was subdued, almost a whisper. Little Dusty rested on Jack's hip and looked over his shoulder at the large, scary man in the living room who stared back at the child with obvious malice.

"What? You want me to feed him?" Sara asked, aghast.

"Seems like he and Simpson fell out, and Dix left him on the side of the road. He's got nothing on him and has nowhere to stay."

"Oh, shit!" Sarah squealed, then hushed herself. "You want him to sleep here, too?" Her eyes flashed with more fear than anger.

"Maybe just for a night or so. Look, Sarah, this guy's nuts, and I'm afraid to kick him out."

"Well, I'm afraid to let him stay," Sarah countered.

"Me, too. But what else can we do? He's got a short temper. Today, after the mess with Dix, he's likely to be hotter than usual. Maybe we can get him drunk until he passes out."

"Great thinking, Jack," Sarah dripped with sarcasm. "Let's liquor up a goon with a violent streak and see if that calms him down or revs him up." She rolled her eyes. "No. That's an idiotic idea."

"Fine, then you tell him he has to leave."

Sarah paused, trying to picture herself engaging the behemoth. "Okay, I'll feed him. A big turkey sandwich." She reached into the bag she had just brought home. "Turkey is supposed to make people sleepy, isn't it? Maybe we can get him to take a nap without liquor."

CHAPTER 83

When Joe pulled onto the farmhouse property, he noticed immediately that his grandmother's Taurus was missing, and he guessed that Inga must have taken off for the hospital with Chelsea.

He went into the house and found the confirming note on the kitchen table.

Third —
Chelsea and I went to Moberly. Wait here. We'll call you when we get there.

Gram

Since Joe had been living in Sylvia these months, he'd seldom seen his grandmother drive her car. She preferred that he drive her. He wondered why she seemed to avoid it, and why she chose to drive this time.

Because it's an emergency, came the answer in his head. Chelsea's parents might die.

A half-pot of cold coffee sat in the coffee maker. Joe poured himself a mug and heated it in the microwave. Nothing to do now but wait.

There was a long list of things that needed to be done. He could refresh the water for the livestock. He could shovel chicken droppings. He could pull down a bale of hay for the cows. But all those things would take him away from the phone, and he wanted to hear it when it rang.

He took his coffee from the microwave and looked around the kitchen. It was a mess. Dishes were piled up and the waffle iron was crusty with dried batter. Leaving a mess in the kitchen was so unlike Grams, that Joe had to marvel. She and Chelsea must have left in a hurry.

At least Joe could do something helpful that kept him within reach of the phone.

He rinsed the dirty dishes, put them in the dishwasher, and turned it on. Then he tackled the waffle iron.

He removed the waffle plates and soaked them in hot soapy water, then washed out the frame that the plates sit in. As he worked, he thought of Moberly and what Chelsea would discover there.

When the pieces were dry, he reassembled the waffle iron and clamped down the lid. He didn't know where Grams kept the appliance. She was so tidy that the iron had its own corner to occupy, but Joe was clueless as to where. So, he picked it up to set it on the counter. *Holy crap,* he thought, taking a sip of coffee. *That thing must weigh ten pounds when it's put together.*

The phone rang. Joe nearly dumped the warmed coffee all over himself in his haste to answer it. Surely Grams and Chelsea couldn't be in Moberly already, so maybe it was Gramps calling with news.

"Yes, hello, Gramps?" Joe said in the phone.

"No, Joey, it's just me." Joe recognized his father's voice.

"Hi, Dad, what is it?"

"That's some greeting. Can't I call my son when I want to?"

"Sure. You just never seem to want to. And I'm kind of in the middle here. Expecting a call. You want to call later when Gramps and Grams are here?"

"What are you in the middle of?" his father pressed.

"Just . . . some stuff has been going on and it kind of hit the fan last night. I'm waiting to hear from Grams. She and Gramps are in Moberly."

"At the hospital?"

"Yes."

"Why?" Joe's father sounded concerned.

"They're okay, but some people we know were injured in the storm last night," Joe explained.

"Your grandmother was telling me a little bit about one of your so-called friends being in trouble," his father said.

"Why does it have to be a so-called friend?" Joe asked.

"Sorry, I just meant that she said it was your girlfriend who was in trouble."

"She's not — I mean, I don't think she's going to be a girlfriend, just a friend," Joe said.

"Well, anyway, I hope it all comes out okay for her,"

"I don't think it will be okay no matter what happens," Joe replied. "The father's a real asshole."

"Wow, Joey. I'm ashamed of you for saying that. No one deserves that. Was it a nice house in a good neighborhood?"

"No, no, and no. You don't know what you're talking about."

"Then tell me so we both know."

Joe paused before saying, "No, I don't think so. It's private, and none of your business. Look, Dad, I need to go and keep this line clear for Grams to call me."

He could sense the reluctance in his father's silence, and knew he wouldn't be allowed to hang up that easily. "Look, Dad," he continued. "Can I give anyone a message?"

"No, I guess not," his father said. Joe heard his father sigh.

"How's Liz?"

"She's fine. She's moving back in right now."

"That's great, Dad. How'd you get her back? I'm really glad to know that."

"Let's just say I'll be flossing crow out of my teeth for a long time."

"So long as it's not Jim Crow," the boy retorted.

"I don't know what that means. Anyway, she's giving me another chance. I think she wants something I can't give her, so I'm not sure this will all stick, but I'm trying."

"What does she want that you can't give?" Joe asked.

"She wants me to change who I am. I don't think I can."

"People can change, Dad, if they want to. I think I've changed. You learn certain stuff and it changes you."

"I'm sure you'd like me to change also, wouldn't you?"

Joe let that question hang in the air for several seconds before he answered, "Damned straight."

"I'm sorry I've been so disappointing to you, son."

Joe's father had had enough of perceiving himself as a failure. But if he were to save his family, he would have to eat that crow, or at least appear to eat it. He was aware that he was being a little disingenuous, but it was for a good cause.

"I've always needed something you couldn't give me, Dad, that's all," Joe began. "Just like Liz."

"What didn't I give you?"

"Something to believe in," Joe answered. Before his father could respond, he said, "Look, I'll tell Grams and Gramps you called. I just want to keep this line open in case they call."

Joe's father relented. "Okay, Joey, I'll let you go. I think maybe Liz and I will come up and see you real soon, okay?"

"Sure, Dad, whatever you say. Talk about it later. Bye."

When he disconnected, Joe II thought about the conversation. Liz came through the front door carrying a load of clothes in a cardboard box. She started up the stairs.

"What's going on?" she asked. "You have a funny look on your face."

"Let's unpack your boxes later," he stated. She looked at him curiously. "Right now . . . road trip!"

CHAPTER 84

The turkey sandwich was satisfying to Soto. He parked his large frame on the Sample's unfurnished living room floor, and settled in for the duration.

Sarah was uncomfortable with his presence, but she shared Jack's hesitancy to ask him to leave. Jack, for his part, recognized that there was no point courting Soto and Simpson as buyers for his meth. The reason for tolerating the brute now was simply a matter of personal safety.

Jack noticed that as Soto sat on the floor with the small, grainy TV on, he watched little Dustin with a strange look on his face. He wondered what that was all about. Sarah was up and down stairs, in and out of rooms, searching for tasks to distract her, ignore Soto and dismiss his presence from her thoughts. His long, beefy legs sprawled out on the floor made that a little harder, but she played with the baby in the playpen, her back to Soto, until he interrupted her.

"I thought you'd be packing to leave," he said.

"I'm sorry. I didn't understand you. What did you say?" Sarah asked.

"I thought you'd be packing to leave this place. Surprised you're hanging around here."

"Why would I leave? I live here."

Soto stared at the baby. Sarah became uneasy. "Why are you looking at Dusty like that?"

"Cute," Soto replied. "Just cute, that's all."

Sarah's fear ratcheted up a couple of notches, and she forgot the cryptic remark about leaving the house. She picked the baby up and took him into the kitchen, settled him into the high chair, and prepared a bottle of apple juice.

CHAPTER 85

Lindsey Ollman, the sheriff's grieving wife, closed herself off from Mitch since Emily's death. She knew that many marriages didn't survive the death of a child, and she should make an effort to reconnect with her husband to prevent that eventuality. But, the future was a black, empty abyss. Life was pointless.

After the accident, the house had been structurally stabilized to allow anything salvageable to be removed. The home would be demolished and new construction could begin. The Ollmans were supposed to schedule the demolition and reconstruction, but in their grief, they had not done so.

The first time Lindsey had gone into the demolished laundry room, her eyes rested on a laundry basket full of Emily's clothes surrounded by the fallen debris.

Lindsey had dissolved into yet more uncontrollable sobs. The laundry represented a storehouse of unbearable memories.

The house still held features she shuddered to dismiss. The empty little bedroom full of toys and books, with the lavender wallpaper sporting tiny white flowers became an unbreachable fortress at the end of the hall, a haunting specter of agonies. Lindsey couldn't stand the thought of getting rid of these things. It would be like getting rid of Emily. Yet, she couldn't bear to keep them, or even look at them.

Lindsey and Mitch moved in with Dottie, their older daughter, until things were settled. Dottie, of course, had plenty of room since her husband's death. The family members provided some comfort for each other, but the pain still raged in Lindsey. It was physically debilitating. Simple tasks seemed impossible and talking to Mitch about her despair was out of the question. That's why the voice of reason Lindsey might have provided if she had known of Mitch's plan to exact vengeance was never heard.

The two were grieving separately, and as Lindsey's grief had become pain, Mitch's grief had evolved into uncontrollable, boiling fury.

While Lindsey stayed home, crying and considering the black void that marked the future, Mitch was across town in his own grieving process. His mood was dour, yet excited. He planned to be at the Sample home by ten p.m., reasoning that he would find his target at home with a minimum of visitors. Ollman had nothing concrete on which to base his theory, but planning this offensive had been underway since the night of Emily's death, and his sour mood was attributable to the conflict within him. He had a job to do that was counter to all his training. Ollman was a peace officer, after all, and trained to use non-violent means rather than weaponry to settle disputes. But,   this was different.

That afternoon, he was in a restaurant in Macon having a large meal. The owner, Bert Billings, was a good friend, and his store-front steak house had been the venue for many Ollman family meals. Emily, Mitch thought, had really liked the surf and turf, so he ordered his last meal as a free man in his daughter's honor.

"Hey, Mitch, great to see you," Bert greeted as he came out of the kitchen and saw his good friend in a booth. "How are you doing, man? I'm happy to see you out and about after everything, um, that's happened. And how is Lindsey doing? Has she gone back to work yet?"

The question was difficult for Mitch to address. Lindsey's grief was so palpable, it unnerved him, making the fight with his own sadness more burdensome.

Mitch considered the timeless purgatory he and Lindsey were in and realized he couldn't answer his friend. He had no idea how Lindsey was doing. He could only see her through the filter of his own grief, and draw conclusions with questionable accuracy.

He knew he should have reached out to help his wife before now, but all of the things she had said and done, was saying and doing, revealed that any help he would offer would not be wanted.

Now, it was too late. By this time tomorrow he would be dead or in jail, and there would be no help left to offer. That was too bad, but he felt no guilt. He wasn't the one who caused this.

To his friend, Bert, he merely said, "It's a process. You know," and let it go. Bert clasped Mitch's shoulder for a moment, and left the man alone.

Mitch lingered over his lunch. He supposed it was delicious, as Bert's meals always were, but this afternoon, his food was tasteless. Still, it was worth savoring, given what the future had in store.

He ordered another beer.

When the check came, he paid the young woman who served him, and tipped her handsomely, tucking a twenty- dollar bill under the empty beer mug. He left with a regretful tugging of his heartstrings, walked across Macon's main drag, against the light, and marched into Shelby Sporting Goods. He would need shells for his service weapon—lots of them.

CHAPTER 86

"Hello," Inga trilled to the redhead wearing the pretty green blouse at the information desk. "My name is Inga MacDonald, and we're here to visit my daughter, Virginia Christmas, in the ICU. This is my granddaughter, Chelsea." As she spoke to the young woman, she saw her husband out of the corner of her eye. He spotted her at the same time and strode across the hospital lobby toward her. She subtly raised a hand to stop him. He noticed the gesture and stopped in his tracks.

"Yes ma'am," replied the receptionist, Roxy. "Just a moment while I get the information." Her eyes were glued to the computer monitor and Inga gestured to Joe to sit down. He complied.

"Yes, here she is," Roxy said after a moment. "Mrs. Christmas is in grave condition. I'm very sorry. She's in Room 8 of the ICU. You'll need to check in at the desk there. Take the elevator to the third floor, turn right and follow the signs to the ICU."

Inga thanked the woman and proceeded across the lobby to the elevators, holding Chelsea by her elbow. As she passed the sofa where Joe sat, she motioned him to follow.

Out of sight of the reception desk, Joe kissed his wife and nodded a greeting to Chelsea. "How're you doin', young lady?"

"Okay," she replied in a small voice. "Mrs. MacDonald told me my dad is in ICU, too."

"Yeah, girl, he is. It's a lot to handle. Will you be okay?" Joe asked.

"I don't know yet. I'm still awful scared."

"Sure." He met Inga's eyes. Inga hugged the girl and explained the next move.

"I'm gonna call Third and tell him you made it." He turned to Chelsea, "Are there any blood relatives we should call for you?"

"I don't think so. My real grandparents are dead, and I only have one great aunt in Kansas City, and she's been married so many times I don't even know her last name. Oh, God, if my mom dies, and I'm just with Dad . . ."

"Let's cross that bridge when we get to it, girl," Joe said. His gaze met Inga's again and she nodded. "I'm gonna find a phone. Then I'll wait for you here."

When the two women got on the elevator and the door closed behind them, Joe went to a pay phone in the lobby and called home. Young Joe answered right away, and issued an audible sigh of relief when he heard his grandfather's voice.

"What's the latest, Gramps?"

"Not much to tell, son. Inga and Chelsea got here a few minutes ago and they're headed to see Chelsea's mom. Her mother's in pretty bad shape, but we don't know much more than that."

"What about her dad?"

"He's here, too. Badly hurt, but not as badly."

"Okay, that's good. Do you understand now what I mean?" Joe asked his grandfather.

"About what?"

"About the things that happen—the little things that happen and change everything else. Like that time I was able to lead the sheriff to the drug dealer only because I got beat up at a party."

Gramps was quiet, not certain where his grandson was going with this.

Joe continued. "Then, yesterday, that government woman scared Chelsea out of her own house, and she came to our house. If she hadn't, if she'd stayed home, she might be dead or in ICU, too. The tiniest decision can change everything."

"Yeah, you're right about that. Thank God, she bolted from that house. Look here, about what you said before, I'm kinda sorry you aren't attracted to her just 'cause of what she's been goin' through. Not sure that's right—you know, to act like she's dirty or somethin."

"I don't know if I think that exactly. I still think she's beautiful—the most beautiful girl I've ever seen. It's more like, I don't know, it's bad enough that I know what's happened. But she knows that I know, so if I wanted to talk to her or anything, she might think that I think she's, you know, easy."

"I understand, Third. Listen, we may not be home for a while. We'll stay here with Chelsea until her mother improves and stabilizes, or goes the other way. You should fix yourself something when you get hungry, and I'll call you again when we're ready to come home. There ain't no point in you comin' back down here. There's nothing you can do but wait.

"There's another storm on its way tonight. Be careful coming home."

"All right."

CHAPTER 87

"Are you ever going to tell me where we're going?" Liz said to her husband as he hopped on the highway out of St. Louis. He'd been cryptic, and Liz had to wonder if a future with him would be filled with more off-putting sudden behaviors.

"I suppose. We're going to Sylvia," Joe responded.

"Sylvia! Why on earth? Joe, I didn't bring a toothbrush or a change of clothes or anything. This is nuts. What are you doing?"

"We'll stop at a Walgreens and get a toothbrush."

"Why are we doing this?"

"Because something is wrong up there, and Joey won't tell me what it is. He says it's none of my business. It's my family, yet it's none of my business. Can you believe that kid?"

Liz measured her words before responding. "You know, Joe, he's making friends up there. Maybe it isn't about your family and it really isn't any of our business."

"Joey told me that there's something wrong about one of his friends, but wouldn't say what. I just think — no, I'm sure — there's something I need to see about. We're going," he said.

"It's too late to go up there and come back tonight. That means staying the night, and if something is wrong, the last thing Inga needs is unexpected company. Let's go home. We'll call up there again and try to get something to put your mind at ease, but I'm not going to show up on the doorstep when they already have a lot on their plate. It's inconsiderate."

Her husband gritted his teeth, but he exited the highway and turned the car around.

CHAPTER 88

Jack Sample summoned whatever courage he possessed and approached Ernesto Soto. "Where are you going to spend the night?" he asked. He hoped the suggestion that he was unwanted at the Sample home would be sufficient to send the man on his way. Soto didn't take the hint, and the interruption only served to annoy him.

"I'm gonna stay right here. Where's dinner?" Soto replied, unmoved.

"We only have one bed," Jack countered, "and you won't be comfortable on the floor."

"Yeah, I guess I'll just have to sleep in the bed." Soto stared at Jack and jutted his chin forward with a sardonic smile that said volumes.

Jack started to object, but then the joke about the eight hundred-pound gorilla popped into his head. Where does it sleep? Wherever it wants. Soto, too, would sleep where he wanted.

"Man? You can't kick Sarah and me out of our bed. Look, I'm trying to be cool with you, but you barge in here . . ."

"Look," Soto said, standing up and towering over Jack. "I'm the least of your problems. You got me for one night. Not even one night, cause the night'll be a short one. You're too stinkin' stupid to know you're about to get raided. The sheriff is onto you and he's coming to get you in the morning. I intend to be gone, and you'll be too if you got any sense."

The color washed out of Jack's face. "How'd you know that?" he stammered.

"What they say in your country? A little bird?"

"What little bird? Please, Ernesto, tell me what's going on and how you know all this."

Soto walked toward Sample, reaching into his waistband and removing the loaded pistol. He brandished it in Jack's face. He grimaced at Jack, and spat between clenched teeth, "Dix has been paying off a deputy in the sheriff's department. A Jap named Nakamura or something. When Dix dumped me, I caught up with the guy. He told me the raid is planned for the morning. Where's that woman?"

"What woman?"

"Your woman, idiot. I expect a good hot meal for once and some sleep, and then we'll all head out. Together. We're a team now," he sneered.

Sarah stood at the top of the basement stairs, a basket of laundry under one arm. She was listening with interest. As she stepped to the landing, she saw the gun. She looked at Soto who snarled at her and said, "Make me something to eat. Now!"

She hesitated, fearful of making the wrong move.

"I guess you don't understand the word *now* do you, bitch?" Soto bared his teeth in an ugly grimace. "I'll explain it to you." He stepped to the playpen where baby Dustin had been roused by Soto's loud voice. Soto reached into the playpen with one immense hand, wrapped it around the baby's neck and lifted the child out by the head. Still holding the handgun in his other hand, he pointed it at the baby's head, touching Dustin with the barrel. "Do you understand this any better, bitch?"

"Nooooo!" Sarah shrieked. Dustin joined her with shrieks of his own.

"Oh, no, Ernesto, please. Please don't hurt the baby. We'll do anything you want. Dinner. Sure. What would you like to eat? Sarah and I will make it for you, just please don't hurt us. Please, man," Jack pleaded.

The attempt to placate the thug only seemed to empower him. His chest puffed with pride.

The baby, of course, continued squalling in pain and distress. Soto regarded the screaming, wriggling baby with an expression of disgust, as if he was holding something distasteful, like a filthy diaper or a dead squirrel.

"I hate these things," he muttered under his breath. "But, I guess I'm stuck with this one for now. Lead the way, man. We'll all go to the kitchen and make dinner." He waved the gun at the two, motioning them toward the kitchen door.

Once in the kitchen, Ernesto took a seat facing the couple. He held Dustin in his lap with one hand around his little waist, bouncing him on his knee as the child's crying settled down. If it weren't for the gun, an outside observer would think he was behaving like a loving, doting uncle instead of a maniac who was holding the child hostage. He had seen Rufina do this with her own children, and sometimes it quieted the squalling.

Sarah was paralyzed with fear, but she forced one foot in front of the other, forced each movement of her hands as she began dinner preparations. As the minutes slowed, punctuated by the occasional cries of her child, she prepared a meal for Soto while an equally terrified Jack Sample stood in a corner of the kitchen watching Soto's every move.

Dusty's a good baby. I hope nothing happens to him, Jack thought. At that moment, Jack realized he wasn't high. He didn't know whether his last dose had worn off, or if he'd been scared sober, but the familiar craving for his drug was starting anew.

The baby began to cry again.

"What in hell is the matter with this thing now?" Ernesto growled.

"He's hungry," Sarah answered. "And he probably needs a diaper."

"Okay, feed it and change it," he ordered. "But do it here on the floor where I can watch you. This gun will be pointed at its head the whole time, capeesh?"

Sarah washed her hands, left the food she was preparing, took the baby from Soto's knee and fell to her knees with him. She turned away from Soto as much as she dared, opened her shirt, and coaxed the baby to begin feeding. Soto leered with great interest as Sarah felt his eyes on her.

Jack reached into a cabinet and removed a disposable diaper. He set it on the table near Sarah.

Soto, following Jack with his eyes, sneered, "I'm hungry, asshole." He turned his attention back to Sarah's exposed breast.

As Jack resumed dinner preparation with direction from Sarah, he searched for things around him he could use as a weapon if the opportunity presented, but there weren't many. Most of the kitchenware was still in boxes, and Jack was a man predisposed to compliance and cowardice more than confrontation or heroism.

Spaghetti and meatballs were well underway by the time Dustin was fed and changed. Soto reached down between his feet and scooped up the baby again. Sarah began to cry. "Please, please don't hurt my baby," she began babbling. Fear drove the tears, but they only served to enrage Soto.

"Shut up, bitch. What time is it?"

"A little after nine," Jack responded, glancing at the clock on the stove.

"Where's the beer? You got more beer?"

Jack opened the refrigerator, took out a beer and tried to hand it to Soto. Without a free hand, Soto commanded, "Open it," and Jack complied.

Soto's hands were full, but the man with the immense grip managed to hold the gun and the beer in the same hand. This effort, with the potential for unintended gunfire, scared Sarah more than anything that had happened yet.

Soto took a long draw from his beer, licked his lips and leaned back in his seat. "I figure I'll sleep with the baby so you two won't try any tricks. You can sleep on the floor. If I hear a word from either of you, somebody will die, got it?"

The two nodded.

"We gotta be out early, so if you got an alarm clock, set it. That car in the driveway, it runs?"

The two nodded again. "Okay, then we'll take it. We leave here by six in the morning. You're driving, Jack. Your woman and the kid ride in the back with me. Now, how long before dinner?"

Sarah's hands trembled as she maneuvered pots and pans.

"Soto," Jack said, "How does the sheriff know that we live here? We went to a lot of trouble to hide out here. No one knew where we were."

"Some dude at the sheriff's office told him. A kid, I think. I think his name is Joe MacDonald. You know him?"

Sarah froze, only for a few seconds, but the pause was long enough to alert Jack. He turned to her.

"You know this guy, Sarah?"

She took a deep breath. "Sort of. A little. He gave me a ride a couple of times."

"Where does he stay?" Soto demanded.

"I never went to his house," Sarah explained. "I'm pretty sure he lives in Sylvia."

"Get a phone book," Soto demanded. "I want to know a street address. "We'll need new digs, and this house is going to become useless in a few hours. Do it!"

Jack left the room to find an old phone book that the previous tenant had left. Knowing Jack wouldn't pull any stunts while out of the room, Soto positioned the baby on his left hip with the gun in the same hand and walked over to Sarah at the stove. He leered at her, standing at her side.

Soto freed his right hand, reached forward and ripped open Sarah's shirt. "Let's have another look at 'em," he sneered.

CHAPTER 89

The youngest MacDonald tired of pacing the floor. As he put away dishes, Joe noticed something that gave him an idea. He pulled open a drawer and identified it as a junk drawer. That's what Liz called it anyway. Every kitchen has one. This one held a box of kitchen matches, assorted batteries, an ice pick, a box of paper clips and another of thumb tacks, an allen wrench, a flashlight, a stapler, and a wound-up phone cord.

Yeah, I thought I saw this in here, Joe thought. He reasoned that there were endless chores he could do if he just wasn't out of earshot of the cordless phone. The extra cord wouldn't help, though, without… there it was. A coupler to connect the two cords.

He connected two cords he needed and tested the phone outside. He had twenty more feet of phone line and a dial tone. Success! He did a test call to Jamal.

When Jamal answered the phone, Joe said, "Hey, man, how are you?"

"Hey, man, I was just gonna call you."

"Yeah, what for?"

"I dunno. What you doing?" Jamal asked.

"Look, I need a favor real quick. Can you call me?"

"Why would I call you when I got you on the phone already?"

"Oh, man, it's a long story. I want you to call me so I can test how far I can get from the base of this cordless phone and still get a ring. Okay?"

"Uh, sure, man. Hang up."

Joe disconnected and took the handset with him as he walked out toward the barn and across the yard. The phone rang, and continued to do so all the way to the water spigot.

"Hey, man, thanks," he said into the phone.

"No problem."

"What'd you want when you said you were about to call me?" Joe asked.

"Oh, uh, I just wondered if you got anything going on."

"That's a loaded question. My folks are at the hospital and I'm—"

"Oh, wow," Jamal interrupted. "What's up? They okay?"

"Yeah, they are," Joe explained. "But Chelsea's not." He explained the situation with the damaged house and the injuries to her parents.

"Yeah, okay," Jamal said, "So, you want some company while you wait? My mom's lying down with the baby, and I got her car and nothing to do."

"Oh, man! That'd be great! Come on over."

As he waited for Jamal's arrival, Joe drained the water trough for the cattle and ran fresh water in it. While the trough was filling, he whistled at Susie the Holstein, and she lumbered over to the fence, her calf alongside.

Joe petted the cow on her head, but what he really wanted was her calf.

Over the weeks he had lived in Sylvia, Susie had learned to come to Joe's whistle as Gramps had promised, and the calf came with her. Joe had loved the little calf from the first moment she had quietly walked up behind him in the field and licked the back of his bare knee. He had named the youngster Domino because of her black and white blotches.

He knelt on the grass and reached through the fence. He petted the side of her face with the tips of his fingers. She was soft, much softer than he ever expected a cow to be. A well of warmth and love rose in Joe and climbed up into his eyes, which watered with a swirl of emotions he didn't understand. Affection for his calf, but also for his farm and his grandparents, and for the life he was living now.

He wasn't anxious to go back to St. Louis. He didn't want to leave the animals, or the farm, or Gramps and Grams, or any of it.

He thought of his friends in St. Louis and the network there of sports and girls and occasional recreational substances that awaited his return, and the tug of war in his soul began.

Joe wiped his eyes and stood up. He gave Susie one last pat on her forehead and went back into the barn. The orange tabby cat, perched on a ceiling joist in the barn, meowed at him.

"Hi, Mary Lou," he spoke to her. "Where're the kids?" He looked around for kittens as the little black one, now two months old, came out from behind a bale.

It darted away as Joe approached, but Mary Lou climbed down off the joist and came to him. She rubbed her body against his leg, so he picked her up. Her purr was loud and pleasant. She patted his face with her paw.

This is a good place, he told himself. This family, this town, this farm.

CHAPTER 90

Sarah's slow, unstoppable climb towards panic accelerated when Ernesto Soto climbed into Sarah's bed with her baby. She thought of all the things that could go wrong, and each exacerbated her feelings of helplessness. Soto could roll over in his sleep and suffocate Dustin. He could lose his temper and kill Dustin. He could become incensed about nothing in particular, and hurt Dustin just for fun.

Adding to her panic, she couldn't call the police to remove Soto; the phone wasn't turned on yet, and even if it were, there was the matter of the basement full of methamphetamine equipment. She couldn't ask him to play nice and not hurt her child. She couldn't motivate Jack to do anything at all. She was on her own, and the drive to rid herself of the despicable criminal was becoming more acute by the minute.

Sarah's lifelong habit of burying her head in the sand and pushing obvious problems aside was reaching the end of its tenure. The fact filled her field of vision: she needed rid of Jack and his meth. She should have acted before Dusty was born, but she didn't, and now it was too late to pretend there was no problem.

She lay still on the living room carpet with a bath towel as a blanket, and stared at the ceiling. Jack, next to her, was completely zonked out. Down from his days-long high, the fatigue had caught up with him, and, she reasoned, a nuclear bomb would be insufficient to rouse him.

Sarah had never felt this alone. Overwhelming fear gripped her. There was no way, her instincts told her, that this was going to come out okay. Her home would be raided in a few hours, she and Jack had not concealed their criminal enterprise from anybody, and Ernest Soto was a very loose cannon. Sarah lay frozen, afraid to move and unable to focus on any options she might have. Her fear for Dustin alone, aside from what could happen to her and Jack, tightened its talons around her.

There would be no sleep for her. She would spend the next hours, while Soto slept, flitting mentally from one horrible scenario to the next. Sarah's unrest, in contrast to her snoring partner, magnified her fear with resentment, anger, and crushing responsibility.

A car came up the street, and as it rounded the corner, its headlights glinted on the ceiling over her head. The tree outside, bare of leaves because it was dying, was caught in the headlights and threw a shadow across her ceiling. The shadow of bare tree branches looked to the young woman like a cluster of bony, grasping hands, the shadowy manifestations of her worst fears, reaching out with gnarled fingers clutching at her.

Sarah squeezed her eyes shut.

CHAPTER 91

Okie Joe had come upstairs to the waiting room outside the ICU. Chelsea and Inga had gone inside shortly after Inga's arrival.

The ICU rules allowed for two family members at a time to visit for only ten minutes once an hour. As Joe waited, the two were inside on their third ten-minute visit. He considered his options. He should call Third. He'd do that as soon as his wife came out of the ICU. It was getting late, the hospital cafeteria was closed, and he was sure they were all hungry. He might need to find a place in town to get some sandwiches. The thought distracted Okie Joe from the worst-case scenario that had preoccupied him. According to the last doctor Inga talked to, the situation looked dire for Mrs. Christmas. Less so for the father, but if he recovered, he'd be in rehab for the foreseeable future.

Inside the ICU room, Chelsea sat in a chair at her mother's bedside. She held Virginia's hand and cried softly as she talked to her mother in hushed tones. "Please be okay, Mommy. Please get better."

Inga offered silent prayers for God's richest mercies from a discreet distance.

An Asian man in a white lab coat entered the room. He identified himself as Dr. Nakamura. He smiled at the young woman and her assumed grandmother.

"Where do you live?" he asked Chelsea.

"I'm from Monroe City, or I was before last night's storm."

"Ah, I see. And where will you be staying now?"

Inga wondered where this doctor was going with these questions. She didn't wait long for her answer.

"I'll be staying with Mr. and Mrs. — um, my grandparents. They live in Sylvia."

"Ah, yes," the doctor nodded. "Shelby County. I have relatives there.

"I want to be sure you have a place to stay. Your mother is in grave condition." He looked at Virginia's still form in the bed, her monitors blinking. "She is bleeding internally," he continued, "and I regret that our efforts to stop the bleeding have not been effective."

"What are you saying?" Inga asked. "What should we expect?"

Chelsea buried her face in her hands and sobbed.

"I'm afraid that she is unlikely to improve," the doctor said gently. "We're doing everything in our power."

Nakamura tightened and untightened his fist. For all his good intentions, he deeply disliked giving families news like this. He had been known to get hives when disclosing the imminent death of a patient.

"Your father, however, Miss Christmas," he continued will certainly improve. "His back is broken and he will have a long road ahead and need lots of rehabilitation therapy, but he'll be able to return to work eventually."

The doctor expected some sign of relief from Chelsea's body language, and wondered why it wasn't forthcoming.

The nurse entered the room to record the monitor readings. She and the doctor exchanged glances. "It's time for you both to step out," she reported. "You can visit again later."

Inga noticed the doctor's face and knew Virginia Christmas was going to die. "We'd like to stay a while longer," she said. "Just in case."

"That will be fine, nurse," the doctor agreed. The nurse nodded her understanding and left without a word. Nothing was to be gained by sending family out of the room.

"Miss Christmas," the doctor said to Chelsea, "there is no social worker on duty at this hour, but I think you should consider making arrangements for your mother's . . ." he trailed off. He paused, looking for the words that wouldn't come to him.

Inga sat a few minutes, unsure of her next move. She glanced up at the clock. It was ten o'clock. The three of them had been there for hours. Chelsea needed to eat something. The waffles she had prepared for Chelsea seemed like a long time ago.

"Chelsea?" she began.

Chelsea didn't respond at first. Her face was still buried in her hands. When she did look up, she looked only at her unconscious mother.

She stood, ignoring Inga, and leaned down close to her mother's graying face. She whispered something Inga couldn't hear, kissed her mother, and cried. "Please wake up, Mommy. Please, just once."

There was no response, of course. Inga stood, went to the bedside, squeezed Chelsea's arm. "I'll be back in a few minutes, Chelsea. I want to let Joe know what's going on." Chelsea nodded, eyes still on her mother.

CHAPTER 92

Joe called the only pizza delivery place within ten miles and ordered dinner for himself and Jamal. When it arrived, he mused to himself that this pizza, with pepperoni, sausage, mushrooms, shrimp, and pineapple, promised to be the worst meal he'd had in months.

Not much was on the television, but the two teens found a station out of Paris that played rotating reruns of Seinfeld, Roseanne, and The Cosby Show. Mostly it was background noise as the two conversed.

Joe discovered over the course of the evening that The Cranberries were Jamal's favorite white band, and though they were Irish, he found their alternative grunge rock appealing.

The boys debated about the popular female singers. Joe thought Mariah Carey was sexier than Whitney, but Whitney had the superior voice.

Michael Jackson was the best guy out there who could sing and dance, Jamal offered.

There was talk on the topic of the best-looking girl in Joe's high school and her knockers.

And so on.

"So, what's going to happen, man?" Jamal said as they started in on the pizza.

"To what?" Joe asked.

"To your girlfriend and her parents."

"I don't know. I'm waiting on a call to find out something."

"What d'ya think's gonna happen?"

"I think she'll end up staying here with us."

"Ah, man, you lucky bastard," Jamal quipped. "How do I never get that lucky?"

"It's not like that. I mean, sure I'd like to, but stuff has happened to the girl and, I dunno, it doesn't really . . . I mean . . . I don't really see myself . . . "

"You said she was hot," Jamal interrupted, losing patience with Joe's reticence.

"Oh, she is, she is," he assured his friend. "But she's got a lot of stuff to deal with, and I'm not going to talk about it until I know more. If she comes and stays here, then I'll feel responsible for her privacy, okay?"

"I don't know what in hell you're talking about," Jamal said, cracking a grin.

The phone rang, and Joe snatched it up.

"Third, it's me," came Gram's unmistakable voice. "How are you doing?"

"Fine, Gram. Jamal's here and we're hanging out waiting for you. What's going on there?"

"Well," Grams replied, "there's a lot to tell. Chelsea's father will be okay, but not for a long, long time. He'll have to go into rehab, and may not walk for a long while.

"Chelsea's mother, I'm afraid, is much worse and may not make it. I am praying for her every minute, but the doctor has left us with little hope."

"That's too bad, Grams. What about Chelsea? How's she dealing?"

"Well, Third, this is a troubling time. I don't know how she'll come out of this, but, for now, um, we'll give her the best support we can."

Joe replied. "Maybe I'll pray, too."

CHAPTER 93

Mitch Ollman hesitated before approaching the Sample front door. His first mistake, he noted, leaving his headlights on. As he turned into Sample's driveway, he'd forgotten to turn them off. He quenched them as soon as they shone straight through Sample's front window. Yet, he hoped, this late on at night, with an empty street, the occupants were asleep, and his plan was undetected.

He was off-kilter tonight — nervous, uncomfortable, and fully aware that the course of actions he planned for Jack Sample were illegal at least, and immoral at most.

Ollman hadn't seen the inside of the new Sample home, of course. He didn't know what the layout would be, or that when he entered, the living room would be on the left of the entryway, and the bedroom on the right. When he broke through the front door with a mighty heave of his shoulder, the door banged open with little resistance, but that would be the end of his element of surprise.

Gun drawn, he marched in and immediately saw Sarah in the living room on his left. She wore shorts and a tee shirt and had a brown towel wrapped around her. Jack Sample was asleep next to her. Even the sharp sound of the door banging open didn't arouse the meth addict.

Sarah, however, was wide awake, and the surprise on her face was coupled with a level of fear Ollman didn't expect. He tightened his grip on his pistol and pointed it at Sarah. Her fear mounted. Here it was, in living color, she was thinking — one of the dreaded scenarios she had just been sifting through her sleepless imagination.

Mitch stepped into the living room. In so doing, he turned his back on the closed door to the right of the entryway.

Almost immediately, the bedroom door opened, and Ernesto Soto stepped out. He wore nothing but boxer shorts. His brown skin, smooth and flawless, stretched over a huge frame. To the untrained eye, Soto's size may have suggested fat, but bare-chested, there was no question about his toned musculature.

He curled his massive hand into a hard fist and punched Mitch in the side of the head. Mitch went down, and his gun flew across the room.

Sarah recognized the sheriff from local bus stop benches and from the gold minivan she had noticed down the block. Certain doom was upon her. The panic within her that she thought could not possibly become worse did exactly that.

She glanced over at Jack. His snoring continued uninterrupted.

Then she looked up at Ernesto. When their eyes met, Soto flew into a rage, spewing a loud, long string of curses in Spanish.

The baby began to cry from the bedroom and to Sarah's dismay, the sound vexed Soto even more.

He kicked the delirious Ollman in the ribs repeatedly as the sheriff languished on the floor, each kick bringing more unintelligible cursing.

Mitch lay very still, faking unconsciousness and gathering himself. He wondered if Soto realized he'd brought a gun. Between the darkness in the room, the silencing quality of the carpet, and Soto's irrational rage, it was possible that Mitch may still have an advantage.

"Who is this ass hole?" Soto bellowed at her over and over.

"I don't know," she lied. "I really don't know. I swear. God, Soto, leave him alone. Let me go to Dustin. Please?"

The commotion finally broke through Jack's consciousness. "What's going on?" he asked, rubbing sleep from his eyes. Then, a moment later, "Who's this guy?"

"I don't know, Jack," Sarah cried. "He just broke through the front door."

Mitch lay still, clutching his bruised ribs. He cautiously opened his eyes and looked around, spotting his gun a few feet away. If he moved forward as little as ten or twelve inches, he might reach it. He said a silent prayer that the woman would keep Soto distracted just long enough to give him the chance.

"Yeah, get up," Soto barked. "We're leaving! Now!"

Soto turned back into the bedroom, and Mitch took a chance. He pushed himself forward, reached under the chair, and grabbed his pistol. Almost blinded by the pain, he struggled to his feet.

Jack and Sarah saw the gun at the same time. Their faces changed together. But they remained quiet. For Sarah, the gun meant a potential escape from this hoodlum whose presence was a much larger threat than the gun itself.

Jack's position was foggier. He didn't go much farther than vaguely wishing he was somewhere else.

Mitch held his right rib cage with his left hand while waving the gun at Jack and Sarah. He motioned them quiet, and they both nodded in collusion. As Mitch's eyes met Sarah's, he realized that she wanted rid of Soto every bit as much as he did.

It was at that moment that Soto returned to the living room wearing pants. He spotted Mitch's gun and without hesitation, he drew his own gun and fired, catching Mitch in his right shoulder.

Mitch fell, screaming. His gun dropped from his hand, and Soto stepped forward and picked it up.

"How many people know you're here?" he bellowed at Mitch. "How many?" He punctuated his query with a sharp blow to Mitch's wounded shoulder with the butt of the gun. Blood gushed from the shoulder and soaking into the beige carpet.

Mitch gasped in pain, but didn't answer.

Sarah began to cry.

Jack, fully awake now, pleaded, "Ernesto, just leave him alone. He can't do anything. Don't make it worse. Please."

"Here's what's gonna happen, you stupid, girly man. You're gonna pick him up and get him in your car. Get in the car with this bitch. I'm gonna hold the brat and sit in the front seat while you drive. And bring the rest of the beer. And some snacks if you can find any."

Soto eased Mitch's gun and his own into his waistband. Then he stepped back into the bedroom and picked up the screaming baby.

While he did that, Sarah dropped to her knees and grabbed the towel she had been using as a blanket. She tied it firmly around Mitch's shoulder and tightened it into a knot. It was something she'd seen in a movie somewhere.

Mitch cringed and took a deep breath. The pain was immense, but he knew the bleeding had to be stopped.

"What are you doing?" Soto snarled.

"Trying to stop him from bleeding to death," she said.

"No, bitch, I want him to bleed to death."

Sarah looked at the sheriff and he looked at her. "No, Soto, you don't. You'll need him for another hostage. Take him with us."

Soto considered the suggestion. "Yeah, you're right. This way he can't call for help. Get him in the car."

"Where are we going?" Sarah asked.

"We're gonna go see your friend, Joe MacDonald, bitch," Soto retorted. "From the address in the phone book, it sounds like a quiet place in the country. Not so many neighbors."

Sarah spoke to Mitch. "I'm gonna put my hand right here. You lean on me, okay?" She noticed the deep expression of pain on Mitch's face and tried to articulate her regret with a sympathetic expression of her own. "Help me, Jack," she ordered.

Jack complied, his knees wobbly as much from fatigue as fear. He put his arm under the bad shoulder.

The sheriff screamed in pain.

"Come on," she said, "Let's get you to the car."

CHAPTER 94

"This is Cow-Pie Radio broadcasting to you from Sylvia in Shelby County. I'm Mark Stevens. Tonight's forecast is another scary one, folks. Let's hope we don't have a repeat of last night, but we just might. The National Weather Service predicts violent storms for the three-county area, and a tornado watch is in effect until 2:00 a.m. Keep your radio dial right here on 890 AM, Cow-Pie Radio, Sylvia. I'll let you know the minute I get an update.

"Folks, be ready to take shelter against these storms. Possible tornadoes have been spotted with at least three systems moving east through the Highway 36 corridor."

CHAPTER 95

Chelsea sat on the edge of her mother's hospital bed, gazing at the comatose woman, and silently pleading with her to live. The monitors beeped and hummed softly a monotone melody Chelsea would remember for the rest of her life.

She sat in this position for at least an hour, not moving. She noted that a fierce storm had begun, as pelting rain assaulted the dark window. She heard grumbling thunder, and it matched her sense of doom. Chelsea stood, circled the room, looked out the window, and returned to her seat. The nurses left her alone, as did Inga, who went out to the waiting room and sat with Joe. The two held hands, each lost in thought, as they considered actions to take based on a variety of contingencies.

Abruptly, Joe asked, "Did you talk to the county about us taking care of Chelsea?"

"Yes, I did," Inga responded. "The woman I talked to said that the storm damage would leave many families homeless, and so she would fast-track our foster care application so she could concentrate on storm victims."

"That's good," Joe answered.

"But for now, she told me that Chelsea should stay with us until this crisis is past. Then we can expect a visitor or an inspector of some kind. "There'll be paperwork down the road, too," she remarked.

"We'll cross that bridge then."

More silence between the two as the minutes ticked by. Inga stood and checked on the girl three or four times through the glass door.

After the fourth trip, she sat with her husband and said, "Do you think we should call Third again?"

"There's nothing to tell him. You said he was hanging out with Jamal. They'll be fine. Maybe he's taught Jamal to shovel chicken shit." He cracked a smile as he thought of the Detroit teen who had, no doubt, never done such a thing in his life.

Inga, reading his mind, said, "Third had never shoveled shit either when he came to us." She smiled.

"Yeah, it was funny then, too."

"A lot of water's gone under the bridge since then."

"What's the best part, you think?"

"Part of what? Third staying with us? To tell you the truth, Joe, I love the boy. I do. But the best part is that we're a lot closer now to reconciling with our boy because of Third."

"I was thinkin' the same thing," Joe said. "But it's been mostly on you. I guess it's my turn to make some peace between us if I can."

"That would be a very good thing to do," his wife agreed. "It's been a long time."

On the other side of the glass door in Room 8 of the ICU, Chelsea continued to gaze at her mother's face and hold her hand. She was startled when Virginia's eyes opened. When she saw Chelsea, a spark of recognition lit her eyes.

"Momma?"

Virginia closed her eyes again and the heart monitor flat-lined.

Chelsea ran from the room and screamed, "Help! Help!" at the nurse station. Then she dashed back in the room, moments ahead of two nurses. One of them pushed Chelsea out of the way as a cart with a defibrillator was pushed up next to the bed.

Chelsea stood in a corner, crying, as the staff attempted to get Virginia back. But the defibrillator failed. One of the nurses called the time. "Ten twenty-seven p.m."

Bitter reality enveloped Chelsea. She sobbed as never sobbed before . The reality closed in on her, of her father's abuse, her hopeless poverty, her mother's failing business, and her empty future. Her mother had been her only friend, only resource, only bright spot in her ugly young life. Despair gripped her.

CHAPTER 96

Joe and Jamal finished the pizza and settled in with a VHS tape of Die Hard 2: Die Harder, laughing at Bruce Willis' improbable stunts.

Joe answered the phone before the first ring was done.

"Hello?"

"Oh, hey, Joe," the smooth, masculine voice of Don Armstead answered. "This is Chief Don, Jamal's dad."

"Hey, Chief. Hold on. Jamal's in the can."

"That's okay. I'll talk to you until he gets out. What're you all doing tonight?"

"We're watching a movie," Joe replied. "It's pretty good. You like Die Hard?"

"Sure. That guy would o' been killed fifty times in those movies if they were real, though."

"Yeah, right. We were just saying that. Hey, look, my family isn't back from the hospital yet, and I have nothing to do but wait for them. Can I ask Jamal to stay the night and keep me company?"

"You're a little old for sleepovers, aren't you?"

"Yeah, I guess, but as long as Jamal's here, I can keep my mind off of other things."

"Well, let me talk to Jamal first and then decide, okay?"

"Uh, sure. Here he is," Joe said handing the phone to his friend with his hand covering the mouthpiece. He whispered, "Tell your dad you wanna spend the night."

"I do?"

"Yeah, man. I already asked him."

Jamal stood over his friend on the sofa. "Hi, Dad. Look, Joe wants me to sleep over. Can I?"

"No, son, why don't you come on home now?"

"Aw, why, Dad? I'd like to stay and keep Joe company."

"I know, but some other time. I'd like you home tonight. There's another storm fixin' to roll through, and it looks like it'll be another bad one."

"Joe's okay. We're not doing anything wrong."

"I know that, Jamal. Come home anyway. This storm system may be worse than last night and I want you home safe."

"Oh, okay. I'm on the way."

Jamal disconnected and looked at Joe. "Sorry, man. My dad is real worried about this storm. Says it may be worse than last night."

"Wow. I may have to go to the cellar. I've been down there a lot this summer."

"Yeah, I know," Jamal agreed. "I talked to this dude in Shelbina who lives out on a farm, and they have a storm cellar. This dude is sixteen, and he said he's lived there since birth and had never gone to the cellar for a storm this many times, until this year, and he's been down there four times since May."

"Wow," Joe repeated, "I guess it's right what everyone says, that the weather this summer is freaky weird." He walked his friend to the door and opened it.

"Hey, thanks for coming over and hanging out with me."

"No problemo, man. I hope everything comes out all right with your girlfriend and her family."

"Yeah."

"Next time we hang out, 'Total Recall,' okay?"

CHAPTER 97

Liz MacDonald had spent the previous hours trying to convince her husband that they shouldn't go to Sylvia.

It was rude and inconsiderate to Inga, she thought, to drop in late in the evening, expecting to be fed and housed with no prior warning.

"Liz, okay, I hear you. But, my mom is always ready for company, and we aren't really company anyway; we're family.

"Joe, you went years not really talking to your folks. Now you have a chance to reconnect. Don't you want to even start by being considerate? Let's call ahead."

Liz made her case as best she could. Whatever was afoot in Sylvia could only be made worse by their arrival, she and Joe could be walking into a mess that would embarrass and upset the parties involved.

Her husband countered. "That's exactly why we should go," he argued. "Something was going on, and I want to pitch in and help."

Liz repeated that Joe and Inga were obviously fine and had not solicited assistance from him.

Truthfully, Joe acknowledged only to himself, he had felt so isolated from his family for so many years that the recent re-con-necting of his life with theirs because of Joey had made him crave the intimacy he had missed for so long. Add to that, he knew his parents, and he knew that helping others was part and parcel of the MacDonald paradigm he had rejected for so many years. He want-ed the feeling of belonging again. He wanted to help them help, to show them he was still one of them.

He never admitted to Liz that he was embracing his failure and trying to atone. He just insisted she get in the car.

Liz, in a last ditch effort, suggested they phone Sylvia before starting out, but Joe would have none of it . He had formed a self-ag-grandizing scenario in his mind where, upon arrival in Sylvia, his presence would somehow be a godsend to his family. He wanted the element of surprise.

CHAPTER 98

It was about eleven-thirty when Chelsea and the elder MacDonalds pulled onto the property in Sylvia. Joe was still up, pacing the floor. He needed no explanation for what had happened at the hospital. The entire story was on Chelsea's face when she entered the house. Her puffy red eyes said it all. Joe didn't know what to do, but Inga did.

"Are you hungry, Chelsea? You haven't had a decent meal since this morning. You must be hungry. What would you like to eat?"

"I'm not sure if I'm hungry or not, Mrs. MacDonald," she replied. "My stomach is pretty much in knots."

"I understand. I've found at times like these that it's best to listen to your body. What would you like to do right now? Sit up and talk? Sit up alone? Try to get some sleep? We're here to help you however we can."

"I don't know."

"Okay, dear. Tell me if you need anything. I'm going to turn in if you don't mind. I'll see you in the morning. Wait. What's going on?"

A vehicle pulled onto the MacDonald property and parked in front of the house. Inga looked out the front window. She didn't recognize the rusty sedan, nor any of the people who began to get out.

"Joe!" she called upstairs. "Come down here, please. We've got company."

Joe came down the stairs fastening the bolt on the shoulder of his overalls. As he did, a loud clap of thunder sounded.

Inga winced.

"Do you know that car?" his wife asked him as she peered out the window again. Joe joined her at the window, and shook his head.

"Maybe they're out of gas or something," Inga said. "Oh, look, someone is hurt. Three men and a woman. And one of them has a baby." Inga described the visitors in detail for her husband. As the rain began falling in torrents and lightning lit the sky, there was a brief flash of illumination, and in that moment, Okie Joe could see well enough to know he didn't recognize the visitors.

Most Sylvians didn't lock their doors. There was no need. Sylvia was peaceful, and serious crime was unheard of. It didn't occur to Okie Joe or Inga to run to the door and bolt it.

Inga's misplaced concern as the visitors came up the steps was getting them in and away from the storm. Wind was whistling and whipping around the house as thunder grumbled overhead.

Water sprayed the windows, obscuring Inga's view. She was barely able to make out the visitors and describe them to Joe. One man and the woman eased the sick or injured man up the steps while the very large man with a baby followed behind. He held the baby in one arm. The other arm was at his side. In his hand, it looked like he had a gun. She processed what she saw as best she could, even explained it to Joe. But it was foreign and out of context.

Young Joe appeared at the bottom of the stairs. "What's going on?" he asked, watching his grandparents at the window.

"Nothing good," his grandfather told him. "We've got company, and one of them seems to be armed." Gramps' tone was more curious than alarmed.

"What? What on earth? Is the door locked? I'm calling the police."

Joe made his point, but not in time. Ernest Soto lurched across the screened porch and pushed the door open with no resistance from the residents. Another boom of thunder punctuated his entrance.

He stepped into the entryway, brandishing the gun. "Hey, nice to meet you," he grinned sardonically with his thick Mexican accent. "I'll be staying here for a while."

Jack and Sarah brought up the rear as they eased Mitch Ollman into the entryway with Sarah's shoulder under Ollman's good one. Jack wore an ambiguous expression of apology and fear.

As the two cleared the door, Mitch looked up and his eyes met the elder MacDonald. A simultaneous look of recognition and a plea for anonymity passed between the two. Okie Joe put on his best poker face. He grasped Inga by the elbow and guided her into the kitchen with young Joe and Chelsea. Young Joe's demeanor was one of more worry and panic, while Chelsea looked to Inga like she would collapse from stress, exhaustion and horror at any moment.

When the group entered the large kitchen, Soto ordered the MacDonalds and Chelsea to line up next to the counter.

"Put your buddy in that chair," he ordered Sarah. Sarah, obliging, lowered the sheriff into a kitchen chair that stood at the table. "Keep your hands where I can see 'em. That's all of you, get it?"

His eyes rested on Chelsea. "What's the matter with you?" he snarled,. When she didn't answer, he demanded, "Huh? What's the matter with you?"

"My mom just died," she whispered.

"Well, ain't that a bitch?" More mocking smiles. "You're a fine girl, though. Pretty fine." He looked her up and down, his eyes lingering on her chest.

The storm was intensifying, and Inga desperately wanted to move away from the kitchen window. She craved the comfort of her storm cellar, but she'd have to calm her fears with the steel of her own will.

Just then, another loud clap startled her. Inga looked out the window and into the sky.

As the continual lightning lit up the sky, Inga saw a thick black cloud start to rotate. It formed a tornado before her eyes.

As she watched, the panic became a metallic taste in her mouth. She couldn't tear her eyes away from the monster in the sky. Her husband noticed it, too, and color drained from his face. He guessed the twister was two, maybe three miles across the corn fields and headed straight toward them. He couldn't gauge how much time they had before it got to the house, but it wasn't a lot.

Paralyzed though she was, Inga's attention returned to the kitchen where the immense man presented a more imminent threat. This must be, she noted, the one time when a tornado approaching her home was not the worst threat ahead of her. She forced herself to concentrate instead on the menace before her in her kitchen. The look on Soto's face frightened Chelsea, but it horrified Inga. There was something about him that seemed familiar. Distant memories she preferred to keep buried surfaced, increasing her fear ten-fold.

"There any beer in that fridge, old man?" Soto asked, turning his attention to Okie Joe.

"No. We don't keep any liquor in the house," he lied.

"Any food?" Soto continued.

No one said anything. Instead, the baby began crying again, and Soto, exasperated with the noise, bellowed, "Is the little shit hungry again?"

The hypocrisy was lost on no one that Soto resented the baby crying for food when he had, in essence, done the same thing a moment earlier. In another circumstance, it would be laughable.

"Yes, I guess so," Sarah put in. She stepped toward Soto, arms outstretched, anxious to take the baby from him, but Soto pulled the baby back.

"No, you kneel here and feed it so's I can get a good look at those titties this time." He leered at her. "Do it!"

Sarah forced a halt to her tears as she unbuttoned her shirt and prepared to nurse the baby. The others looked away in an empty attempt to offer her privacy.

As the baby fed, and Soto grinned lecherously at Sarah's exposed breast, the whooshing of storm water against the window reached a momentary zenith.

"Uh, mister," Okie Joe began, "we're really not safe here. There's a twister I can see from the window, and it's coming this way . . . "

"Shut up, ass hole!" bellowed the giant.

He then turned his gaze on Chelsea. "C'mere, little girl," he commanded. "You a fine little girl, I tell you that. Let's have a look at your titties, too, huh?"

At that moment, a clap of thunder sounded loudly as if it were right over the house. There was a palpable shaking of the house foundation, and everyone started. But Soto seemed oblivious.

The baby, the most startled, shrieked.

"Madre de Dios, make it shut up!" Soto bellowed . "Jesus, God, I've had enough of that noise." With that, he grabbed little Dustin under his chin, lifted him away from Sarah, and tossed the baby across the floor with his left hand. His right hand still held the gun, lifted it, and fired at the shrieking baby.

"No! No!" Sarah howled. She pitched herself across the floor toward the child. The baby's midsection was laid open. Sarah pressed her hand over the child's wound, but his shrieking quieted to eternal stillness, and Sarah howled and roared her empty protests as grief consumed her. The others gasped and moved closer together as if becoming one solid mass could save them from a similar fate.

Jack Sample stared, shaking his head. "Oh, God, what'd you do that for? Oh, God, oh, God."

Soto, still brandishing the gun, stepped toward Jack, and leaned down into his face. "You gonna start whining, too? I can put another shell in your gut just as easy." He pointed the gun at Jack's jaw.

Mitch Ollman had flinched with the impulse to help when the gun went off, but he recognized his helplessness . He sized up the scene. He had civilians, unarmed, elderly in some cases, and no firearm. Sitting in silence, he watched Soto, calculating, waiting for an opportunity to act. He watched the gun as the killer waved it about. It was a compact Glock nine millimeter, and held fifteen rounds. Soto had more than enough firepower to kill everyone in the house, unless he had already fired off some rounds before the confrontation at Sample's house. But Mitch had no way to know if he had, and he guessed Soto wouldn't be sharing the knowledge. In his condition, with the bleeding slowed, but the pain searing his shoulder, there was little chance he could overcome Soto without the help of the MacDonald men.

Soto not only had his nine-millimeter Glock, but also Mitch's gun, he reminded himself. As Mitch analyzed and assessed all permutations and possibilities for mounting a coup against this maniac, Inga and Chelsea did their best to mute their cries of anguish over the murder of the infant.

But Chelsea's efforts, on top of all she had endured that day, were not enough. She gasped and whimpered, calling Ernesto's attention back to her. He turned and moved toward Chelsea. He grabbed her right breast and squeezed. He pointed the gun at her cheek. The young girl froze with panic. "Take it off," he whispered. "The shirt. Take it off."

"Wait just a minute!" Okie Joe objected.

"Look, jack ass, this is real easy," Soto interrupted. "I have the piece." He waved the gun at Okie Joe. "And if I want to get me a piece right now, I will. I can take what I want or I can kill this girl and you while I'm at it. Makes me no difference. All I need is one hostage. The rest of you people are just, how do you Americanos say, baggage?"

Turning back to Chelsea, he commanded, "Take off your clothes and lie down on the floor."

Chelsea burst into tears, but she complied. She'd been through this before. Not exactly this, but close enough. Her tears fell as they often did when her father had made a similar demand, because the lesson learned was that fighting back just made it worse.

As she stripped off her tee shirt and jeans, Soto, using his free hand, extracted Mitch Ollman's gun from his waistband and set it in a kitchen drawer. Any attempt to retrieve it would be stopped by one of his own bullets.

Soto then unfastened his pants and positioned himself over Chelsea.

Inga, watching, appeared hypnotized by the Mexican, as he somehow connected her to her distant past. Buried memories flooded into her conscious mind and reawakened the fear and loathing from her own childhood. And the heroism.

Outside, the sounds of the storm grew louder—rhythmic, like a nearby freight train racing along its track.

"Mister, that twister's almost here," Okie Joe said. "It's comin' right at us. We need to take shelter."

Soto ignored him. He knelt between Chelsea's legs as she whimpered. She shut her eyes, wincing in dread.

"You all don't move or I'm gonna put a bullet in her head, right?" The brute leaned on the hand with the gun in it, pointing it at Chelsea's head, as he lowered his body.

Inga felt faint. She had to do something to stop this. Her fear and rage melded together with her memories.

She glanced around for a weapon. Third, she noted, had cleaned up the kitchen and put all the knives in drawers. But then she saw the waffle iron on the counter near her.

Knowing its heft, she clasped it with both weak, arthritic hands and lifted it.

Some distant voice in her head acknowledged the danger to Chelsea of possibly causing the gun to go off, but Inga's careful observation suggested that the beast was too intent on his actions to note that his gun had shifted in direction.

She brought the heavy appliance down on the back of Soto's head and it made a wet awful thunk. Blood spurted immediately as the brute fell on Chelsea, unconscious.

As he did, the gun went off. Okie Joe screamed, "Ah, God, I'm hit!"

Inga could see in her mind's eye her own mother so many decades ago pounding Inga's own rapist with a shovel, pounding and pounding. The memory drove her. She lifted the waffle iron and hit Soto a second time, a third.

The rest of the room became a blur of motion. Third grabbed the waffle iron from Grams and set it back on the counter while she ran to her husband. Blood shot from Soto's wound. Chelsea was squirming her way out from under him.

Okie Joe fell to the floor and grasped his bleeding ankle. It looked like a superficial graze, and Inga thanked the Lord.

Mitch Ollman struggled to his feet and spoke, "Where are you hit, Okie Joe?"

"My ankle caught it, Mitch. I'll be okay. We gotta get out of here now!"

"I know, Joe."

Sarah, kneeling by her baby's corpse, lifted it into her arms and rose to her feet. Her sobs were uncontrolled.

Jack Sample stood by, frozen, lethargic from his days without rest and the residual effects of his beloved chemical companion.

Mitch turned to Jack. His sworn enemy, the chemist whom Mitch had gone to Elsa to kill, was now no more than a pathetic loser. His anger remained. His little girl was still lost, but Jack was no threat. He was a brown recluse spider — poisonous, but easy to swat.

Mitch spat, "Sample, be useful for once in your life and help Mr. MacDonald."

Chelsea was wiggling back into her clothes. As she zipped her jeans, she looked at Joe, embarrassed and helpless.

Joe took that as his cue. He grasped Grams' panic and Gramps' injury and recognized his new standing as the ranking uninjured MacDonald, and the onus was on him to save these people.

He spun around and flung open the junk drawer, extracting the flashlight. He slid it across the table and into Chelsea's hands.

"Out the back door and to the right," Joe commanded, struggling to be heard over the storm. "You'll see it, Chels. It's just a little ways. About twenty feet or so. Get the door to the cellar open. Hurry!"

"The storm's coming from the west," Okie Joe shouted to the others. "That means the house is between it and the cellar. We can make it, but we've got to go. It's just about on us!

"Baby, baby, you go with Chelsea and get under cover," Okie Joe said to Inga. "I'll be all right." Now on his feet with Jack's help, he took a halting step with a wince of pain. Blood was soaking his sock and shoe, as the sticky wetness melded his sock to his flesh. He opened another drawer, yanked out a handful of dishtowels, and shoved them in his pockets.

Getting to the cellar would be a challenge, but his most pressing task was to get everyone underground. He nudged Inga toward Chelsea who was opening the door. As she did, a blast of wind that seemed alive and sentient roared into the kitchen, bringing rain and debris with it.

Jack, heeding the sheriff's demand, wrapped his skinny, poorly muscled arm around the elder MacDonald's waist and moved him toward the door. Joe leaned on the dealer and hobbled toward the exit. Young Joe helped the sheriff, as Sarah carried her baby's lifeless body.

As the group exited the kitchen, a tree branch hit the kitchen window, shattering it. Glass flew and caught the sheriff in the face as he lurched toward the door. It caught Sarah, too, lacerating her forehead next to her eye. Numbed by grief and panic, she showed no reaction. Like a robot, one foot stepped in front of the other without cognition.

Together the group filed out the door and struggled to the cellar, as they were soaked with cold rainwater, and the wind threatened to take them off their feet. Inga glanced behind her at the tornado, an immense cloud of boiling fury, too big for her to see its perimeter. It was nearly on them, and Inga felt her feet try to lift off the ground. Sleet and hail pummeled the group.

Inga reached the storm cellar a step or two behind Chelsea. She would wonder later how she was able to function at all in her terror. Together, the two eased the two by four off the hooks on the door and swung it open. Inga tossed the board down the two stairs and followed it. The sound of the tornado was deafening and she saw motion in the black sky. The wind blew sideways, catching debris and posing an additional threat. The twister was on her property, enveloping her house, mere feet away, as the force of wind tried to pull her back out of the cellar. She could become airborne at any second.

Chelsea was right behind her.

Inga turned around and cried out through the open door, "Joe! Joe!" Hail pelted her in the face. Her voice was carried away by the wind. She couldn't even hear herself, let alone expect her husband to hear her.

"We're here, Gram's," Third yelled, as he eased the sheriff down into the cellar. Jack, holding Okie Joe, descended the two plank stairs behind him.

Once everyone was in, the younger Joe closed the door, and fastened it tight.

The rush of wind, the clacketing of hail on the door, the distinctive freight train sound and the bellowing thunder drowned out the whimpering and crying of Chelsea, Inga, and Sarah. Okie Joe held Inga in his arms as she sobbed. Young Joe stood near Chelsea but didn't dare to touch her.

Mitch eased himself onto the floor as Sarah sat near him. She turned her back to Jack.

"If that Mexican wakes up, he'll kill us all," Chelsea sobbed.

"Yeah, he will," put in Mitch, "but I'm pretty sure he's not going to. I think Inga fixed him pretty good."

No one spoke as the group listened to the violence outside. Flying debris banged against the door to their shelter and provided a cacophony of frightening sounds—shattered glass, tortured tree branches, ripping and tearing.

After a few minutes, Okie Joe's adrenalin settled. "Hey, I got a question," he winced. He was wrapping a towel around his bloody ankle and handed another towel to Sarah as he motioned to indicate the blood on her face.

He turned to the sheriff. "What in the hell happened, Mitch? How'd that mess end up at my door?"

"Joe, I'm sorry. I really am. I'd never have brought this on you. The department has known for a while that we have a mole—someone telling the drug dealers what we're planning. We believe the mole told Soto–that's the gunman's name—we were planning a raid on his supplier's place in the morning." He looked straight at Sample and narrowed his eyes.

"Wait! What? You're the sheriff?" Jack asked.

Sarah shook her head in exasperation even as she continued sobbing. "Jack, you clueless bastard. You stupid, clueless ass, you killed my baby!"

Jack stepped forward, arms outstretched as if to hug her. She pushed him away roughly. As Jack stepped back, he stepped on Dustin's lifeless little hand where Sarah had set him on the dirt floor. He jerked his foot away, but not before Sarah saw it.

"Sarah, Ernesto killed Dusty. You know that. You saw him."

"Ernesto is a crazy man. I blame you! You had to hook up with that maniac and his friend. This is on you, Jack," she screamed, dissolving into renewed cries. She stood in the dark room and punched her fists into Jack's shoulders and stomach. Her small stature made little effect physically, but Jack embraced her message.

When she collapsed in more tears, Sample turned to the sheriff. "Um, sir," he began, "what do you think it would get me if I told you who your mole is?"

"How would you know?" Mitch asked with great interest.

"Soto told us his partner, Dix, had been paying off one of your deputies."

"Which deputy?"

"See, that's what I'm saying, man. What can I get for the information? I know I'm going away for a long time. I'm just trying to get a little consideration from the cops."

Jack's outrageous appeal for clemency enraged Mitch. But without his gun, trapped in a cellar, with terrifying noises outside and no escape in sight, Mitch had few resources. He heaved a heavy sigh and resigned himself to a continuance of his own vengeance. Instead, Mitch turned to Sarah. "Sarah, you blame him for killing your son. Well, I blame him for killing my daughter, so you and I have a common thread, don't you think?"

Sarah looked at the sheriff for several seconds before she replied in a tone that was menacing in its serenity. "Yes, Sheriff Ollman, I do think we're connected. Your mole is a guy named Nakamura." With that, she turned and glared at Jack in disgust.

Mitch's lips parted in unmasked surprise. He had thought highly of Nakamura. So had Bill Fast. They would never have guessed.

"Sarah," Jack whispered. "Why would you tell him that?" But he knew even as her name left his mouth that any connection he had to her died with Dustin.

The noises outside the cellar intensified, and Inga's panic reached a zenith. What she heard was not just pelting hail and cracking thunder. She felt certain she could hear the trembling crack of wood. She pictured her home being demolished with each thunderclap while she trembled helplessly. She winced and jumped with every sound. She held her husband's hand.

"Baby," he said. "We're alive and we're here. Third is here with us. No matter what goes on outside, we're safe. In the morning, we'll see how bad it is, but for now, it's okay. Do you hear me? We're going to be okay."

"Do you mean we have to stay here all night?" Chelsea asked Gramps.

"No way to know, miss. Better settle in." He lowered himself to the floor and tugged on Inga's hand to indicate she should join him.

Seven people crowded inside the cellar was way beyond its capacity. The seven sat close together under the bare forty-watt bulb.

The air was moist and hot. All were breathing hard from panic and adrenaline, soaking the air further.

"Let's all try our best to stay calm," Okie Joe advised. "The air in here will get stale fast with all these people, so let's make it last. I think, if we open the door and let in more air, the wind'll catch it and we'll never get it closed. We've got to hope and pray this storm passes quickly so we can get out. Meantime, there's nothin' to be gained by blame and accusations." He glanced at Mitch as he spoke the last.

The noises outside intensified and culminated in a huge banging thud against the door.

"What in hell was that?" Mitch asked.

"I don't know," the younger Joe replied, "but I'm gonna find out."

He unfastened the door and pushed up on it slowly, just enough to get a look. He was expecting it to blow open on its own, but it didn't. He couldn't heave it open with the best of his strength.

Jack Sample, trying to redeem himself, joined in. The two young men braced themselves under the door and lifted, but the door only came up a couple of inches — just enough for Joe to see that a large tree had fallen across the door. "All right, down," he said to Jack as he lowered the door back into place. Turning to his grandparents, he stated the fact. "It looks like that elm tree is no longer, well, a tree. We talked about cutting it down, Gramps. Now we won't have to. The bad news is that it fell right on us and we're trapped. We can't get out." He looked around him at the somber expressions in the tiny room. He took a breath. "Gramps is right, folks. Let's settle in."

CHAPTER 99

Joe and Liz MacDonald arrived in Hannibal close to midnight. They had spent two hours sitting at a truck stop off of Highway 61 waiting for the storm to pass. Visibility was awful, and they had long ago abandoned all hope of reaching Sylvia at a civilized hour.

Liz had scarcely said a word to her willful husband since they left St. Louis. She wanted to go home. She was tired. She was irritated at him for insisting on this impulsive trip, and she didn't know why they were there.

She had claimed victory earlier in the day when she had convinced him to turn the car around, but she knew the fight wasn't finished. After dinner, he had insisted again that they make the trip. It was as if some force outside both of them was tugging at him, drawing him to Sylvia. His decision to go was that of an undisciplined child.

Liz had told him about the forecast. Shelby County was expecting multiple tornados.

"All the more reason to go," Joe had told her. "I could be there to comfort my mom. She hates storms."

"Well, why haven't you wanted to comfort her during storms for the last twenty years? It's never been an interest of yours before. Why now?"

Joe hadn't had an answer, which made the decision to drive up here at this time of night even more ridiculous to Liz. But here they were, still an hour out of Sylvia with wind gusts up to eighty miles per hour and a highway that was devolving into a debris field.

"Let's compromise, Lizzy," he had offered. "Let's get a hotel room here in Hannibal and drive into Sylvia tomorrow in daylight."

"Fine, but we better hurry. With the storms, rooms are likely to be at a premium soon."

Liz was right. The first place they stopped in Hannibal had doubled its room rate in anticipation, but Joe, having second thoughts about dragging Liz on this trip against her will and into hazardous conditions, slapped down his credit card without a squeak of protest.

The hotel room was unremarkable, but Liz was too tired to care. She plopped on the bed with a sigh, while Joe sat on the other side and picked up the phone. After a few moments, he hung up. "There's no answer at Mom's house," he announced. "That's unusual."

"Don't you suppose they're sound asleep, Joe? It's midnight."

"I know, but my mom answers the phone at all hours. She always has."

CHAPTER 100

The seven people hiding in the storm cellar had utilized an old bucket to relieve themselves, thus adding to the various fragrances of hot, sweaty people in close quarters.

The air was hot and close. Sarah remarked that her mold allergy was subject to trouble her after this episode. Inga, meanwhile, was not feeling well. The stale air, heat and humidity were hitting her the hardest.

They sat on the dirt floor fearing they wouldn't be rescued.

Mitch regretted his part in the assault on the house in Elsa. He had embarked surreptitiously on the plan, and not a soul on earth knew where he had gone.

Jack Sample spent the hours considering how he could save himself or at least shave time off a long prison sentence. The relationship with Sarah was over, and that made him angry. She blamed him for the death of the baby, but he hadn't invited Soto there. The maniac showed up on his own, so he wondered how this was his fault.

Sarah gave no thought to her partner. Her thoughts were devoted to Dustin. She held his little hand in the dark as it grew stiffer and colder with each hour that passed. She saw him in her mind's eye, giggling and playing. She heard his voice singing the nursery rhymes she had been trying to teach him. Her predicament in this cellar, she thought, was perfect. Even if she were outdoors, she would still feel suffocated and lost in a dark abyss.

Third did not allow himself to lose hope. He would get out of this room. He would breathe fresh air again, and so would his family.

Okie Joe turned to the sheriff for answers. "Mitch, tell me again how this raging animal got to my house."

"I told you, Joe. It was Nakamura who told Soto and Simpson who you are. Or, rather, who your grandson is."

"And who am I as far as this guy is concerned? I didn't do anything to him." Third was indignant.

Sarah, sitting on the floor of the cellar, rested her head gently on her knee, careful to avoid reopening the wound. The bleeding had long since stopped, but without an emergency room visit and stitches, she was resigned to an unattractive scar. It hardly mattered. She looked up and said, "Mr. MacDonald, I think this was my fault. I know Joe from town and he knew that Jack was cooking meth in our house. So, when Ernesto came to our house earlier and we found out it was about to be raided, Ernesto decided to come here. He wanted back at Joe, I guess."

Sarah spoke in a monotone. All emotion had drained out of her. She glanced at Dustin's lifeless body, wrapped in an old shirt of Joe's. She was glad, in a way, that it was too dark to see him. It was horrible enough knowing he was there.

Jack Sample addressed the group. "Hey, I got a question, too, man. How in hell are we going to get out of here?"

"I've been thinking about that, too," said Okie Joe. "Maybe if we all pushed on the door, we could budge the tree. Or, maybe we could wedge it open just far enough for one of us to get out and call for help."

"Not a good idea, Gramps," Joe protested. "The smallest of us is Chelsea, and I don't want her unprotected out there when that guy could be on the loose."

"Well, that's something I hadn't thought about," Gramps admitted.

"The phones probably went out with the electricity anyway, Joe," Mitch reminded him.

"How long do you think before someone finds us?" Chelsea asked. "The hospital has the number here but there's no reason for them to call unless it's about my dad."

"Us neither," Sample said, "We sure weren't expecting anyone to come by the house, so no one's looking for us, either."

"And even if they did and found you gone and your kitchen in the basement, I'll bet a dollar that friends like yours don't call the police willingly." Mitch Ollman's smirk was invisible in the dark, but his voice carried it.

"Well, we know that house will be visited by the deputies in the morning, but they won't know where you folks went."

"It could be days before we're found," Okie Joe admitted defeatedly.

Joe took a seat on the floor, "I guess the danger now is flooding. If this room fills with rainwater, we could be in big trouble. 'Til then, there's nothing to do but wait."

"It's really getting hot in here," Chelsea complained. "I'm feeling a little faint."

"No surprise there," Mitch agreed. "Seven people, no air flow, at the end of July."

"Try harder, Third. "You and this, uh, Jack, need to get us out of here." Gramps sounded worried.

CHAPTER 101

True to his plan, Bill Fast assembled his teams at six a.m., armed them, inspected their body armor, and did the coach's pep talk before heading out for Elsa. He was curious when Sheriff Oll-man did not attend, but he assumed that his absence was part of the plan to protect the prosecutor's case. He gave it no more thought than that. "Nakamura, you've got the front door. My team will enter through the basement door. Remember that a young child and a woman are probably in the house.

Drive carefully. Travel will be slow. As you know from your drive over here, the highway is a debris field. Fifteen roads are completely impassible . That can help us or hurt us. It will possibly contain the suspects, but also hinder our movements. Dismissed."

An hour later, two unmarked vans with headlights off rounded the corner and parked down the block from the salmon-colored home at the top of the hill.

The deputies silently exited their vehicles. Fast had packed the long-sought warrant in his back pocket. The warrant had been acquired with great effort from Judge Harlem Bennett whose cooperation had, at best, been tantamount to extracting teeth using a putty knife. Fast was still secretly shaking his head in exasperation at the routine softness on crime this judge showed.

Reisman, Danvers and Spann followed Fast around the house to the back door.

At seven o'clock, Nakamura inserted the key, provided by the landlord, into the front door lock, and led his team in, weapons drawn. At the same time, Fast's team burst through the basement door.

Both teams were met with silence. Fast's team found the methamphetamine lab. Cold burners, Pyrex bowls and stacks of charcoal starter, peroxide, driveway cleaner and boxes of cold pills littered the basement.

Bill and his team made their way up the staircase to the upper floor.

Fast turned the corner at the landing and was met by Nakamura. The two looked at each other in surprise.

Fast stepped into the living room and found the beige rug soaked with blood. "What the hell happened in here? Looks like blood." He wouldn't know until much later that the blood was that of his friend and boss.

Nakamura confirmed the assumption after kneeling for a sample.

The teams searched the deserted house. There was a small amount of crystal meth, but otherwise, nothing.

"They knew we were coming, Hiro," Fast said to Nakamura, "Looks like they left in a hurry. This kitchen is a mess. Food left out. Dirty dishes. It's like they knew we were coming."

Nakamura had no response. He joined the rest of the team for another sweep of the small structure. There was no vehicle in the Sample driveway and there was no sign that anyone would return home soon. The abandoned food, the television on in the bedroom, the deserted meth lab in the basement—all were clear indicators that the home's residents had fled in a hurry. Jack Sample had been tipped off, and he had taken his family and fled like the cowardly butt wipe that he is, Fast told himself. Whoever the mole was in the department, he'd like to get his hands on him.

Frustrated, the acting sheriff ordered his men back to Sylvia.

At seven-forty a.m., Fast walked into the sheriff's office, picked up the phone and dialed Mitch's number by heart.

"Hi, Lindsey. Bill Fast. Sorry to call so early. I need to holler at Mitch for just a minute."

"What? No! I thought he was with you." she said.

"You did?"

"Yeah, he hasn't been home all night. I thought he pulled a graveyard. I was surprised, though. I thought he was on leave for a while longer."

"Lindsey, no. He's not due back here until the day after tomorrow. I haven't seen him either."

The phone was silent as neither could answer the other's questions.

"All right, Lindsey. Please call me if you hear from him and I'll do the same."

CHAPTER 102

"This is your seven a.m. wake-up, sir," the receptionist at the front desk of the Holiday Inn said when Joe picked up the phone.

"Thank you." Joe disconnected. He kissed his wife and said, "Sleepy-head? Time to rise and shine."

The cute clichés irritated Liz. She was still put off by the idiocy of this trip. The sooner it was over, the better. She rose, showered, and put her jeans and tee shirt back on. Her husband skipped his shower, anxious to get underway. They picked up breakfast sandwiches at a fast food drive-through and started out west on Highway 36.

"Holy crap," Joe said as he headed toward his parent's home. "This looks like a battlefield."

"Joe, I hope they're okay, your parents and Joey. This looks real bad. Look out!"

Joe slowed the SUV and steered around the loose cow that had sauntered out of her fallen fence and was lumbering across the two-lane highway.

"This is going to be an ordeal," Liz said through clenched teeth.

And so, it was. The normal speed limit on the way to Sylvia was slowed by various obstructions to an average twenty miles per hour as Joe picked his way over debris and around unfettered livestock. As the miles passed, however, Liz became less anxious to go home, but more anxious about the state of her stepson and her in-laws.

It was close to three hours out of Hannibal when Joe and Liz pulled onto his parents' property. They gasped in unison.

An uprooted poplar tree from somebody else's property was horizontal and lying inside the home's living room, having speared the window like a toothpick stabbing an olive.

The kitchen windows were broken by what appeared to be a piece of the barn's roof and part of another tree that laid halfway in the window jam.

The second floor appeared to have been spared as the shutters had been nailed down tight, but another look showed the white aluminum siding that covered the house was missing from the upper floor and a portion of that roof had also been torn away.

The couple stared in disbelief. Liz was the first to speak. "Joe, we've got to get in there and see if anyone is alive!"

"They're not in there, honey," he told her with confidence. He backed up and drove across the debris-scattered lawn and around to the back of the house. When he saw the old elm tree he had climbed as a child lying shattered across the rear of the property, Joe panicked. The main portion of its trunk lay on top of the cellar door, a homemade affair that sat on a thirty-degree angle to the ground.

Joe slammed the SUV into park, leaped out and sprinted to the door. "Dad! Dad! Are you in there? Momma!"

He heard numerous voices from inside the cellar. They all called for help. He heard both his parents and the familiar voice of his own son calling to him. He heard the voices of strangers as well.

"Dad! Is anyone left in the house? Dad? Is there anyone inside? The place is pretty damaged. Is there anyone in there to worry about?"

The muffled voice of Joe's father came from within. "Yes, son, we left a man inside, but, well, he's probably not our first worry. It's a long story. Don't go in there and don't try to help him. If he's alive, he's dangerous."

The stockbroker attempted to process this non-sequitur. He muttered an expletive to himself and concentrated on the matter at hand.

"Dad, what do you want me to do?"

"Son, is the barn standing?"

"Yes, it is," cried out Liz who had come up behind her husband. "It's missing part of its roof which is now in your kitchen. And the windows are all broken."

"Okay, son, we need to hurry. The air is sticky and humid. Hard to breathe. We've all been here all night."

"How many?"

"Seven."

"Oh, my God."

"Son, you've got to cut up this door and get us out. There's a chainsaw in the barn."

"Dad, no. The tree is the problem. Cutting the door won't help at this point. There won't be enough room for you to get out. Plus, Dad, there's no power. The house is dark."

"Son, the chainsaw runs on gasoline, but there may not be much in its little tank."

Joe looked around. "Liz, stay here. Talk to them. Don't leave them. I'll be back." He sprinted away toward the barn.

The tree trunk that sealed the cellar door was huge. It would take a while to get through it, no matter what he used. Joe, knowing this, flew into the garage. The barn was illuminated slightly by the missing piece of roof. He looked around but couldn't find the chainsaw. He cursed himself for not getting more specific guidance from his father. If he could find it, he could siphon gas from the SUV. In desperation, he grabbed a large handsaw and a rubber hose and ran back to the cellar door with an item in each hand.

"Dad. I can't find the chainsaw," he bellowed at the door. "It's too dark in there. Tell me exactly. I'll send Liz while I start here."

He placed the saw blade against the tree trunk on one side of the door and began sawing, but it wasn't more than a minute before he realized this would take hours on a trunk this size. He needed the chainsaw.

Joe's heart sank when Liz returned from the barn with the chainsaw in hand.

It was small, more suitable for cutting hedges or tall bushes, and no match for the job at hand.

To her husband's surprise, though, Liz pulled the cord on the chainsaw, and as it revved to life, she plunged into the task of sawing the tree in half.

He watched her for a moment, and then reapplied the handsaw.

The work was arduous. Liz made better progress, but the thickness of the tree and the inadequacy of the tools assured both of them that this was going to be a long job. Joe was already soaked with sweat and his muscles were aching, but he kept at it.

As he worked, Joe considered sending Liz into town for help. But it seemed more than reasonable that there would be no help to find . Emergency crews would be burdened with other people's problems, and she would certainly return empty handed. Neighbors would be dealing with their own troubles too. No, Joe told himself. He and Liz were on their own.

"Joe, I don't want to make this harder, but, son, your mother isn't doing well in this heat," His father's worried voice sent Joe into a renewed frenzy of sawing. He looked up at the sun that was beginning to bake the farm and imagined how hot it must be in the cramped quarters.

Liz's chainsaw sputtered to stillness. She tried repeatedly to re-start it.

"Liz," Joe panted. "Take the rubber hose. Do you think you can siphon the gas tank on the Bronco?"

"Got it." Liz took the hose and ran toward the SUV. Winded and running out of steam, desperation pushed Joe to keep going.

As the saw blade got duller, Joe's frustration grew. He needed better tools. Where was Liz? He got up and started toward the car just as Liz returned.

"I got it," she told him. She triggered the chainsaw and it roared back to life. "But the teeth aren't that sharp," she told him.

The two, standing back from the tree and the cellar door, had a clear view of the daunting task before them.

Joe had an idea.

"Liz, listen. Let's work on the smaller branches. Look at the tree. It's mostly trunk, and if the smaller branches were gone, well, we might get it to just roll off. That chainsaw will work much faster on the small branches."

"I'll get started," she replied.

Joe ran back to the barn. The sun, rising in the sky, threw more light into the barn than it had a few minutes ago. He went to the corner where he remembered his father had always kept a thick, long chain for pulling tree stumps. It was still there, buried under a tarp and electrical cords. It was rusty now, but if he could attach it to the trailer hitch on the back of the Bronco, his plan might work.

"Joey! Can you hear me?" he bellowed as he ran toward the cellar.

"Yes! Dad! I hear you!"

"Can you lift the door at all?"

"We tried last night. It only lifts a little."

"Then lift a little when I tell you. Do the best you can." As he barked orders, Liz was cutting through a branch that would be a suitable size for his purpose.

In the cellar, Joe and Jack put their shoulders into the door and created a two-inch gap between it and the jam. The relatively cool air from the outside felt great to those trapped. Joe's father wedged the tree branch into the opening to hold the door open.

Joe took the saw from Liz and resumed sawing the smaller branches, but only those on the left side of the door. He hoped to pivot the tree and get it to roll. Again, it was only minutes until the chain saw's engine weakened and died. Joe cursed.

Liz took off running toward the house. Her husband didn't notice her.

"Joe! You okay?" the eldest MacDonald yelled from within.

"Yeah, Dad, the saw is out of gas again." He assumed Liz had gone for more when he looked up and she was gone.

"Son, your mother is losing consciousness."

Joe picked up the handsaw and went at the tree with fury.

Suddenly, Liz was at his side with a plastic bowl full of ice cubes.

"You went in the house?"

"Yeah. It's a mess, but I was able to get to the fridge. Problem is, I don't know how to get this ice inside there unless I hand it one cube at a time."

She knelt at the opening. "Joey? I'm going to hand you some ice cubes. Try to cool off your grandmother first and the rest of you."

"Liz!" bellowed her father-in-law. "Don't go in the house. I told you not to go in the house!"

"Too late. I saw the man you said was inside."

A long silence emanated from inside the cellar. Joey spoke first. "Liz? What was he, um, like?"

"Looks like he got hit in the head by the tree branch that came through the kitchen window. He's kind of buried and not . . . conscious. He's got a pulse, but I'm most worried about you ."

"Yeah," Okie Joe agreed. "He got hit in the head. Son, there's a guy in here, the sheriff, he's lost a lot of blood. He's not conscious. I know you're doing your best, but . . ."

Joe, sweating and trembling, stopped sawing and took a deep breath. He turned to Liz. "Wait here. I wanna try something." Liz nodded. She was handing ice cubes into the opening.

He jumped into the Bronco, and backed it up near the cellar door. He wrapped the chain around the trailer hitch. Then he wrapped it around the tree trunk where it was free of branches.

He thought that if he could pull one end of the tree off of the cellar door, he could at least free enough of the door to saw through it.

Joe wished his hands would stop shaking as he rigged the chain.

"Liz?"

"I know what to do."

"Do you?"

"Yes, I'm driving."

"And I'm pushing."

Joe stepped up on the top of the cellar door and got to his knees behind the trunk. As his wife got in behind the wheel, he braced his feet and pushed as hard as he could against the tree. His intent was to roll it forward and down the cellar door.

The exhaust pipe was inches from his face, but he held his breath and focused all his strength as Liz pressed the accelerator. The strain of the engine against the large, heavy cargo was audible, but still insufficient to move the tree. Joe needed more leverage and a better angle.

Joe flipped over on his back and applied his shoulders to the trunk. Then, with his feet, he pushed his body backwards against the trunk. He felt the trunk give, but only slightly. Then the engine relaxed.

"Joe?" came the voice of his wife.

"Yeah, what?"

"I'm going to tear up this transmission the way this is going."

"Then tear it up. Go ahead. No! Wait! I want to try one more thing." Joe stood and ran back to the barn one last time. His arms and shoulders were screaming already, but he ignored their cries. In the garage, he found a shovel.

Returning to the cellar, he heard his father call out to him. "Son, what's going on?"

"Just a few more minutes, Dad," Joe yelled through the door. "Just a bit longer. I'm gonna get you out. Just hold on. How's Mom?"

"I'm afraid she fainted. Chelsea's putting ice cubes on her face."

Joe's frenzy to rescue his mother left no time for him to ponder the many questions he had. Why was there a guy in the house who might be dangerous? Who was Chelsea, and who else was in the shelter? He brushed those thoughts away. Not now.

He wedged the tip of the shovel under the tree and leaned on the handle to apply the entirety of his weight. He yelled for Liz to try it again.

Liz pressed the accelerator and the engine roared. At last the tree trunk moved, but only so far as to free itself from the shovel tip. The shovel collapsed down with Joe's hands wrapped around it and his knuckles hit the door hard. The skin on his knuckles was scraped off and he began bleeding. He cursed with the pain.

"Joe, talk to me," yelled his father from the cellar.

"Had a little trouble with the shovel."

"Are you okay?"

"Yeah, I'm just a bit bloody. Liz! Try again." Joe forced the shovel tip back into place. He thought they had gained a few inches with the first effort.

Liz hit the gas pedal. The engine strained again, but then the wheels of the SUV, having worn away the grass on the wet ground, began to spin in the mud beneath.

"This is useless," Liz hollered. "I've got no traction." She hopped down from the SUV and then noticed her husband's bloody hands.

"What happened!" she demanded.

"I got an owee. Get back in the truck."

"Joe, I told you there's no traction."

"I don't care. We've almost got it. We're this close. Try again."

"There's no point."

"Goddammit!" Joe yelled. He looked up from the cellar at the SUV stuck in the mud. Frustrated, he walked to the Bronco and pulled the chain off of the trailer hitch, then he got in and put the vehicle in gear. He eased the Bronco forward and backward, , using a rocking motion like he did when there was snow. After a few minutes, he was able to ease the vehicle back onto grass.

As Liz watched, Joe got out and reattached the chain to the Bronco, stretching all the slack from it.

The pain in his hands and shoulders was growing, but he ignored it.

Joe returned to the cellar door. He spoke to Liz. "One more time."

She got back into the Bronco, and eased it forward as Joe pushed down on the shovel handle.

The tree trunk began to slide. As Joe expected, it pivoted on an angle, but as it did, the rusty old chain broke. The loose end flew up in the air and hit Joe in the eye and nose.

"Ow! Goddammit!" he howled, as he grabbed his bloody face with his bloody hands.

"Are you all right?" Liz and his father yelled in unison.

"No!" he answered. "I think I broke my nose, and I'm bleeding a lot. Shit! All right, Liz, that gave us some room." As he wiped his bleeding nose with his shirt, he saw that the effort before the chain broke had cleared enough of the wooden door to allow him to cut an opening large enough for a human to get through.

He set to work with the chainsaw as blood ran down his face. Liz attempted to wipe the blood with a towel from the Bronco, but Joe waved her away. "I need to see what I'm doing with this chainsaw."

"But, Joe, your hands are full of blood. They're slippery. At least wipe off your hands." She offered him the towel again. He set the saw down and wiped his hands and face. The towel reddened, but Joe continued.

Within minutes the chainsaw was out of gas again and Liz's efforts to siphon more were fruitless. She cried to those in the cellar, "I'm so sorry. I can't get more gas out. We were low when we got here, and . . ."

Meanwhile, the conversation continued with the seven people trapped in the storm cellar.

"Dad! Dad!" yelled Joey.

"Yes, what?"

"Our truck in the barn has almost half a tank."

"We don't have a truck in the barn. Our truck is here and out of gas."

"Yes, we do. Of course, we do. Our truck. The truck that belongs to the farm."

"Oh, right."

Joe glanced at Liz who nodded and took off running toward the barn as her husband wiped blood from his face.

"Jeez, Dad," Joe yelled to his father. "I'm sorry this is taking forever. How are you all in there?"

"I won't lie, Son. We need to get out. We're getting some air, but it's real hot in here. Your mother can't stand up, so she's lying in mud. We emptied out the water bottle a few hours ago."

"What if I ran a garden hose to you? Would that help?"

"Sure would."

The spigot was next to the back door with the hose attached. Joe could only pray that it would reach the cellar door. It did, with five feet to spare. He fed the five feet into the opening he had created. He then ran back to the house and turned the water on to trickle.

As he did, Liz returned with the chainsaw.

"Dad," Joe yelled. "I need you all to step back from the door. I'm going to start cutting it apart."

"Okay, Son, go ahead."

The chainsaw with the dull teeth struggled against the heavy plywood door, but it was easy compared to the task of cutting up the tree trunk. Within minutes Joe had cut a square hole in the door. He turned off the machine with a fatigued gasp of air.

The eldest Joe said to his son, "Joe, I'm sending your mother out first. That'll be easiest. I got me a little gunshot wound and so does the sheriff, so we'll go last."

"You got what?" Joe barked.

"Here comes your mother. You're gonna have to lift her out by the shoulders."

"Okay, Dad, we'll do our best, but I'm about wasted and a little banged up myself. I'll need help from your end."

As Inga's head and shoulders popped out of the opening, she breathed deeply. As warm as the day was to Joe and Liz, the air seemed fresh and cool to Inga after languishing in the dank, humid room below.

Her son lifted her, and once a knee had cleared the opening, she pushed herself up. She blinked against the bright sunlight. "Thank you, dear," she said to her rescuer.

Quickly, Okie Joe assisted the others in exiting the cellar beginning with the two young men. He knew they would be the most help lifting the females, the sheriff, and himself.

Jack came out and then Third. Sarah stepped to the doorway holding Dustin's remains. She handed him up through the hole, but when she saw Jack prepared to take the little body, she snatched it back. "No!" she shrieked.

Jack stepped out of the way and allowed Third to receive the baby. To him, it was a grim reminder of the nightmare this day has been.

Liz's head was spinning with astonishment and curiosity as her stepson handed her, of all things, a dead infant.

Chelsea came next, then the sheriff. Jack Sample, trying to ingratiate himself, and Third pitched in to free the sheriff, mindful of his injuries.

At last, Okie Joe poked his head out and, breathing hard, boosted himself out of the cellar, dragging his injured ankle.

"We need to get all of you to a hospital," Liz stated, as Sarah took the dead child from her . Liz stared at Sarah as she handed off the corpse, a million questions and fears on her face. Sarah averted her eyes.

"Yeah, the nearest hospital is in Macon, isn't it Dad?"

"I'll drive the Taurus," the youngest Joe offered. "I can get five people in it."

"No, Third, you won't," Gramps said. "You're dehydrated and sick like the rest of us. Your mom will drive our car and your daddy can drive his. We'll all have a ride."

"No," Sheriff Ollman interrupted. "Leave the SUV. It might not have enough gas anyway. I'm gonna ride with Sample, in his car. That way I'm sure he gets where he needs to go." He looked at Jack with disgust. "I'd like you to drive that car, if you will, sir," he said to the middle Joe. "And we'll take Sarah. The other five ride with your wife." Mitch left no room for argument.

Third nodded his assent to the sheriff. He pulled the hose out of the cellar and returned to the spigot to turn it off. As he did, he took a long drink.

"Okie Joe, you and your family get in your car and get going. I gotta check one thing," Mitch said. "Be right back." He hobbled off toward the house holding his injured arm.

When he entered the kitchen, his heart sank. The tree that had shattered the window and the wall was big and heavy. He knew he had little arm strength, but he needed to retrieve both guns, and the tree blocked any access. Mitch fell to his knees with difficulty, pain still searing his shoulder, and felt with his good hand under the tree branches.

There was Soto's hand all right. His pulse was weak, but there was a sign of life. Mitch would have to send an ambulance as soon as possible. He felt around near the hand until he touched metal. Soto's gun. He removed it and set it aside.

Struggling to his feet, Mitch attempted to open the drawer in which Soto had placed the other gun, but it wouldn't budge. The tree barred the drawer shut. Mitch felt faint; he had lost a lot of blood, but he wanted his gun. "Damn," he said to himself. "I used to like trees."

He would have to come back for it later. He couldn't delay the trip to the hospital any longer. Anyway, no one could get in that drawer. Not until that tree was removed. He picked up Soto's gun.

Chapter 103

"Lindsey." Mitch's voice at the other end of the phone was as welcome as the dew in a desert.

"Where are you, Mitch? I've been worried sick all night, especially after Bill told me you weren't at work," Lindsey answered. Her voice cracked.

"I'm at the hospital in Macon. I've been shot."

"What? Bill said you weren't at work."

"It's a long story. Really long. Can you come? I need to call Bill while I still have the strength. I've lost a lot of blood, Lindsey. They're transfusing me now, but I'm going into surgery. Once they give me a shot, I won't be coherent."

"I'll be there as soon as I can, Mitch, but I'll call Bill Fast first so you don't have to. I'm sure he'll get there about the time I do."

"No, baby, I gotta call him no matter what. There're a few matters I'll need him to take care of. A couple of people he'll have to arrest."

"Who on earth is there to arrest?" asked Lindsey.

"Jack Sample, for one. Me, for another."

CHAPTER 104

"Bill? Mitch."

The same wave of relief that had washed over Lindsey when she heard her husband's voice now washed over Bill Fast.

"Good to hear from you, Sheriff. Where are you?"

"I'm in Macon at the hospital. I was shot, lost some blood — long story. Look here, I know where Ernie Soto is. If he's still alive, I'll need you to pick him up. He may not be alive, but take care just in case."

"Yeah, this sounds like a long story. I've got one myself about the Jack Sample raid."

"You got there and there wasn't a soul in sight, right? Empty house. They knew you were coming, right?"

"How'd you know?"

"I got there before you did, Bill. I went there to kill the son of a bitch, but I was ambushed by Soto. He shot me."

"Okay, where is he now?"

"Do you know where the MacDonald farm is on Rural Route 4 south of Sylvia?"

"Uh, yeah, sure. What's he doing out there?"

"Bleeding, probably. Or dead. Send at least two men and an ambulance. The house was pretty torn up by that tornado—"

"So was a good part of the town," Fast interrupted. "We had four tornadoes last night. Lots of damage all over three counties. And Mitch, there are no ambulances. All of 'em are on calls."

"Well, one hit the MacDonald property. Anyway, Inga MacDonald clobbered Soto pretty good, but I don't know if he bled out or what. She's the one hero we got in all this. When I checked him he was alive, but not by much," Mitch explained.

"All right," Bill assented, knowing there was more story to hear. "I'll send Nakamura and Jeckle out there when they start their tour."

"No, Bill, you won't. Instead, arrest Nakamura and charge him with accepting bribes. He's our mole. Soto and Simpson have been paying him off for months."

"No shit! I've thought the world of that guy. Holy shit! Can't wait until you feel better and we can talk this through. I'm pretty confused right now," Fast admitted. "I'll be there in twenty minutes. Oh, one thing. Since you know all about this, where is Simpson?"

"That, I don't know, Bill. Uh, one more thing. I'll be turning myself in as soon as the hospital releases me."

CHAPTER 105

The eldest Joe MacDonald, with his foot wrapped up and wearing a walking boot, sat at Inga's bedside, holding her hand. She was tethered to an IV that was administering fluids. The room was air conditioned, and Inga had begun to feel much better.

Third sat near the bed in a cushioned chair. Chelsea Christmas slept in a corner, her head propped in her hand.

"I want to get back to the house," Third announced. "If we've got any animals left, I'll take care of them. I want to see what kind of damage we have. Joe looked at his grandfather, but Gramps didn't answer.

The teenager considered the work at his house, and the prospect of doing it without Gramps for the foreseeable. The burden and challenge rested on him.

"I guess, then,' he remarked, "I've got a lot to do in three weeks."

With that, he stood, jingled the Taurus keys in his pocket, and headed for the door.

"Joe," his grandfather said, "Stay out of the house."

Joe smiled. "I'll be careful. But I gotta see about Susie and Domino and the others."

When he had left, Inga turned to her husband. "We don't even know if the house is livable. Have you checked with the insurance folks?"

"Yeah, they're sending someone tomorrow. We shouldn't have anyone there until, you know, the sheriff's office says it's okay."

Memories of their ordeal were preoccupying both of the MacDonalds.

A moment later, the door opened and Joe II walked in with Liz. Joe wore a white bandage across his nose. His eyes were swollen and his face was beginning to sport an ugly collage of purples, blues, and blacks.

He walked directly to his mother's bedside and gathered her up in an extended embrace.

As Joe stepped back, his father reached forward, clasped his son's hand, and shook it heartily. "So, the obvious question for you is: what the hell were you doing in Sylvia?"

"That's gratitude for you," Joe said to Liz. "I saved his life and he asks me that. I don't believe this guy."

Inga intervened. "Joe, lighten up! That's not what he meant, but it's an honest question. How did you end up at the farm? It's a good thing you did. We would've all been dead before we were found. You saved us all. Thank you."

"I'm really not sure why I came. You said on the phone that a lot was going on up here, but you didn't tell me what, and, I don't know, I just didn't want to be so left out. Anyway, Momma, who all did I save? Who are all those people? How are they connected to you?" As he spoke, he noticed Chelsea in the corner. She stirred at the sound of voices.

Inga smiled at her son as she explained how she and Third had met and befriended Chelsea and what had happened to her parents. She left out the story of her father's abuse, sufficing to say he was still in the hospital. Inga explained the visitors, Soto, and how everyone got to the cellar.

Liz and Joe were incredulous. Joe shook his head. "All this trouble was brought on by my son making friends with a drug kingpin and his girlfriend. This kid. Jeez. If there is a wrong thing to do, a wrong way to act, a mistake that can be found, he'll find it. He's as consistent as sunrise."

"It wasn't Joe's fault," interrupted Chelsea. "The dirty cop gave the drug lord Joe's name. Joe didn't do anything wrong. He's been a great guy to me, and I can't stand you dissing him!"

To Joe's great surprise, Chelsea began weeping after all she had been through.

"Joseph, Chelsea is telling it right," Inga put in. "Our grandson has been a huge gift to your father and me. None of what has happened was brought on by him, and don't think for a moment that he shares any blame for this. Do you understand me?"

"Yes, exactly!" the weepy Chelsea exclaimed. "He didn't do anything wrong."

"Yeah, all right, miss," Joe relented. It wasn't this girl's business, whoever she was. The stockbroker had difficulty forgiving his son for the many bad choices and misjudgments of the boy's young life. He ticked away the running roster of malfeasances in his head.

CHAPTER 106

Joe pulled the Taurus onto the MacDonald property, parked, and looked around. He went into the barn first. Mary Lou and the kittens were okay, at least. He went into the pasture near the house and took a census on the cattle. Two head down and under debris. He whistled for Susie again and again. She was a skittish cow, he reminded himself, and almost as timid of storms as Grams. But he couldn't quit looking until he found her and Domino. He prayed that Domino was okay. Joe couldn't remember having ever prayed before.

Well, he thought, as he looked around at the debris and damage to the house, if there was a time to start praying, it would have been when that storm and those people descended on the MacDonald farm. He'd missed doing it then. Better late than never.

As he gazed across the flat pasture around him, he heard a noise. He spun around, startled, and saw his little black and white calf sauntering over to him.

"Domino!" he cried with relief. "How are you, girl? Are you all right?"

He knelt and examined his pet. He touched her all over. She seemed to be okay. "Where's your momma, Dommie?"

Joe heard the sound of crunching gravel, and looked up to see a Shelby County sheriff's car. Joe walked over to meet it. A tall, lanky, dark-haired deputy was getting out of the car. Joe recognized him from his visit to the sheriff's office.

"Hi," he said to the visitor. Joe's experience as a budding criminal had left him wary of law enforcement in general, and that attitude was hard to shake off.

"Hey, how're you doin,' kid?" Jeckle said. He looked around at the property damage. "Wow. You all right? How're your grandparents? We heard they're in the hospital. You wanna tell me what happened?"

Joe described the events of the previous two days, concluding with, "So, we think the Mexican guy is still in the house, but he's hurt real bad. I'm glad deputies are here."

"That's what we're here about," Jeckle said. "Brett, you ready?"

Brett Fishman stepped out of the squad car adjusting his belt which struggled to contain his girth.

Joe was reminded of Sheriff MacAfee and noted to himself that the donut-hog cliché lives.

"Fast said the guy might be armed. Is that right, Joe?"

"Oh, yeah. He has a handgun of his own, and he took the sheriff's gun, too. I hope he's still knocked out. But I don't know."

"You stay here. We're gonna bring him out in handcuffs or on a stretcher, but you steer clear. Go in the barn or someplace. Better yet, get in your vehicle and head into town. If you wait for us in the sheriff's office, you'll know when it's safe to come home."

Joe resisted, but his personal experience had taught him the value of obeying the police. Or appearing to.

"Uh, okay. I'll do some chores in the barn, okay? I've got plenty to do around here."

"Out of sight, kid," Fishman cautioned.

The three walked together to the back of the house. Joe parted from them and walked in the direction of the barn as the two deputies approached the kitchen door with their hands on their guns. Jeckle opened the door with his left hand and stepped inside.

The mess there was convincing. A large sheet of wood from the barn was jutted into the kitchen through the window. It rested precariously on the edge of the kitchen table which seemed to be buckling under the strain. There was a huge tree limb underneath the barn section. Glass cabinet doors were shattered and shards from the dishes were strewn everywhere as well. Mud covered the floor, stove, and most counters. Debris, filth and water were everywhere. Beneath the tree branch and assorted debris, Jeckle noticed a thick, muscular hand sticking out.

"Here we go," he said to Fishman. He hunkered down and grasped the wrist of the suspect.

"He's alive. There's a pulse, a pretty good one. He's cold as a mackerel, though. Let's get him out from under there."

The two deputies began to remove the debris, sending it back out through the window. The tree limb was large and bushy and the branches hid the body of the suspect. The two lifted, but getting the section of the tree out was not as easy as the rest. The branches caught in the window jam. A script ran through Jeckle's mind of the normal perpetrator protocol. It called for him to kneel on the shoulder of the malefactor. But Jeckle couldn't get to the shoulder. No worries, though. This guy was down for the count. Still, his training nagged him.

"I'll go outside and pull," Fishman told Jeckle.

That did the trick. The deputy lifted the limb, stepped back, and the branch came free. That done, he rejoined his partner in the kitchen.

Joe stood in the barn door watching Deputy Fishman. Several things didn't feel right.

As Fishman struggled with the tree limb, Joe thought of Ernesto Soto. He recalled the events of last night, the courage his grams had shown, and the evil of that man. He shuddered, remembering the thud of the waffle iron impacting the thug's head.

Soto was huge and strong, and while he had been clobbered pretty well, Joe felt a creepy sense of his own limitations. The dark house seemed ominous and silent, and the killer inside was a specter, a lurking monster. The creepy feeling began to evolve into palpable fear and dread. Yes, he reminded himself, the cops were here.

But the cops didn't know this monster the way Joe did.

Joe leaned the shovel he was holding against the barn door. He trotted around to the front door of the house , and pushed it open.

"He's got a head wound," Jeckle was telling Fishman, "but he isn't bleeding anymore. A lot of blood loss, though. I can't tell where the blood stops and the mud starts on this floor. Let's turn him over so we can get cuffs on him."

Turning the huge beefy man was no small task. The two deputies grunted with exertion, made worse by the fact that the suspect was lying on his right arm. Still, with great effort, Jeckle pushed and Fishman lifted and the suspect was flipped onto his back.

With one fluid motion, Soto opened his eyes and pointed the gun in his right hand at the two deputies.

"Thanks for straightening me up," the Mexican sneered. "I got one mother of a headache. But not so hurt as you thought, eh? Anybody got an aspirin?" He laughed to himself. "Don't make a move to those guns, fuckers." Soto sat up, still brandishing the gun.

"You," he said to Jeckle. "Very slow now, set the gun on the floor and kick it over here to me. I'm on you, sucker. Don't try anything or you and your partner will catch it. Slow. You, stay real still." The last was to Fishman. "Your cop friend couldn't get the drawer open to get the other gun, but I could. Tell him for me to work out." Soto's smile was mean."

Jeckle complied, removing his gun from the leather holster, placing it slowly on the floor and kicking it across the room. Of course, it didn't go far in the mud.

"Now you," Soto barked. "Same deal.

"Whichever one of you drove, toss the car keys to me. Now! Do it right. If I miss catching them, you'll die."

Jeckle complied again, aggravated at himself for trusting that the perp was out cold as he seemed to be. This is why the protocol is the protocol.

Fishman began to sweat. Criminals such as Soto did not leave survivors to follow him. Soto's best shot was to disappear in the squad car, and by the time the two were missed, he'd have stolen another car.

Dean Jeckle, trying to stay clear-headed and focused, ran through the events of the last few minutes. Surely, the perp seemed unconscious. Now, evidently, had he not only been conscious, but able to get out from under the tree, get a gun out of a drawer, and resume hiding in plain sight. Damn! He'd probably been waiting four hours, stranded, waiting for a cavalier cop, making assumptions, to bring him a car.

As Jeckle mused, Soto reached the same conclusion Fishman had. There was no point in keeping these cops. He sneered and pulled the trigger. The gunshot caught Fishman in his ample gut. He stumbled back, screaming.

Jeckle dove out of the way, terrified and helpless without his piece. The bullet intended for him left Soto's gun noisily.

It was at that moment that Joe appeared in the kitchen door with the shotgun from the hall closet. He took aim and fired, not giving himself even a half second to think about it, fearful he would chicken out.

At the moment the shotgun fired, Joe knew his life was changing forever. He was a murderer, and he couldn't call the shot back. He was committed. But the few minutes he had spent with the lunatic the evening before had been enough to convince him there was no talking the guy down.

Jeckle, after a moment of terrified confusion, grasped that he was somehow uninjured. After a moment, he got to his feet and tried to contain his tears of relief.

Soto's head was nearly gone. The splatter of blood and gore touched every surface of the kitchen. Jeckle's stomach, already in knots, was nauseated by the sight.

He heard a thud and saw Joe, collapsed on his knees, still holding the butt of the shot gun.

"It's okay, son. It's over now."

He checked Fishman who was groaning in pain and bleeding from the midsection. "I'll be back. I'll radio for help. Keep still, Brett."

As he headed toward the back door, he lifted the shotgun out of Joe's hand and took it with him. "Are you okay, son?"

Joe, kneeling on the floor behind the corpse, leaned on his wrists and vomited.

CHAPTER 107

"Hiro? Come in the office for a minute," Bill Fast ordered.

Nakamura strode into the office

He smiled at Fast. "Yes, sir?" He glanced around the room. Two of his fellow deputies were with Fast, and they looked uneasy. Scott Dansbury looked at the floor, avoiding eye contact with Nakamura.

Hiro swallowed hard and tried to control his breathing. As he took a step, his knee tried to buckle, but he steeled himself as best he could. It seemed chilly in the office and the deputy shivered.

"Hiro," Fast began, "You are under arrest. I think you know why, and I think you know your rights. Dansbury, tell them to him anyway."

As the Miranda rights were recited, Nakamura showed no reaction. The smile remained frozen on his face; his movements had ceased; he stared glassy-eyed at no one in particular.

Fast took his badge and Dansbury removed Nakamura's service revolver from its holster and set it down on Fast's desk.

"Okay, Scott," Fast said to Dansbury. "Find him a private cell. "

Scott Dansbury cursed under his breath as he guided his friend and colleague out of the room.

CHAPTER 108

Joe stayed at the farm until nightfall, piling debris into a large mound away from the house. He would start a bonfire later when he had his gramps to help him.

Joe worked as hard as he ever had, intent on driving the memory of earlier events out of his head. He had killed a man in a most grisly way, and the memory of it replayed in his mind over and over with no relief. The feel of the shotgun in his hand, the recoil, the sound, the spraying of gore all over the room—it was all a horrible B movie that repeated through his mind until Joe thought he would scream in frustration.

He thought of Chelsea to distract himself.

He thought of Jamal.

He cried in spurts, but then dove into the task at hand.

Sure, he reasoned, the guy was awful. He was about to kill another person when Joe pulled the trigger. Deputy Fishman, shot in the stomach, was in the ICU in Moberly recovering, and Detective Jeckle would be dead had Joe not acted.

There hadn't been any discussion of arresting him or even any further investigation with regard to the shooting.

But that wasn't the point. The moment the life-changing decision had been made could not be undone. It would give him nightmares, he knew.

Trying to erase the mind's-eye images he walked the farm and found most of the missing animals. Lady was fast asleep in the barn. When he called her name, she awoke and strolled over to him. He fell to his knees and hugged the dog for a long time, scratching her ears, kissing her head, and letting his tears run into her coat. He reminded himself to tell Grams that their dog was okay.

Joe counted cattle and chickens. The hen house had been pretty well protected, and the storm had done little to decimate Inga's flock. At least it looked that way by the amount of chicken droppings there were to shovel.

Late in the day, Susie wandered back toward the barn. The fence that normally contained her was down for fifteen feet.

She walked toward him slowly when he called to her, but as she neared, his heart broke.

Susie's left ear had caught some flying piece of debris and was hanging loose. Blood covered her head, neck, and part of her chest.

Joe patted his cow and spoke to her with soothing tones even as he wept for her pain. "Let's go home, sweet girl, come on. We'll get you cleaned up."

He led the cow to the barn and locked her inside. He went into the house, and returned with peroxide and a towel. Joe washed the wound and realized it could have been much worse. He reunited Domino with her mother and left them to rest.

Grams would call the vet in the morning after he saw her. He wondered how many other animals were injured or lost in these counties.

When darkness fell, Joe headed to town to rejoin his grandparents at the hospital. He thought about the work he'd done today. Hours and hours of labor, and at the end of the day, he had not even scratched the surface of what there was to do. This would take months, he told himself.

CHAPTER 109

"Mitch, I don't want to arrest you, and I'm not gonna do it. Okay, so maybe it's a little good ole' boy corruption. I don't care."

"Bill, I went to Sample's place to kill him. There's no way out of that. If that behemoth hadn't stopped me, I'd have let Sample have it. Lock me up."

"Sorry, boss, you lose," Bill said. "I have a statement here from Sarah Dednum who was with you from the moment you showed up at the Sample home until you were brought to the hospital.

"Ms. Dednum states that you were nothing but heroic during the siege on the Sample residence, and that you strove at great personal risk to save her and her child from the actions of the perpetrator. You're a hero, Mitch, and no one needs question that heroism."

"But I went there to kill him."

"But you didn't kill him."

"Bill, I can't do this. I've stood by my principles all my career and I can't take a freebie just because I wasn't successful in committing a crime."

Bill looked at his friend. "I understand, Sheriff. I do. But I don't much care. Jack Sample is in your jail. We have all we need on him. Dednum has lost her child, and to me, that's punishment enough. Soto, tough as he was, is finally dead and out of our hair. It's all good."

"You didn't find Simpson, did you?" Mitch asked.

"Actually, Mitch, I did. Dix Simpson is in Mesa, Arizona with his wife. Did you know he had a wife? He has a daughter, too, age nine. I searched on the computer and saw charges against him there. He owes child support out the yin-yang and the authorities there found him in the home and took him into custody for failure to pay, initially. He was facing a hearing about the money he owes until I called down there. I reported the evidence we have against him, including the connection to the cartel.

"A woman at the college in Columbia provided a statement that she witnessed Simpson giving meth amphetamine to her daughter, age eleven. There are two other witnesses who had received meth on the Columbia campus and fingered Simpson. We also have the testimony of Dednum against Sample, Soto, and Simpson. This one is tied up with a pretty red bow, Sheriff."

"None of that mitigates what I did, er, intended to do, Bill," Mitch reminded him.

"Fine. If you insist, take yourself to the prosecutor's office and turn yourself into him. See if you can make him press charges. From where I sit, you were instrumental in saving the lives of the MacDonalds, that Christmas girl, and everyone else in that cellar. You're a hero."

"No, I'm not."

CHAPTER 110

"Hi," Third said to his grandparents with stoic dispatch. "I'm back. How are you guys doing?"

As he entered the hospital room, both Grams and Gramps perked up, but found their grandson's demeanor disturbing. There was a sadness, almost a depression, that they had not seen before. Joe sat on the bed next to his grams and held her hand.

"Grams, the pets are OK, but we lost four chickens and two head of cattle that I know of," he announced, sounding detached. "Susie's ear is hurt, she'l need Dr Economon to come look at her. I cleaned up the blood. There's a lot of damage, although it could have been worse. The south fence is down for about fifteen feet, and I don't know what I need to repair it. I'll need help with that and—"

Suddenly the young man's rambling stopped and he dissolved into sobs. His grandparents looked at him, and then at each other.

"Third?" Grams asked. "We'll put the farm back together. I'm sorry about the livestock, but Third . . ."

Joe muttered something unintelligible between sobs.

Gramps grabbed a box of tissues off the side table and handed it to his grandson.

The couple waited while their grandson calmed down. "Third, you're worrying me. Please talk to us," Grams pleaded.

Gramps spoke. "Third, we can replace the animals. I know you care about them a lot. Oh! Is Domino okay?"

The youngster nodded, his face in his hands.

"And what happened to Susie?"

"Her ear is torn off," the young man gasped. "I took peroxide to it." He stared in his lap for countless seconds. The couple waited for their grandson to regain his composure.

"Tell us what it is, then!" Inga cried. Her tone startled the young man.

He took several deep breaths until he thought he could talk. "I killed that man."

"What man?" Gramps exclaimed.

"That Mexican. He's dead. I killed him."

The three sat in silence for a few minutes. Grams spoke. "Third, I'm pretty sure it was me who killed him. I hit him hard. I think he was dead before we left the kitchen, and I—"

"No. You didn't kill him. He was still alive when the sherriffs got to the farm today. They tried to arrest him, and . . . Grams . . ."

"What?" Grams cried. "What are you talking about?" Her voice raised in pitch and volume.

"I'll tell you," Joe assured her. "I'm gonna tell you."

Slowly, between tears, Joe told the tale of Ernesto Soto surprising the deputies, and how he approached the criminal from behind with the hall closet shotgun.

"I've never killed anybody before," he concluded.

"Well I certainly hope not," Gramps remarked.

Grams shushed him. "Third, I don't think you had any choice. He was a horrible man, and I can't tell you I'm sorry he's dead." Then she paused. "Thank God you acted, Joe. Thank God you ended that dreadful danger."

He looked at her. She had never called him "Joe" before. She only called her husband that. Joe took that appellation as an honor and a vindication. It lifted him as nothing else could.

Joe buried his face in her shoulder. After a few minutes, he looked up at her and said, "How did your mom do it? Deal with killing a man?"

Grams took both his hands in hers. "I don't know, Third. I've never known."

CHAPTER 111

"Momma, come home with me and let me take care of you. Joey's coming home and we'll spend some family time together," Joe II told his mother on the day she was released from the hospital.

"There's our spare bedroom waiting for you. I know Dad won't come—he's got the farm—but you should take some time away."

Inga looked at her son with hat shrewd, knowing expression she was famous for. The five MacDonalds were headed back to Sylvia to assess the storm damage.

As they pulled onto the property, Inga's expression turned to one of sorrow and exhaustion. Sure, the tree was no longer in the kitchen window. The pile of debris Joe had stacked up lay waiting for a match to light it, but it was obvious that he had only made a dent.

Inga bowed her head in prayer. "Father, thank you so very much for your mercy and care of us. This could have been so much worse. We could so easily have lost our lives. Instead, we have You to thank for just this small amount of inconvenience."

Her husband squeezed her hand.

The five got out and surveyed the scene. "Gramps, I think we should start by rebuilding the fences so we can contain the livestock," Joe suggested. "I noticed the other day that most of the cattle are staying on the property, but we've got to get them penned. If you make a list of materials we need, I'll go to that warehouse in Shelbina and start picking up the supplies. Okay?"

His father turned to him. "Joey, school starts in less than three weeks. Don't you want to come home with Liz and me and spend a little of what's left of your vacation in St. Louis?"

The possible sarcastic remarks he could make flitted through the young man's mind: "Oh, so now you want me, huh, Dad? What changed?" Or perhaps, "According to you I am on vacation, so what difference does it make if I'm here or in St. Louis?" But Joe, having matured since the beginning of the summer, said nothing. He had plenty on his mind, and the topic would have to come up soon, but he wasn't ready.

"Oh, by the way, Joey," Liz advised, "Coach Nichols called for you last week. He's starting try-outs for the team a week before school starts."

"I'm already on the team, Liz," Joe reminded his stepmom.

"Yes, but he'd like you there for tryouts to, you know, be there and encourage the newbies. And to get back into the groove, I guess, with practices and what-not."

Again, Joe said nothing.

"So, it might be easiest if you packed up what you can get to in the house and go home with us now. That way we don't have to come back and get you in two weeks."

Liz had a machination of her own—to get the youngster into some counseling about the shooting. She was afraid that the trauma would turn into an excuse to be even more hostile and detached from his father.

Joe, however, couldn't help but think his dad and stepmother were in collusion. She wanted him to go home because his father had told her to want it. It didn't matter. On one hand, Joe was irritated at the suggestion that he should abandon his grandparents at the time of their greatest need. And it bugged him that his parents had every intention of doing so. They should stay and help too, his emotional side railed, and to hell with their stupid, pointless jobs! He looked inside himself at the selfish, spoiled boy who had arrived in Sylvia last May and tamped the boy down.

His matured side had hoped to work straight through these three weeks and get as much done as he could before returning to high school. He had also discovered that strenuous physical labor was excellent therapy.

But, now it didn't matter. One way or other, Liz had forced the issue.

"No, Liz, you won't have to pick me up in two or three weeks," Joe said. "I was hoping to do this differently and avoid putting Grams and Gramps on the spot.

I've been thinking about St. Louis, and what there is to do there, like graduate from high school. And I've been thinking about Sylvia, and what there is to do here—"

"Get to the point," his father barked. The middle Joe smelled a rat, an uneasy fear of what might be coming."

"Okay, fine, Dad. Don't hear me out, as usual. Here it is. I'm staying here. I'm finishing high school here. And if Gramps will help me, I'll learn to be a farmer."

"What about college?" Liz said.

"I'll go to college, Liz," he answered. "You've been after me for months to think about what I'll major in. I guess I'll get some kind of degree in agriculture. There's a program at the university in Columbia. Anyway, I've thought about this a lot and, well, I'm needed here. I'm not needed in St. Louis. You can tell me I am, but we both know better. I've got work to do, and I want to do it with my grandfather. That's my decision. There's no point in arguing."

"Joey, you have no interest in farming. You told me that yourself," Liz said.

"Don't worry, Liz," her husband put in. "I give this another month and he'll be calling, begging for a ride home. What do you think, Dad? I guess the kid never even asked you if you and Mom want a permanent house guest."

The five stood near the MacDonald SUV in silence. Grams and Gramps wished they had not been brought into this discussion. It was a discussion Third should have had first with his parents.

Gramps thought how to word his answer. "Well, son, I think this is something you and Third need to work out. I just want you to know that whatever you decide is fine by us. Third would be most welcomed to stay. We can certainly use the help, but it's up to you."

That was as careful and diplomatic as Gramps could manage. He didn't expect his wife to put in two cents.

But Grams spoke. "Joseph, I want Third to stay here with us. That's what I want. I want him to be a basketball star. I want him to help us put back together our farm. I want him to continue putting together his life.

Third has grown to be a wonderful young man, Joseph. But he has more growing to do, and I believe that your father and I can help him do that. In other words, we need Third, and Third needs us, and that's what I want."

"Okay, Momma, but what I hear you saying is that you don't think I'm a very good parent, and that you can do a better job raising my boy than I can. Frankly, I resent that."

Inga replied, "I didn't mean it —"

"Well I mean it that way," Third interrupted. "Dad, you're not a good parent. You may be a good stockbroker, and I thank you for breaking your nose to get us out of the cellar, but let's be real. You and I have had no relationship since Mom died. I can't get near you and you don't want to get near me. I'm staying here, and I don't care what you say about it."

Third's voice ratcheted up in timbre and volume as he grew angry.

"Well, you've done quite a lot wrong," Joe II said, but he knew it was a lame attempt. The stockbroker was tentative, unsure how to communicate with the teenager who was recovering from an ordeal that he, himself, could not fathom.

"And why do you think I did so much wrong? I'm not blaming you because I stole that car. I blame myself for that. But, looking back, I wanted you to notice me, and you never did, unless I was doing something stupid. I just wanted you to, I don't know, be my dad! Now you want me to go back to St. Louis so you can continue to ignore me? No thanks. I'm already home. I live here!"

By this point, the teen was yelling, and everyone was embarrassed. Third was fighting off tears of anger and sorrow, but meant every cruel word he said.

When the diatribe ended, the five stood in uncomfortable silence.

At last, Liz spoke up. "Why don't we go inside and see if we can do anything to put that kitchen back together?"

"The cleaning crew has been here already?" Third asked.

"Yes, they were very quick and thorough," Grams answered. "And Third, I want to thank you for keeping me out of it. The sheriff's department called me at the hospital and explained what they were up against, and, well, I'm glad I listened to you."

Joe II had calmed after the scene and spoke to his father. "Dad, didn't I see a big piece of plywood in the barn when I was in there?"

"Sure did," Gramps replied, surprised. "It's left over from the cellar door."

"Let's go board up that kitchen window."

CHAPTER 112

Chelsea Christmas stood in the boutique she now owned in downtown Monroe City. She considered whether she could run it by herself and make enough money to live.

She walked back and forth through the small storefront, as ideas and panic swept through her.

She went into the bathroom. It was a pretty large bathroom, Chelsea thought, for a place this small. If she had to, she could sponge bathe in the sink, and spread out some blankets on the floor in the storage room where she could sleep. Inga MacDonald had offered her a place to live, but Mrs. MacDonald hardly had a place to live herself right now.

No, she'd stay here at least until it was more convenient for the MacDonalds. With luck, Bonnie Wallace and her colleagues would assume Chelsea was still at the farm .

Chelsea lifted the phone to dial the MacDonalds' number, but then remembered that they didn't have power yet. She'd have to wait until they came and got her before she told them to go on back without her. Never mind, anyway. There was a lot to do. She had to start with her mother's books and teach herself to run a small business.

Chelsea took a sheet of paper from the office and a black marking pen.

Closed Temporarily

Due To Family Emergency

Come Again Soon

That simple act brought a flood of emotions to the teenager. The sign was an act of ownership—of her boutique, and of her new life. She wept for her mother, but forced herself to cut her grieving short. There were responsibilities to shoulder, and no one to help her but herself.

The doctors had told her that her father would be in rehab until long after her eighteenth birthday.

In addition to her father's medical issues, there would surely be prison time–punishment for all those times he . . . she shut her eyes in an attempt to wipe her mind free of the images.

Yes, she told herself. She was free. It would be a long road ahead, long and hard. But the worst part of her life was over.

She opened a filing cabinet and started reading.

CHAPTER 113

In return for Sarah Dednum providing Sheriff Mitch Ollman everything she knew about competing drug factories, their locations, and who ran them; the names and locations of addicts she knew; the process for quick, easy, meth production, and everything she knew about Dix Simpson and his dealings in the surrounding counties, Sheriff Ollman did not arrest her. He considered her a confidential informant, and as such, she was much more valuable as a free woman. Sarah passed a polygraph exam and agreed to testify at the trials of Jack Sample and Dix Simpson.

Homeless, jobless and helpless, Sarah was in dire need of any assistance she could get. She grieved the loss of Dustin, and her emptiness without him was a constant ache.

Mitch had invited her to stay with him and Dottie. Lindsey had left him, absorbed by her grief, and had gone to live with her parents in Ottumwa, three hours away. Mitch vowed to court his wife back, and grieve with her instead of without her.

Meanwhile, he hired Sarah to be a girl Friday in the sheriff's office. She would go to school at night, learn to type, and use a computer. Mitch decided not to replace Nakamura, freeing up part of the budget.

Sarah and Mitch shared the tragic bond of losing a child in a drug war. Sarah blossomed into an outspoken foe of meth and other narcotics. As a veteran of the drug life, she could honestly and plainly speak to youth groups. Mitch believed she could become an asset to the department.

"I think you're going to be okay, Sarah," he said to her one Saturday afternoon, as the two sat at home watching television.

"I hope so," she replied. "A lot has changed in a few weeks, and I have a future now, thanks to you."

Mitch was silent.

"I never thought much about a future before," she continued. "I had always let life just happen, and if it was bad, I didn't think about it. But you have to steer your own life. I see that now."

CHAPTER 114

"Hi, Aunt Ruby, this is Jamal, in Missouri. Is John home?"

Jamal's aunt in Detroit was happy to hear from her nephew.

"Sure, Jamal. He's here. How's your father? I don't hear from him much."

"He's okay. He had to be in the hospital a month or so ago. He got too much smoke running into a burning house, but it came out okay. Can I talk to John?"

"Sure, sweetie."

Jamal could hear a muffled sound as his aunt called his cousin to the phone.

"Yeah," John said into the phone.

"Hey, J.B. It's Jamal."

"What you up to, man? Glad you called. Whaddup in that little town...what's it called?"

"Sylvia. Sylvia, Missouri, and there's a lot up here. We've been having terrible weather. Terrible storms and a lot of folks got their houses torn up. The whole place is in reconstruction mode. My best friend got his home real damaged, and me and my dad have been helping them put it back together."

"Yeah, your dad is good at construction. I remember he built my mom's new kitchen before you all moved," J.B. replied.

J.B., short for John Brown, was two years older than Jamal, and the son of his dad's remaining living sister. The two young men had been close before the Armsteads moved to Missouri.

"Yeah, now he's building another kitchen for my friend, Joe's, family. I'm learning a lot. He's teaching me to hang drywall, and showed me some stuff about electricity and plumbing. He even had me wire the light switch by myself. I mean, he watched me, but I did it myself." Talking about his father filled Jamal with pride.

"Where were you when this storm happened?" J.B. asked.

"I was home, but I'd just got home from Joe's. I was gonna stay the night, but my dad called and wanted me home. Glad I went cause Joe's whole family ended up trapped in the cellar and could've died in there. They got rescued just in time. If I'd stayed, I'd have been trapped in there too."

"Wow. Who rescued them?"

"Joe's dad showed up out of nowhere. He drove up from St. Louis, and no one knew he was coming. He came to take Joe back, but Joe wouldn't go. If he hadn't come up here when he did, and if I hadn't gone home that night, I'd be dead now."

"Holy shit," J.B. exclaimed. "Sometimes the most random little things that happen make a big difference in what comes after."

"Yeah," Jamal agreed. "Joe says that all the time. Now he lives here and will start school here in a few days. He's gonna farm his grand-dad's farm and play basketball on our team, and finish his senior year while he puts the farm back together after the tornado hit it."

"Wow. That's a lot to do."

"Yeah, and I'm helping. Dad thinks I have what you call spacial dimension cognition. It means I naturally understand space and how things fit in it."

"Okay, whatever. So, is this gonna turn into a job?" J.B. asked.

"I'm thinking it could. I wanna keep working with my dad and learning stuff and after high school, I might try to get work with a construction company.

"Okay, so this guy Joe, where'd you meet him?"

"Oh, uh, he goes to my parents' church. He's a white dude."

"Wow, man, you're friends with a white dude. I never thought you'd say that, man," J.B. teased.

"Yeah, but Joe comes from St. Louis. He's pretty cool. His dad got real pissed when he said he was staying here instead of going back there," Jamal said.

"What about you, man? You ever coming back to Detroit?"

"I don't know. I guess. Dad wants me to go to college, and there are schools in Detroit that have majors in music management, cause, you know, it's Detroit."

"Yeah, man, I know it's a musical town. I live here," J.B. reminded him. "You wanna go into music?"

"I might. Music management and maybe production. But I'd hate to leave here."

"What? You'd hate to leave that stupid little town? You shittin' me, man? You hated that place from the moment you got there. What changed?"

"Well, a lot. It's a lot better when you got people. I mean, I always had my dad, and Lynae, after my dad married her. And now I got a little brother. But I got other people here and stuff to do. I'm needed and being needed means a lot. Really a lot.

"Life's gonna be okay in Sylvia for a while."

www.ingramcontent.com/pod-product-compliance
Lightning Source LLC
Chambersburg PA
CBHW051937090426
42741CB00008B/1181